A PLUME BOOK

TURN RIGHT AT MACHU PICCHU

MARK ADAMS is the author of the acclaimed history *Mr. America*, which the *Washington Post* named a Best Book of 2009. A writer for many national magazines, including *GQ*, *Outside*, and *National Geographic Adventure*, he lives near New York City with his wife and children.

Praise for *Turn Right at Machu Picchu*

"Mark Adams crisscrossed the Andes and has returned with a superb and important tale of adventure and archaeology. The Inca ruins at Machu Picchu are one of the world's enduring mysteries, and Adams has written such a bold, compelling account that I'm sure many of us will soon be trekking up those same outrageous mountains to see them for ourselves. It is a beautiful and profound world that he has entered, and his readers are immeasurably the richer for it."
—Sebastian Junger, author of *The Perfect Storm* and *War*

"In this book you will certainly learn more about Peru, Inca culture, half-sane pith-helmeted explorers of the twentieth century, zero-sane Australian travel guides of the twenty-first, and the mysteries of Machu Picchu than you ever knew before. But you will also learn more about Mark Adams, a hugely funny and thoughtful writer, diligent researcher, and unexpected man of action who climbs up from soft middle age to the dizzying, thin air of adventure. You will want to go with him."
—John Hodgman, *The Daily Show* resident expert and author of *The Areas of My Expertise*

"After reading Mark Adams's book, I did two things. First, I checked airfare to Machu Picchu. Second, I told my friends they had to read this amazing and entertaining tale about explorers, stolen treasures,

Amelia Earhart, and the controversial professor who—according to new evidence Adams found—just may be the model for Indiana Jones."

—A. J. Jacobs, author of *The Year of Living Biblically* and *The Know-It-All*

"Mark Adams's ebullient *Turn Right at Machu Picchu* . . . seamlessly joins three narrative threads . . . [An] engaging and sometimes hilarious book."

—*The New York Times Book Review*

"Adams's *Turn Right at Machu Picchu* is a serious (and seriously funny) travelogue, a smart and tightly written history, and an investigative report into perhaps the greatest archaeological discovery in the last century."

—NationalGeographic.com

"In *Turn Right at Machu Picchu*, Adams proves an engaging, informative guide to all things Inca."

—*Entertainment Weekly*

"A story that hooks readers early and then sails along so interestingly that it's one of those 'can't put it down' books. What more could armchair adventurers want?"

—Associated Press

"Like all great travelogues (and this is certainly one), *Turn Right* . . . should come with a fedora and a rucksack."

—*Men's Journal*, Best Nonfiction of 2011

"Adams deftly weaves together Inca history, Bingham's story, and his own less heroic escapade. . . . Those favoring a quirkier retelling [of Bingham's exploits] will relish Mr. Adams's wry, revealing romp through the Andes."

The Wall Street Journal

"Quite funny and unpretentiously well informed . . . Short of actually traveling to Machu Picchu yourself, it's the perfect way to acknowledge the lost city's one hundredth birthday as a modern-day tourist site."

—*Christian Science Monitor* ("Editor's Choice")

"If you haven't been to Machu Picchu and environs, this book will inspire you to drop everything and go. And if you've already been, *Turn Right at Machu Picchu* will transport you straight back to those soul-soaring heights."

—*National Geographic Traveler* ("Book of the Month")

"With a healthy sense of humor . . . Adams unearths a fascinating story, transporting his readers back to 1911, when Yale professor Hiram Bingham III hiked the Andes and stumbled upon one of South America's most miraculous and cloistered meccas."   —NPR.org

"[An] entirely delightful book."   —*The Washington Post*

"In this fascinating history/travelogue . . . Adams successfully weaves Bingham's tales—as well as resuscitating Bingham's positive reputation and accomplishments—into his own description of difficult but often amusing travels."   —*Publishers Weekly*

"This delightful travelogue is reminiscent of Hugh Thomson's *The White Rock* and Tahir Shah's *Trail of Feathers*. Adams, both funny and insightful, is intrigued by Machu Picchu without seeming New Agey, and the characters he introduces are compelling. Recommended for adventurers and armchair travelers alike."   —*Library Journal*

"The author deftly weaves together two story lines, each peopled with striking characters and astonishing landscapes. . . . Coupled with his keen eye for the absurd and his knowledge of the travel industry, the author gleefully remarks on the excesses of the increasingly commercialized adventure-travel business, while never hesitating to point out his own foibles. A funny, erudite retrospection offering more subtle and lasting rewards than the usual package tour."   —*Kirkus Reviews*

ALSO BY MARK ADAMS

*Mr. America: How Muscular Millionaire Bernarr Macfadden Transformed
the Nation Through Sex, Salad, and the Ultimate Starvation Diet*

TURN RIGHT
at
MACHU PICCHU

REDISCOVERING THE LOST CITY

ONE STEP AT A TIME

MARK ADAMS

A PLUME BOOK

PLUME
Published by the Penguin Group
Penguin Group (USA) Inc., 375 Hudson Street, New York, New York 10014, U.S.A. • Penguin Group
(Canada), 90 Eglinton Avenue East, Suite 700, Toronto, Ontario, Canada M4P 2Y3 (a division of Pearson
Penguin Canada Inc.) • Penguin Books Ltd., 80 Strand, London WC2R 0RL, England • Penguin Ireland,
25 St. Stephen's Green, Dublin 2, Ireland (a division of Penguin Books Ltd.) • Penguin Group
(Australia), 250 Camberwell Road, Camberwell, Victoria 3124, Australia (a division of Pearson
Australia Group Pty. Ltd.) • Penguin Books India Pvt. Ltd., 11 Community Centre, Panchsheel Park,
New Delhi – 110 017, India • Penguin Group (NZ), 67 Apollo Drive, Rosedale, Auckland 0632, New
Zealand (a division of Pearson New Zealand Ltd.) • Penguin Books (South Africa) (Pty.) Ltd., 24 Sturdee
Avenue, Rosebank, Johannesburg 2196, South Africa

Penguin Books Ltd., Registered Offices: 80 Strand, London WC2R 0RL, England

Published by Plume, a member of Penguin Group (USA) Inc.
Previously published in a Dutton edition.

First Plume Printing, May 2012
1   3   5   7   9   10   8   6   4   2

℗ REGISTERED TRADEMARK—MARCA REGISTRADA

The Library of Congress has catalogued the Dutton edition as follows:
Adams, Mark, 1967–
Turn right at Machu Picchu : rediscovering the lost city one step at a time / Mark Adams.
p.   cm.
Includes index.
ISBN 978-0-525-95224-4 (hc.)
ISBN 978-0-452-29798-2 (pbk.)
1. Adams, Mark, 1967– —Travel—Peru—Machu Picchu Site.
2. Machu Picchu Site (Peru)   3. Cultural property—Protection—Peru—Machu
Picchu Site.   4. Bingham, Hiram, 1875–1956.   I. Title.
F3429.1.M3A43   2011
985'.37—dc22   2011010211

Printed in the United States of America
Original hardcover design by Nancy Resnick
Maps by David Cain

*Penguin is committed to publishing works of quality and integrity.
In that spirit, we are proud to offer this book to our readers;
however, the story, the experiences, and the words
are the author's alone.*

For Aurita

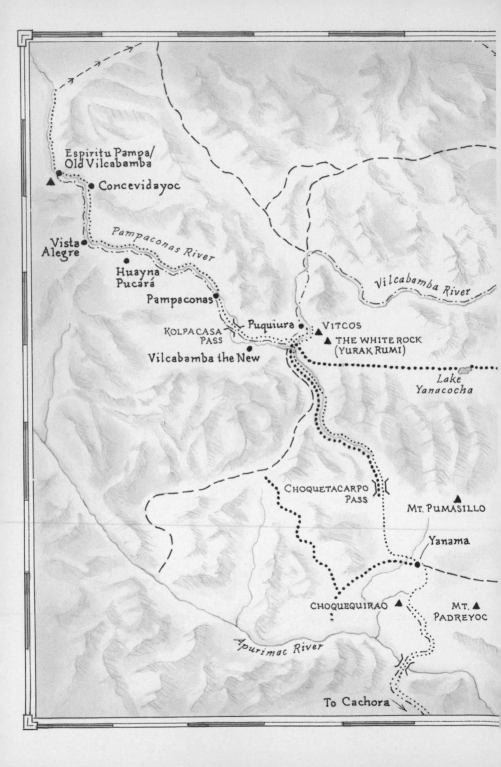

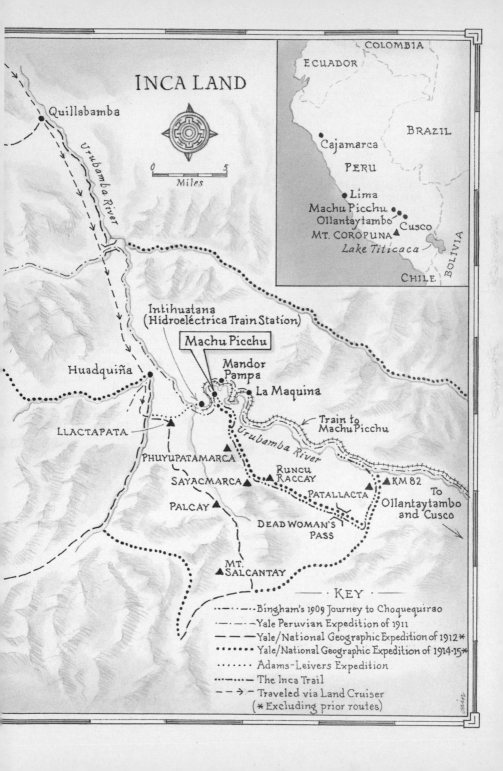

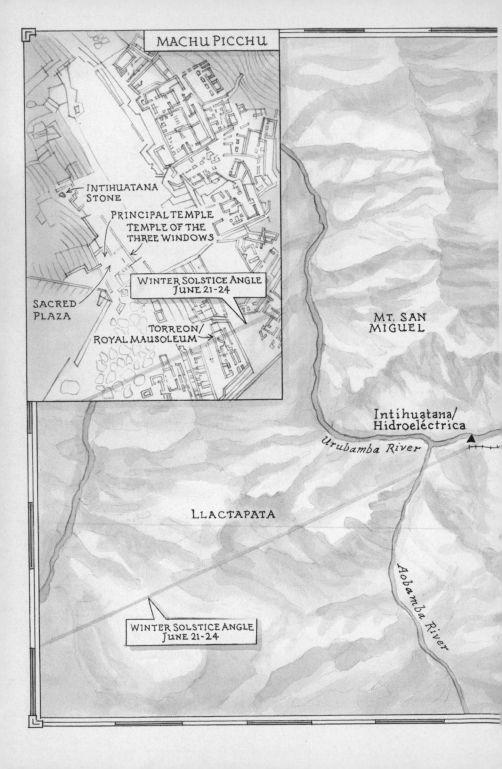

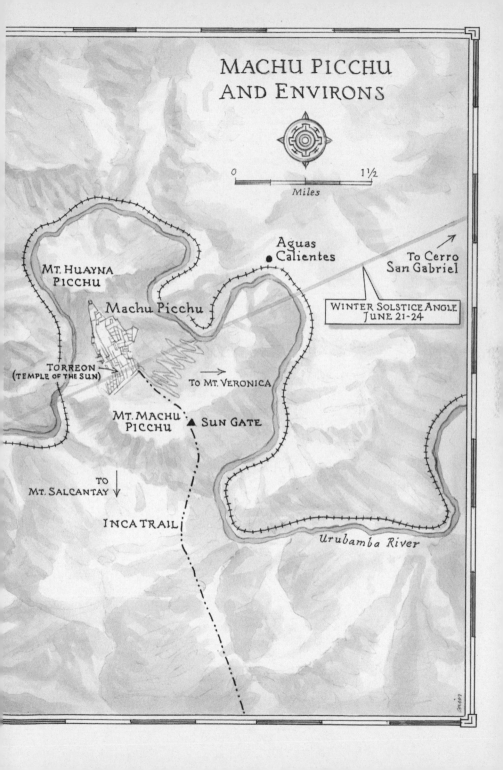

Author's Note

Many place names in Peru have multiple spellings. For simplicity's sake, I have chosen the closest thing there is to a standard spelling for each of these, even when the original printed source uses a different variant. Geographical features of the Andes also tend to have multiple names—for example, the Vilcanota River and the Urubamba River are the same body of water. In such cases, I've chosen the easiest variant, even if someone is speaking. And since it's *still* hard to keep these names straight occasionally, you'll find a glossary on page 297 for quick reference. Anyone who, like me, has absolutely no sense of direction, will also find the maps at the front of the book to be particularly useful.

A few minor details in this story, including some names, have been changed because not everyone I've written about knew they were going to be characters in a book.

TURN RIGHT
at
MACHU PICCHU

ONE

The Man from Oz

Cusco, Peru

A s the man dressed head to toe in khaki turned the corner and began racewalking uphill in my direction, I had to wonder: had we met before? It certainly seemed unlikely. John Leivers was in his late fifties and spent most of his time exploring in remote parts of the Andes, machete in hand, searching for ancient ruins. The overdeveloped pop-culture lobe of my brain noted his passing resemblance to Crocodile Dundee—John wore a vest and a bush hat, and greeted me on the sidewalk outside my hotel with a cheery "Hallo, Mark!" that confirmed deep Australian roots—but there was something else strangely familiar about him.

"Sorry about the delay," he said as we shook hands. "Just got back to Cusco last night."

In a general sort of way, John Leivers reminded me of the professional explorers I'd encountered over the years while working as an editor at various adventure travel magazines in New York City—the kind of men and women who drove dogsleds to the South Pole and combed the ocean floor for sunken treasure. John was extremely fit; dressed as if ready to clamber up the Matterhorn though it was a cloudless, seventy-degree day; and about as unattached as a man could be in the twenty-first century. He had no wife, no children, no permanent mailing address, just a cell phone and a Gmail account. He'd been

recommended to me as one of the best guides in South America, and
it had taken weeks to reach him. But now that he was finally here, sitting down to a late breakfast at my tiny hotel in Cusco, an old colonial
city in the middle of the Peruvian Andes, I wasn't quite sure where to
begin. Because I didn't exactly have a plan.

We ordered coffees, and John started to tell me about himself, occasionally stopping in the middle of a sentence—"When you're traveling alone, you've got to be absolutely, um, *seguro* . . . sorry, it's been a
little while since I've spoken English"—then patting his ear like a swimmer dislodging water, as if a tenacious Spanish verb were stuck in there.
John had started coming to Cusco twenty years ago, when he was
working as an extreme-trip leader, driving fearless globe-trotters across
four continents in an open-back truck. "Back then the shops were still
closed on Sundays and you could go months without seeing an American," he said. During the last decade, a period during which the number of visitors to Cusco had multiplied exponentially because of its
position as the gateway to Machu Picchu, John had seen interest in serious adventure dwindle.

"People used to be *travelers*, Mark," he said, stirring his coffee. "Now
they're *tourists*. People want hotels, cafés, the Internet. They won't even
camp!"

"You're kidding!" I said, a little too loudly. I had already checked my
e-mail at an Internet café twice that morning. The last time I'd slept in
a tent was in 1978, when my father brought an imitation teepee home
from Sears and set it up in our backyard.

And that, more or less, was why I was in Cusco. After years of sitting at a computer in New York and sending writers off on assignment
to Kilimanjaro and Katmandu—places John knew firsthand—I wanted
an adventure of my own. I figured that my near-total lack of outdoor
experience was a subject that John and I could discuss once I'd decided
whether to go through with this.

"So what sort of trip did you have in mind?" John asked. "Paolo says
you're thinking about going after Bingham."

"Yeah, I think so. Something like that."

For most of his life and many decades after his death in 1956, Hiram Bingham III was known as the discoverer of Machu Picchu. The story he told in his adventure classic *Lost City of the Incas*—knockoff editions of which were available in most of the stores that catered to tourists (even on Sundays) in the center of Cusco—was one of the most famous in the annals of exploration. Bingham was a Yale University history lecturer who happened to be passing through Cusco in 1909 when he learned of a four-hundred-year-old unsolved mystery. When the Spanish conquistadors had invaded in the sixteenth century, a group of Incas withdrew to a hidden city high in Peru's impenetrable cloud forest, carrying with them the sacred treasures of their empire. This city and its inhabitants had vanished so long ago that as far as most serious scholars were concerned, legends of its existence were about as credible as tales of Atlantis. Bingham thought the experts were wrong, and he scoured obscure texts and maps for clues to its location. In the dramatic climax of *Lost City of the Incas*, he was on the hunt for this final Inca refuge on July 24, 1911, when he stumbled across the geometric splendor of Machu Picchu instead. The ruins he discovered were so unexpected, so incredible that he wondered, "Will anyone believe what I have found?"

As the hundredth anniversary of Bingham's achievement approached, the explorer was suddenly back in the news. I'd been introduced to John via e-mail through his friend Paolo Greer, an obsessive amateur researcher with an encyclopedic knowledge of Inca history. Paolo also happened to be a retired Alaskan pipeline worker who lived alone in an off-the-grid cabin in the woods outside of Fairbanks. He had found what he claimed was a rare map indicating that someone may have beaten Bingham to the top of Machu Picchu by forty years or more. Just months after Paolo's map made headlines around the globe, Bingham's name began popping up again. The former first lady of Peru had ignited an international incident by demanding that Yale return artifacts that Bingham had excavated at Machu Picchu, on the grounds that the explorer—she preferred the term "grave robber"—and his employer had violated a legal agreement. Yale and Peru had originally planned to jointly open a new museum in Cusco to celebrate the centennial of Bingham's feat. As the hundred-year mark approached, they were suing each other in U.S. courts instead.

In the avalanche of news coverage that followed the filing of Peru's lawsuit, questions kept popping up: Had Bingham lied about discovering Machu Picchu? Had he smuggled artifacts out of the country illegally? A woman in Cusco was even claiming that her family still owned the land on which Machu Picchu sits; was it possible that both Yale and the government of Peru were wrong?

As a magazine editor, I knew the revised version of Bingham's tale had the makings of a great story: hero adventurer exposed as villainous fraud. To get a clearer idea of what had really happened on that mountaintop in 1911, I took a day off and rode the train up to Yale. I spent hours in the library, leafing through Bingham's diaries and expedition journals. While holding the little leather-covered notebook in which Bingham had penciled his first impressions of Machu Picchu, any thoughts of the controversies fell away. Far more interesting was the story of how he had gotten to Machu Picchu in the first place. I'd heard that Bingham had inspired the character Indiana Jones, a connection that was mentioned—without much evidence—in almost every news story about the explorer in the last twenty years. Sitting in the neo-Gothic splendor of Yale's Rare Books and Manuscripts Room, the Indy-Bingham connection made sense for the first time. Bingham's search had been a geographic detective story, one that began as a hunt for the Lost City of the Incas but grew into an all-consuming attempt to solve the mystery of why such a spectacular granite city had been built in such a spellbinding location: high on a secluded mountain ridge, in the misty subtropical zone where the Andes meet the Amazon. Fifty years after Bingham's death, the case had been reopened. And the clues were still out there to be examined by anyone with strong legs and a large block of vacation time.

"What's your take on Bingham?" I asked John.

"Bit of a martini explorer," he said, employing what I later learned was a euphemism for a traveler who fancies himself tough but who really expects a certain level of comfort. "Not very popular in Peru at the moment. But you can't argue with the things he found."

Like every serious explorer in Peru, John had all but memorized Bingham's published accounts of his 1911 expedition. During that summer, Bingham had made not one but *three* incredible archaeological discoveries, any one of which would have cemented his reputation as a world-class explorer. In his spare time during that visit, he had managed to squeeze in the first ascent of Peru's twenty-thousand-foot Mount Coropuna, thought at the time to be the highest unclimbed peak in the Western Hemisphere. Bingham found so many ruins during his three major Peru expeditions that many had since been reclaimed by the wilderness. John had helped organize an expedition a few years earlier to *rediscover* a site that Bingham had found within view of Machu Picchu, which had gone missing again for ninety years.

As John sipped his coffee, I floated my idea to him. I wanted to retrace Bingham's route through the Andes on the way to discovering Machu Picchu. I also wanted to see three other important sites that he had visited: the mountaintop citadel of Choquequirao, now considered by many to be Machu Picchu's twin city; Vitcos, site of one of the holiest shrines in the Inca empire; and Espiritu Pampa, the long-lost jungle city where the Incas made their last stand against the Spaniards. Exactly how we were going to accomplish this—buses? trains? llamas?—was a detail I hadn't thought through very well.

"Maybe we could hike the Inca Trail," I said. "That way I could get a taste of Bingham's experience, you know, following the road that leads to Machu Picchu." I had mixed feelings about the Inca Trail. For trekkers, hiking it was like making the hajj to Mecca; you had to do it once in your life. But every story I'd read about the Inca Trail—and when you work at an adventure travel magazine, you read a *lot* of stories about the Inca Trail—made it sound as crowded as the George Washington Bridge at rush hour. The best parts of Bingham's books were those sections describing Peru's natural beauty, and I was hoping to get a sense of Peru as Bingham had seen it, if such a thing still existed.

"You know, Mark, *all* Inca roads lead to Machu Picchu," John said. He reached across the cluttered tabletop for a jam jar. I couldn't help but notice how different our hands were. His had square-cut nails and looked like they'd spent a lifetime hauling lines on a trawler. Mine looked like I'd just visited the salon for a mani-pedi. "If this is Machu Picchu"—here he placed the jar at the center of the table—"and this is Choquequirao"—he aligned the sugar bowl—"then these are Vitcos and Espiritu Pampa." He moved the salt and pepper shakers into position. The four pieces formed a Y shape with Machu Picchu at the bottom.

"There are no roads to most of these places, only trails," John said. "You can still walk pretty much everywhere Bingham went." He reached into one of his vest's many pockets and pulled out a little blue notebook with a plastic cover. "I buy these in Chile—they're essential for traveling in wet areas.

"Now, let's see. You'll need three days in Cusco to acclimatize to the altitude. One day to drive to the trailhead for the hike to Choquequirao. Two days' walk to the ruins. It's not very far but it is a bit steep. Incredible views. We'll have a look around, then continue on to Vitcos—that's about four more days of walking. We'll take a good look at the White Rock, a *very* important religious site that Bingham spent a lot of time trying to figure out. Serious country out there, *serious* Inca trails. You'll need a good sleeping bag because we'll be spending one night near fifteen thousand feet. Might get snowed in.

"We'll take a day or two of rest near Vitcos. Then we go down to the jungle, quite a ways down, actually, toward the Amazon basin. Maybe three more days to get there, depending on the weather, which can be a *little* unpredictable. We get to Espiritu Pampa and walk down the staircase to the old capital of the Inca empire, which Bingham made it to, though he never really understood the importance of what he'd seen. You'll want at least two days there." John paused for a second. "Presumably you want to see Llactapata, too."

"Huh?"

"Llactapata. It's the site Bingham found when he came back to Peru in 1912. I was up there a few years ago. You can look right across the valley to Machu Picchu. Just incredible. It's like what Machu Picchu used to be like before it was cleaned up—hardly been excavated."

"Of course, *that* Llactapata," I said, trying to guess how the name was spelled so that I could look it up later. "*Definitely* can't miss that."

"It'll help you get an idea of how the Inca engineers and priests aligned all these sites with the sun and stars. Brilliant stuff."

If John didn't look like a cum laude graduate of the French Foreign Legion, I'd have sworn we were tiptoeing into New Age territory. Cusco was a magnet for mystics. You couldn't swing a crystal without hitting someone wearing feathers who called himself a spiritual healer. The big draw, of course, was Machu Picchu itself. Something about the cloud-swathed ruins in the sky had a dog-whistle effect on the sorts of New Agers who went in for astrological readings, sweat lodges, and Kabbalah bracelets. Travel brochures that arrived in my magazine office always seemed to imply that the stones of Machu Picchu practically glowed with positive energy. There was no single explanation for *why* the citadel Bingham had found was sacred ground, but that didn't stop thousands of spiritual pilgrims from flocking to the site each year, hoping to experience a personal harmonic convergence.

"All right. So we walk up to Llactapata, come down the far side, and we can either take the train to Aguas Calientes"—he looked at me over his notebook—"that's the town at the base of Machu Picchu. Or we can walk along the rails and save the train fare."

"Is that legal?"

"Well, you know how things work in Peru, Mark. It all depends on who you ask."

"Do a lot of people sign up for this sort of trip?"

"We used to get a few people every year—*serious* travelers. Hardly anyone does it anymore."

"How long would it take?"

"About a month. Maybe less if the weather cooperates."

Represented by jars of breakfast condiments, the trip didn't look especially daunting. About a hundred miles of walking, by my rough calculations. From the sound of what John had described, we'd go north, cut through the mountains, bear left toward the jungle, then double back toward Cusco. For the big finish, all we had to do was follow the river and turn right at Machu Picchu. This last part sounded like a pleasant afternoon stroll, something to kill a few hours and work up an appetite for dinner.

"I know it's a lot to take in," John said. "Any questions so far?"

I could only think of one. "Is this harder than the Inca Trail?"

For a split second, John looked like he didn't understand me. "Mark, this trek is a *lot* harder than the Inca Trail."

TWO

Navel Intelligence

Cusco, continued

John and I agreed to meet the next day for breakfast to coordinate our schedules. He had tentative plans to spend several weeks hiking out to someplace that sounded like it was on the dark side of the moon, and I had commitments of my own. As I was starting to stand up to leave, I felt one of those commitments place a hand on my head. I looked up to see my thirteen-year-old son, Alex, standing over me. This trip to Cusco was both a reconnaissance mission and a father-son adventure. Though we'd both been to Peru many times because Alex's mother is Peruvian (and I suppose by the law of matrilineal descent, so is he), we'd never been to the famous capital of the Inca empire.

"I thought you were going to be down here for half an hour," he said. "That was two hours ago. I'm *starving*."

We walked down to the Plaza de Armas, which had once been the center of pre-Columbian Cusco. The name of the Incas' holiest city translates as "navel of the world." From the plaza four roads led out toward the four regions of Tawantinsuyu—literally, "four parts together"—as the Incas called their empire. At its height from 1438 to 1532, Cusco had been the heart of a kingdom that ruled ten million subjects and stretched twenty-five hundred miles up and down the Andes. In this city so sacred that commoners were expelled each night had stood the Koricancha, the gold-plated temple of the sun. The great nineteenth-century historian William Prescott called it "the most magnificent structure in the New World, and unsurpassed, probably, in the costliness of its decorations by any building in the Old." The absolute ruler of it all was the Sapa Inca, a hereditary monarch whose power derived not only from his parentage but from his religious status as the son of Inti, the sun god. So divine was the Inca's person that everything he touched—whether the clothing he wore only once or the bones of meat he'd consumed—was ritualistically burned each year. Any stray hair that fell from his head was swallowed by one of his beautiful female attendants. Being a god, the Sapa Inca was considered immortal. When he died, his body was mummified, and he continued to reside in the palaces he'd inhabited while alive, providing imperial guidance through special interpreters when needed.

Visitors to Machu Picchu are advised to spend a day or two in Cusco to adjust to the altitude, but it's also a good place to acclimatize to the strangeness of the Andes. Like Hong Kong or Beirut, Cusco is an in-between city where cultures have collided, in this case those of the Incas and the Spaniards. Several epochs now clashed in the plaza where the Incas had once celebrated their military victories by stepping on the necks of their vanquished foes. Vintage VW Beetles cruised the square, passing in front of a McDonald's advertising lattes and Wi-Fi, next to a seventeenth-century Spanish church built with stones cut by Inca masons before Spain existed. (Two blocks away the Koricancha sun temple was now the Santo Domingo monastery.) Small packs of stray dogs jogged through the tight alleyways of an ancient street grid, appearing and disappearing like ghosts. The only certainty was that no matter what restaurant, café, taxi or pharmacy Alex and I entered, some awful song from the 1980s would be playing. When we heard Quiet Riot's "Cum on Feel the Noize" for the third time, Alex turned to me with a pained look and asked, "Is this really what music used to sound like?"

We met John early the following day at a fake English pub.

His "martini explorer" comment had unnerved me a little— compared to Bingham, I was a white-wine spritzer explorer—so before committing to anything, I thought I should mention that it had been a while since I had slept outdoors. What came out of my mouth instead was "I might not be completely up-to-date on the latest tent-erecting methods."

"That's all right," John said. "We'll need mules for a trip like this and the *arrieros*—the muleteers—can set up the tents. How do you feel about food?"

"Sorry?"

"You like cooked food?" John asked. I admitted that I did, in fact, have a weakness for victuals prepared over heat.

"Right. When I travel solo, I usually prepare my own cereal mix and carry that with me. Fantastic stuff—all the nutrition you need. You're going to need a lot of calories out there, maybe twice as many as usual, because the body starts breaking down after three days." John was a serious clean-your-plate man; he'd finished his enormous breakfast, polished off the toast that Alex and I couldn't get down, scraped the remaining yogurt out of everyone's serving dishes and poured all the leftover dairy products into his coffee before downing it.

"So let's say we bring a cook. Shouldn't be too expensive. We'll need maybe four mules to carry the food and gear. Now, do you need a toilet, or can you go in the bush?"

"You go to the bathroom in a bush?" Alex asked, his attention suddenly diverted from CNN's *World Business Today*, the first television he'd seen in a week.

"No, in *the* bush," John said. "Like the forest."

"Oh man, that's gross," Alex said.

I sensed that this was not the correct answer.

"No, no. I can go outside," I said.

Alex's facial expression made clear that this, alternative was no less gross.

"Good! Because a toilet means an extra mule and chemicals sloshing around all over the place. How's your health? Any history of heart trouble, or stroke? People think if you get into trouble out there that you can just pull out the satellite phone and call in a helicopter. They're kidding themselves. That's tough, tough country. You break a leg, even two days from the nearest hospital, and you're walking out."

I assured him that other than a little thickness around the midsection and occasional sore knees, my health was fine.

"You've got about six weeks between now and the time we leave. You've *got* to exercise. Focus on your core, your upper back and your joints. Your body's going to take a lot of abuse on this trip."

When John excused himself for a minute, I turned to Alex. "What do you think of John?"

"I guess he's a little intense. But I like him. And he sure knows a lot more about Peru than you do."

On the way back to the hotel, John dictated a long list of equipment that I needed to buy for our excursion: drip-dry clothing for day, warm clothing for night, walking stick, rain gear, headlamp, sleeping bag liner, rip-proof daypack, waterproof cover for daypack. My pen ran out of ink. We stopped at a stationery store off the plaza to buy a new one. The shopkeeper, standing over a glass display case holding copies of *Lost City of the Incas*, stared at John—dressed, as I soon learned he always was, in full explorer garb—as if she'd seen him before.

"You know who your friend looks like?" she asked me as I handed over my money. "Hiram Bingham."

THREE

The Three Hirams

Honolulu, Hawaii

History's greatest discoveries have usually resulted from explorers' bravery and endurance. Neil Armstrong had to ride a gigantic flaming can of Sterno through the earth's atmosphere before taking his one small step onto the moon; Marco Polo not only walked to China but waited twenty-four years to carry his tales of Kublai Khan's empire back to Venice. Bingham employed a different set of abilities in finding Machu Picchu: organizational skill, careerist ambition and impatience. At a moment when young men were rushing to find the globe's last great places, risk be damned, Bingham outpaced almost all of them by writing up formidable to-do lists and checking off their items at a furious pace.

Bingham's three most important expeditions to Peru—which he managed to squeeze into four years between 1911 and 1915, while raising seven young sons and holding down a teaching job at Yale— coincided with the heyday of Frederick Taylor's new field of "scientific management," the Progressive Era push to make the world a better place through the gospel of efficiency. Bingham's files from that period—which are themselves a marvel of organization—reveal a personality fixated on maintaining total control. The "Official Circular of the Second Yale Peruvian Expedition," which gave explicit instructions to each team member, including some Yale professors who outranked him, is exemplary of his passion for getting things done by

leaving no detail uncovered: "Every one should see to it that his bow-
els have moved at least once a day," he wrote in section 18, note 13B.
"If the day has passed without a movement, one Compound Cathartic
Pill should be taken the next morning a half hour or more before
breakfast."

The other key element of Bingham's winning formula, his ambition, was a gift from his forebears. In greater Polynesia, it is the explorer's namesake grandfather, the Reverend Hiram Bingham I, who's
the famous one in the family. The Reverend Bingham arrived in what
was then called the Sandwich Islands (now Hawaii) as the co-leader of
a group of missionaries who sailed from Boston, landing in late March
1820. Only forty years had passed since the British sea captain James
Cook made a return trip to the archipelago that he had just written
onto the world map, whereupon he was clubbed and stabbed to death
by a mob of islanders. The Reverend Bingham's orders from his home
office were to bring buttoned-up Yankee Christianity to this race of
people who went about naked, swapped sexual partners and saw nothing socially unacceptable about human sacrifice.

The ability to arrive uninvited in an alien land and convince one's
hosts that almost everything they believe is wrong requires a rather
forceful personality. The Reverend Bingham sought to Christianize
Hawaii by bending its inhabitants to his will, which conveniently was
indistinguishable from the will of God. Combining a passion for hard
work with paternalism toward native peoples—other traits he would
pass along to his adventurous grandson—the Reverend Bingham undertook an extraordinary program of church and school building. (His
best-known legacy is the Punahou School, now famous for graduating
President Barack Obama.) His missionaries created a written form of
the Hawaiian language, which they used to translate the Bible into the
native tongue.

Hiram Bingham I did little to hide his revulsion toward the chattering, "almost naked savages" who paddled out to meet him. Their
appearance of "destitution, degradation and barbarism," not to mention their "sunburnt, swarthy skins," was nothing short of "appalling."

Bingham's strong opinions didn't entirely endear him to his fellow missionaries, either. When an illness that struck his wife required them to return to the East Coast, his superiors at the American Board of Commissioners for Foreign Missions inquired of the settlers in Hawaii whether they'd like Bingham to return. The answer was an unambiguous no.[1]

Having put Hawaii on the road to salvation, Hiram Bingham I envisioned his proselytizing heir, Hiram Bingham II, spreading the good word all the way to China; the elder Bingham told his son that he could be "the teacher of the Celestial Empire as your father was of the Kings and Queens of the Sandwich Islands." The son aspired to duplicate his father's success in a locale even more remote and ungodly than Hawaii. In 1856, Hiram II and his wife, Clara (a pair who, judging from their photograph, rivaled his parents as the least fun couple ever to sail the South Seas), embarked for the Gilbert Islands, a string of Pacific specks midway between Hawaii and Australia, where two island clans were engaged in a bloody war over control of the archipelago.

Hiram II did repeat his father's achievements, though on a more modest scale. A *much* more modest scale. He spent thirty-four years translating the Bible from Hebrew into Gilbertese, an idiom spoken by only a few thousand people. In nearly two decades of difficult missionary work, he tallied only a few dozen souls for the Lord, versus the two thousand strong congregation that his father had left behind in Honolulu. In 1875, seeking medical treatment for a crippling case of dysentery, he and the pregnant Clara left the Gilberts for good. The pair landed in Honolulu six days before Clara, age forty, gave birth to a boy on November 19, 1875. Had Hiram Bingham II possessed a stronger constitution, the son he named Hiram III might never have left the South Pacific, let alone found Machu Picchu.

In Honolulu, the Binghams lived in a modest house purchased for

---

1   Among his other achievements, Hiram Bingham I was the first member of the family to inspire a fictional character. The inflexible missionary Abner Hale in James Michener's *Hawaii*, later made into a movie starring Max von Sydow and Julie Andrews, was based on the Reverend Bingham.

them by the missionary board. "There, under the oppressive shadow of the first Hiram and the brooding presence of the second, the third Hiram spent his boyhood," one of Hiram III's sons later wrote. Growing up the only child in a household that contained four pious adults—his parents and his father's two older, childless sisters—Hiram III was never allowed to forget that he was destined for great things. (Or maybe predestined, since the Binghams were strict Calvinists.) The family read the Bible literally, and Hiram II seems to have adopted Proverbs 23:13–14 as an unofficial Eleventh Commandment: "Withhold not correction from the child: for if thou beatest him with the rod, he shall not die. Thou shalt beat him with the rod, and shalt deliver his soul from hell."

It is perhaps not surprising that at a young age, Hiram Bingham III developed a passion for spending time outside of the home.

In *Inca Land*, Hiram III's first book about his discoveries in Peru, he compared the scenery near Machu Picchu to the lush volcanic topography of his native Hawaii. His father had, he wrote, "taught me as a boy to be fond of climbing the mountains of Oahu and Maui and to be appreciative of the views which could be obtained by such expenditure of effort." Also passed down were the Bingham family's wanderlust and distaste for making small plans. At age twelve, Hiram III withdrew $250 he had saved for his college education and bought passage on the steamship *C. W. Bryant*. He'd drawn up a detailed plan. First he'd go to New York City and build a bankroll as a newsboy; then he'd move on to England and, eventually, Africa. When the *Bryant*'s departure was delayed, Bingham's accomplice got cold feet and told his own father of the escape plan.

Hiram III sailed for the mainland a few years later, at age sixteen. His father, having finally completed his Gilbertese Bible, now needed to oversee its publication in New York City. Hiram III was enrolled at Phillips Academy in Andover, Massachusetts, a prep school traditionally favored by America's wealthiest and most powerful families. (Both presidents Bush attended.) Hiram Bingham III paid his own tuition and worked each day in a campus boardinghouse, and later as a tutor, to cover other expenses. A slim, gawky transfer student—"I am not fit for athletics," he wrote as a teenager, after he'd sprouted past six feet in height—whose devout parents forbade him even to dance, he did not make a huge social splash among the children of the Gay Nineties elite. "It is my purpose to save souls for Christ," he wrote to his approving parents back in Hawaii.

In the autumn of 1894, Hiram III matriculated at Yale, his father's alma mater. By the end of his first year he'd made a name for himself on campus by helping the freshman debate team defeat Harvard. The unlikeliness of this victory, Yale's first in debate against its most hated rival, may be guessed at by a headline in *The Boston Globe*: HARVARD FRESHMEN BEATEN. When Bingham was hoisted onto the shoulders of his classmates, he found that he rather liked the adulation. From that moment he blossomed in New Haven, pledging a fraternity and joining the glee club. He even caved in to social pressure to dance—it would insult party hostesses not to, he reasoned—and begged his mother's forgiveness.

The reason we know these things about Hiram Bingham is that he carefully preserved his correspondence and clipped any news items in which his name appeared, to be saved in an annotated scrapbook. (He'd learned the habit from his mother.) His father, by toiling for decades in obscurity with little to show for it except a Bible that almost no one could read, had taught Hiram III a valuable lesson in the importance of self-promotion. If a man was going to work that hard, the world ought to know about it.

FOUR

How I Met Your *Madre*

New York City

Future scholars of the Adams family are unlikely to unearth much evidence of ambition or adventurous spirit. Any early interest in the outdoors that I might have developed was squelched in the second grade when I was banned from the Cub Scouts due to a late birthday. Seventeen years later, I was splitting my time unenthusiastically between two vocations unlikely to result in a sunburn—tending bar in the Chicago Loop and halfheartedly pursuing a PhD in English literature uptown. One night, my roommate's notoriously pushy girlfriend came into the bar, ordered me to buy her a drink and announced that she'd met an editor from *Outside* magazine that morning and had all but badgered him into offering me an internship, sight unseen. I reported for work a few months later and felt as if I'd landed in a foreign country. I'd had absolutely no idea that so many people were so interested in things like mountain climbing, hiking, and camping.

After six months of apprenticeship, I left to seek my fortune in New York City, a place where I knew no one. I rented a room out of the *Village Voice* classifieds, in the home of an eccentric lawyer who owned a converted firehouse in Brooklyn. Most mornings I awakened to find her morbidly obese house cat sitting on my face. The odd living arrangements came with one excellent fringe benefit: proximity to the lawyer's beautiful niece. Aurita wore cowboy boots and smelled like jasmine and wanted to be a veterinarian. She happened to be Peruvian. She also happened to have a boyfriend. But she was willing to sit for hours and listen to a lonely young would-be writer pour out his guts as he was—unbeknownst to either of them—falling in love. When I moved on to a cat-free apartment, we traded a couple of answering-machine messages and fell out of touch.

My best friend from high school had moved to Bolivia to work on nature documentaries and invited me down to visit. Unless you count a brief pass through the Canadian side of Niagara Falls on the *Maid of the Mist*, I had never been outside of the continental United States. Within hours of landing in La Paz, we were standing in the aisle of a decommissioned school bus with a seating capacity of thirty-two (the little plaque, in English, was still bolted above the driver's head), loaded with at least fifty people and an unknowable number of animals, careening through the Andes down a steep, twisting road that I later learned is a perennial contender for the title of World's Most Dangerous Highway.

For a jet-lagged boy raised in the pancake-flat Midwest, the experience of stepping off that bus and staring up two miles at a twenty-one-thousand-foot peak was akin to seeing the face of God. Intrigued by tales that Aurita had told me of even greater wonders along the Inca Trail, my friend and I tried to enter Peru via the Lake Titicaca ferry but were rebuffed by a menacing teenage soldier carrying an AK-47 and wearing a Barbie backpack. I looked across the water toward Peru and vowed to return one day. Then an old man with a cane picked my pocket.

E. B. White once wrote that a person should only come to New York if he's prepared to be lucky, and as they would for Hiram Bingham in Peru in 1911, the stars aligned for me in my first couple of years in the Big Apple. I found a job with medical benefits and a light-filled apartment two blocks from Central Park. Right before my second Christmas in the city, out of the eight million people I might have col-

lided with on the sidewalk, I bumped into Aurita, who was now single.
We went for coffee and never really separated. By the following Christmas, she was my wife.

It has been said that anyone who takes a Latin American spouse
is essentially marrying the entire extended *familia*. In my case this
brought me into the orbit of Nati Huamani. Nati had started out as
Aurita's nanny and now managed her parents' sprawling beehive of a
home in Washington, D.C., as a sort of full-time personal assistant-
cook-majordomo. Aurita's family was from Lima, the cosmopolitan
capital on Peru's Pacific coast. Lima is a lot like Los Angeles: valet
parking, beaches, smog alerts. Nati was from the Andes, which aren't
even remotely like any other place on earth. She had grown up speaking Quechua, the language of the Incas. Occasionally, loosened up by
a pisco sour, Nati would tell me stories about the mysticism and super-
stitions of the Quechua people in her tiny mountain hometown.

Life in the Andes hadn't changed much since the Spanish Conquest
almost five hundred years ago. People still plowed their fields by hand
with sticks and observed centuries-old rituals to pay their respects to
the Pachamama, or Mother Earth. Older folks kept time by monitor-
ing the shadow cast across a local volcanic peak, which was revered as
an *apu*, or mountain deity. Evil spirits were obstacles to be dealt with
on a daily basis, much as I might have to contend with trying to catch
a taxi on a rainy day. When you had a problem, you could say a prayer
at the Catholic church and then talk to the village *chaman*, a healer
who knew how to broker deals with the *apus*.

Nati was a great believer in the power of omens and dreams, which
often foretold future events. She was perplexed by one image that visited her sleep for weeks.

"I keep dreaming that Aurita has a fruit tree growing in her stomach," she told us.

It was right around then that we found out, quite unexpectedly,
that Aurita was going to have a baby.

FIVE

Itinerant Scholar

Berkeley > Cambridge > Princeton

A photograph taken of Bingham at Yale showed the six feet four, sandy-haired explorer-to-be standing a full head taller than his classmates, looking like a somber, skinny power forward from a Soviet basketball team. He likely had a lot on his mind. After graduating in the spring of 1898, Hiram III returned to Honolulu to join the family business, as superintendent of a mission devoted to aiding the down-and-out. But Bingham's years at Yale had taught him to question his father's fundamentalist faith, and he lasted only six months before tendering his resignation. He later explained that he had left "because I found it impossible to teach the very orthodox beliefs which those in charge of the Mission expected to be taught."

Something else may have been crowding Hiram III's thoughts during those first months back in Honolulu. The previous summer, on a trip to the Yale-Harvard yacht races near New London, Connecticut, he had met a shy, sheltered young woman named Alfreda Mitchell. Her mother, Annie Tiffany Mitchell, was an heiress to the Tiffany jewelry fortune. Annie's husband, Alfred, was an entrepreneur; his peripatetic career prior to settling down comfortably as a man of wealth had included stints operating whaling ships, serving in the Union Army and prospecting for gold in California.

Alfred Mitchell had fond memories of his seafaring days in Hawaii, and around the time Hiram Bingham III began doubting his future as a missionary, the four Mitchells were entering Honolulu Harbor aboard their yacht *Archer*. Two days after their arrival, Bingham paid the first of many social calls at their winter cottage on Waikiki Beach. Considering that Mitchell's father-in-law, Charles Tiffany, had thought Mitchell wasn't good enough for *his* daughter, Bingham might have expected a little more sympathy. Instead, Mitchell packed his daughters off to Japan.

Bingham took the hint, bought a ticket to San Francisco and enrolled as a graduate student at the University of California, Berkeley. He would pursue a master's in history. Annie Tiffany Mitchell cabled encouragement to the new scholar in California: "When you get your M.A., you can have your A. M."

Hiram II, on the other hand, was flabbergasted by his son's secular turn. Hiram III did not help matters by explaining that his love for Alfreda was the light by which he now navigated his life. The elder Bingham, convinced that his son was aboard an express train to hell, reminded him that "the greatest force in a man's life should be supreme love to Jesus, supreme loyalty to the Saviour of the world. . . . If it is not, I have everything to fear for you."

Demonstrating the drive that would later serve him well in his explorations, Bingham fulfilled the requirements for his graduate degree in a single academic year, all while giving a series of lectures on Hawaii and managing to cut something of a figure on the social circuit. The *San Francisco Chronicle* noted his attendance at a private dinner dance, entertaining "a merry group of this season's debutantes." He was, perhaps, a young man in too great a hurry; one grandson noted later that in writing his thesis, Bingham had "copied a number of long passages without the use of quotation marks." By the fall of 1900, Bingham was in Cambridge pursuing a PhD in history at Harvard. He and Alfreda were married at the Mitchell home in New London on November 20, in a ceremony presided over by Yale's former president.

At Harvard, Bingham had chosen to specialize in a new, but potentially important, field of study—South American history. For his PhD dissertation topic, Bingham wrote about the Scots Darien Colony. This ill-fated settlement had been an attempt by Scottish explorers at the end of the seventeenth century to establish a trading beachhead in what is now Panama. Unfortunately, they chose an especially inhospitable spot of jungle, known today as the Darién Gap, which still remains among the least developed areas in the Western Hemisphere. Bingham received his doctorate (and a $10,000 gift from the Mitchells) in 1905. His greatest hope was for a Yale appointment," one son remembered. Bingham repeatedly called on the university's president, Arthur Twining Hadley, to see if there was anything he could do for him. There wasn't. Harvard showed no interest in offering him a teaching position, either.

Unexpectedly, Bingham received an inquiry from Woodrow Wilson—yes, *that* Woodrow Wilson—who was then building his reputation as a brainy, liberal university president at Princeton. Would Bingham consider a position as a "preceptor"—one of Wilson's energetic young faculty leading innovative small discussion groups— teaching history and politics? After seeking permission from his in-laws, who had purchased and furnished a Cambridge mansion for the newlyweds, Bingham accepted the three-year assignment.

Princeton was not a good fit. Bingham struggled to stay on top of his course load. He squabbled with Wilson over special treatment that the president wanted for the son of a wealthy alum. An attack of appendicitis provided Bingham with an excuse to request a year's leave of absence, supposedly to convalesce. Having recently turned thirty, he was more concerned with thinking about his future. As it turned out, both he and Wilson were contemplating major life changes. Wilson was considering a move into politics; Bingham was looking for adventure. Seven years later, under very different circumstances, they would be two of the most famous men in America.

SIX

The Call of the Wild

New York City

Some humans are born great and others achieve greatness, but contrary to what Tony Robbins might tell you, most of us are perfectly content to have slightly-above-averageness thrust upon us. After rushing through my first couple of years in New York on a frantic sprint from extra-innings adolescence to sobering adult responsibility, I spent the next decade on a leisurely slide toward middle age. Aurita became a veterinarian. Alex was joined by two little brothers, Lucas and Magnus. We bought a house in the suburbs, a gas grill, a Volvo wagon. Aurita and the boys and I traveled to Peru almost yearly, but these trips were like my coworkers' weekend visits to Connecticut to see their in-laws. Between the lunches and dinners and cocktail parties at which we saw various cousins and uncles and aunts and close family friends who weren't blood relatives—as far as I could tell—but were called uncles and aunts, we rarely left the city limits of Lima.

My passport probably held some sort of U.S. record for most entry stamps to Peru without managing to visit Machu Picchu.

Any hopes I had of returning to explore the 99.9 percent of South America that exists outside of Lima were sublimated into my work, assigning stories to writers and photographers who got to fly off to the ends of the earth. On paper, I was an adventure expert. My actual boots-on-the-ground experience was somewhat limited. I had never hunted or fished, didn't own a mountain bike and couldn't start a fire without matches if ordered to do so at gunpoint. Back when the Barbie backpack kid had waved his AK at me at Lake Titicaca, it had taken me a few seconds to understand that I even *was* at gunpoint.

And then, as it tends to do, life started sending gentle overdue notices. Turning forty is supposed to be the milestone that kindles a man's urge to buy a Maserati and chase sorority girls. It was the approach of forty-one that got to me. An e-mail from an old boss arrived: a former coworker my age, who had the physique of a ten-thousand-meter champion, had collapsed on the subway when his heart stopped. His life was saved only through a million-to-one coincidence: An off-duty paramedic had been called in to work unexpectedly that day when a plane crash-landed after takeoff, was riding home in a car that happened to be delayed across the platform, stepped off her train to investigate why a crowd had gathered around my unconscious friend, *and* happened to know that they were in one of the few stations in the five boroughs that had a defibrillator.

A few weeks later my wife's Peruvian cousin, who'd just sent us pictures of his adorable newborn daughter, dropped dead of a coronary in Lima, six days after his forty-first birthday.

On my fortieth birthday, it occurred to me that I was now the same age that my mother had been when she found a tumor in her mouth, the first sign of the cancer that took her life before she got around to doing all the things she'd planned to do once her five children finally left the house.

It was around this time that Hiram Bingham's name turned up in the news and Machu Picchu started appearing in my dreams. This in itself wasn't surprising, since I often dream about my work—nightmares about forgotten margarita orders haunted my sleep for years after I hung up my bar rag. I spent my days working in the offices of *Adventure* magazine, a publication that specialized in ambitious trips to far-off places and coverage of extreme expeditions to the earth's remaining frontiers. In other words, the sort of job where someone could spend hours on the Internet indulging his new Machu Picchu obsession without attracting a lot of attention. The dreams continued for weeks and were strangely repetitive; in each one, I'd step onto an escalator in the subway or in a department store and step off onto Machu Picchu's empty, mist-shrouded central plaza. We kept meeting in the strangest places, Machu Picchu and I, like the leads in a romantic comedy.

As piles of Bingham-related material accumulated on my computer's desktop, I noticed that one crucial piece of information seemed to be missing. No one could say with confidence exactly why this extraordinary complex of stone buildings had been constructed in the first place. Was it a fortress? A sun temple? A really elaborate granary? A spiritual portal to the fourth dimension, constructed by extraterrestrial stonemasons? All of these ideas had been floated, but only one person seemed to have definitive answers: Bingham. After making three expeditions to the mountaintop citadel, the explorer was certain that he'd found the legendary Vilcabamba, famous as the Lost City of the Incas, which he described in his best-known book as the "magnificently built sanctuary" to which the surviving Incas escaped when their empire was invaded by Francisco Pizarro and his small army of ruthless Spaniards in 1532. "Here they were shut off from that part of Peru which was under the sway of Pizarro and the conquistadors by mighty precipices, passes three miles high, granite canyons more than a mile in depth, glaciers and tropical jungles, as well as by dangerous rapids."

If there was one thing modern Machu Picchu experts definitely *did* agree on, however, it was that Bingham's theories about the site were ridiculous. The latest hypothesis, which seemed to have been generally accepted, had been conceived by two Yale scholars who'd spent years going over the artifacts that Bingham had excavated. Their conclusion was that Machu Picchu had been something slightly less romantic than the Lost City that Bingham imagined. Rather, it had been the country estate of an Inca emperor.

I thought: That's *it*? The lost summer home of the Incas? There had to be more to the story.

One morning, while procrastinating at my desk on the nineteenth floor of a Manhattan skyscraper, I closed the door to my office and took from my bag a copy of Bingham's *Journal of an Expedition Across Venezuela and Colombia*. The book was Bingham's chronicle of his first great adventure, a 1906–07 trip to South America. (When the librarian handed it to me, she said, "Looks like this one's been on the shelf for a while." The last due date had been stamped in 1914.) Like me, Bingham had been bored with his work. He was toying with the idea of writing a biography of the great South American liberator, Simón Bolívar, while on leave from his dead-end Princeton teaching job. The published sources were woefully inadequate to answer his questions. "I came to the conclusion that if I wished to understand this period in the history of South America," Bingham wrote, library resources would be insufficient. To truly get inside his subject's head and understand his actions, he would have to leave his desk and undertake "an exploration of the route of his most celebrated campaign."

I picked up the phone and called Aurita at her veterinary office.

"Is this important?" she asked. The background noise sounded like a gang war had broken out between cats and dogs. "I'm on the other line with a collie that ate a Ziploc bag. Er, the owner of a collie. You know what I mean."

"What would you say if I told you I wanted to quit my job and go follow in the footsteps of the guy who found Machu Picchu?"

"I guess . . ." She paused. Somewhere in the background, an angry kitten meowed. "I guess I'd say, 'What took you so long?'"

SEVEN

Explorer

Across Venezuela and Colombia

As he convalesced from appendicitis at the Mitchell family estate in Connecticut, Bingham undertook an accounting of his life. He was soon to be a father to his fourth child. He lived like a man of wealth, but in many ways he was a snazzily dressed marionette whose strings were pulled by his in-laws—in particular, Annie Mitchell, an imposing woman who ruled over the affairs of her husband and daughter. Bingham believed more strongly than ever that his unorthodox choice to specialize in South American history had been the right one. The United States' crushing defeat of Spain's decrepit imperial forces in the Spanish-American War of 1898 had made the southward spread of North American influence and commerce inevitable. The U.S. Congress, after seriously considering digging a shipping passageway through Nicaragua, had just voted to take over the financially catastrophic Isthmian Canal project from the French. The conveniently slim nation of Panama had only been founded in 1903 when President Theodore Roosevelt assisted Panamanian revolutionaries in liberating their province from Colombia—a bit of gunboat diplomacy that left many South Americans suspicious of their northern neighbor's motives in the region. Bingham's careerist gamble looked smarter every year.

Bingham didn't really enjoy teaching, though. Professors were anonymous creatures that played to small audiences. It was the research and writing half of academia that he loved. Bingham had inherited a deep respect for books and authors from his father and grandfather; in addition to their translation work, Hiram I had written the 600-page doorstop classic *A Residence of Twenty-one Years in the Sandwich Islands.*[2] If Hiram III used his medical hiatus from Princeton to trace the route of the doomed Scotsmen who settled in the Daríen, he might tack on a fact-finding mission to Venezuela and Colombia to begin researching what would be the first major biography in English of Simón Bolívar.

Alfreda's childbirth in the summer of 1906 was a difficult one, and Bingham accompanied her to New York City for postpartum surgery. While his wife was recuperating in Manhattan, Bingham made the acquaintance of Hamilton Rice, a Boston-born physician with interests strikingly similar to his own. Roughly the same age, Rice, whom *The New York Times* described in his obituary as a man "as much at home in the elegant swirl of Newport society as in the steaming jungles of Brazil," could have been Bingham's more accomplished doppelganger. He had descended from a prestigious lineage, studied medicine at Harvard and later married into one of America's richest families. Rice had already visited the Caucasus and paddled the far reaches of Hudson Bay. He'd also made his first journey to South America, crossing the Andes from Ecuador and traveling down through largely unmapped territory to the Amazon, following the route of the legendary one-eyed sixteenth-century Spanish explorer and conquistador Francisco de Orellana.

To Bingham, Rice's MD would have been less impressive than the letters FRGS, which Rice was allowed to place after his signature as a fellow of the Royal Geographical Society. The RGS was the world's most prestigious explorers club. Its members had included Richard Burton, who had snuck into Mecca disguised as an Arab; David Livingstone, who'd sought the Nile River source (and who was in turn

---

2 Bingham's eldest son, Woodbridge, remembered that Hiram III's father had offered his son $10 if he read Hiram I's book. Hiram III had repeated the offer to his own seven sons. No Bingham was believed to have ever earned the money.

sought by reporter Henry Stanley, who greeted him with the immortal words "Dr. Livingstone, I presume?"); and Charles Darwin, who had done pretty well for himself after his own South American travels.

During Bingham's talks with Rice, the idea emerged that the two men should follow the route of Bolívar's desperate 1819 march across the Andes of Venezuela and Colombia, a military gambit comparable in difficulty and historical impact to Hannibal's elephant parade through the Alps. As he would do again and again in years to come, Bingham rationalized as duty his need to spend six months away from his family. "Let us not complain at our long separation but rejoice in the opportunity to accomplish a good piece of work," he wrote Alfreda from South America. He was more passionate, and perhaps more honest, in writing to his father: "I feel the Bingham blood stirring in my veins as I start for little-known regions, as nearly all my Bingham ancestors for ten generations have done before me."

By the time Bingham and Rice departed Caracas on January 3, 1907, their group had expanded to include two Caribbean assistants who were shepherding one thousand pounds of gear on five mules, supplemented by a wooden cart and two Venezuelan drivers. Bingham had been influenced by an article in *Scribner's Magazine* by the globetrotting celebrity war correspondent Richard Harding Davis that listed items useful on an adventurous journey, including "a folding cot and a folding chair." Dressed in a British pith helmet and riding boots, Bingham looked like he was off to fight the Zulus. The party brought along nearly enough arms to do so: "two Winchester rifles, a Mauser, and two Winchester repeating shotguns, beside three revolvers and a sufficient supply of ammunition."

If Bingham had been hoping for a taste of adventure, he found it. The book that eventually emerged from the journey, *The Journal of an Expedition Across Venezuela and Colombia*, was neither a Bolívar biography nor a scholarly examination of the Darien scheme. It was a chronicle of a perilous trip into a deeply foreign world. Venezuela was a land of leper colonies and colonial ruins, where howler monkeys and screaming macaws populated the upper reaches of trees with trunks that grew up to twenty feet thick. When the party tried to carry its large cache of firearms across the border into Colombia, a squad of four Venezuelan soldiers accused Bingham's group of smuggling arms to Colombian revolutionaries. Bingham's team had to sneak the arsenal out in their luggage. Colombia was even stranger and more dangerous. For days at a time, almost all of the famished team's sustenance—a diet of stringy "storks, cranes and wild birds"—depended on Bingham's skill as a hunter.

Sadly, Bingham's prose does not seem to have been inspired by Richard Harding Davis's vivid war reportage. (A *New York Times* review of a later book could apply to all of Bingham's written work: "His facts are extremely interesting; his presentation of them is clumsy and tedious.") The few bright spots in Bingham's narrative are his first encounters with South American "savages," the Yaruro people, whom he found "very slightly clothed and bearing spears, bows and arrows." He caught one native woman just as she was about to hurl a fresh cow patty at him, presumably trying to stir up trouble. In a friendlier encounter, a Yaruro chief:

> put his hand on my shoulder, patted me on the back, took off my pith helmet, put it on himself, ran his fingers through my hair, said "bonito" [pretty], patted his heart saying "contento" [happy], patted my heart, smiled, and asked for my cartridge belt and then for my gloves.

By journey's end, the group had traveled nearly one thousand miles in 115 days. Bingham was extremely proud of completing what he boasted to *The New York Herald* was not merely an interesting expedition, but "a feat hitherto not accomplished." Rice, who had grown weary of Bingham's sometimes reckless behavior—the novice explorer had been quite willing to unholster his gun to get South Americans' attention—ditched his partner in Bogotá. Rice would concentrate his future explorations in the Amazon, where he played the well-funded foil to the British explorer Colonel Percy Fawcett in the fruitless search for the vanished jungle metropolis that Fawcett called the City of Z. Neither man could have dreamed that the greatest prize in South America actually lay undiscovered less than a hundred miles west of Cusco.

Bingham had faced down "great savages, swollen rivers . . . and the scarcity of everything," including food. The idea of resuming the drudgery of his duties at Princeton, once merely unpleasant, was now unthinkable. Within days of his return from Colombia, he was off to Yale to plead his case with President Hadley once again. Unbeknownst to Bingham, Hadley had already surveyed the members of the history faculty, who had reacted coolly to his inquiries about hiring Bingham as a junior professor in their department.

Hadley presented Bingham with two other possible positions at Yale: assistant professor of geography or lecturer in South American history. The geography job was secure: a full-time salaried position with a full teaching load. The lecturer position would be more or less like a job in the William Morris mailroom—a low-paying gig that might lead to something bigger should the young striver prove himself. It would also allow Bingham fewer teaching responsibilities and more flexibility to continue exploring—a pursuit that Hadley encouraged with gusto. Money wasn't a serious factor, since Alfreda's parents provided free housing and $10,000 annual allowance—about five times the yearly salary of an assistant professor.

Bingham happily accepted the lecturing position. After nearly a decade away, he was returning to his beloved Yale. His timing was perfect.

EIGHT

Legend of the Lost City

Cusco

lmost from the moment he took his new post at Yale, Bingham flourished. A reason to return to South America presented itself when Secretary of State Elihu Root, who had
provided Bingham with an extremely handy letter of introduction on his previous trip, selected him as the youngest U.S. rep-
resentative to the Pan-American Scientific Congress, to be held in
Santiago, Chile, in December 1908. By the end of his first year of teaching in New Haven, Bingham was at the White House shaking hands
with President Theodore Roosevelt, no slouch himself as an adventurer, at a reception for the delegation. Good news continued to arrive:
Bingham had been named a fellow of the Royal Geographical Society
for his work in Venezuela and Colombia.

Aside from attending the Santiago conference, Bingham's plans for
his next trip south were hazy, though typically ambitious. He had another major expedition in mind. This time, he would follow "the most
historic highway in South America, the old trade route between Lima,
Potosí, and Buenos Aires." Bolívar had used the route during some of
his later military campaigns. Beyond that, it seems that Bingham just
wanted to have a good look around.

The travelogue that Bingham published after the journey, *Across
South America*, reads like two books welded together. The first half,
presumably written with his political sponsors in mind, is devoted to

tabulating business opportunities for American companies and making Twain-like observations such as "I have been in eight South American capitals and in none have I seen such bad manners as in Buenos Aires." One of his Yale students, Huntington "Coot" Smith Jr., joined him for this first leg of the journey. After a one-thousand-mile train ride through Argentina, the pair encountered "two rough looking Anglo-Saxons" at the border with Bolivia. One of the men, a robber "driven out of the United States by the force of law and order and hounded to death all over the world by Pinkerton detectives" was likely an associate of Butch Cassidy and the Sundance Kid. The gang leaders had been killed days before in a shoot-out with the Bolivian Army. Bingham's guide took advantage of the opportunity and bought the bandits' mules.

In Bolivia, Bingham had his first exposure to the two primary indigenous peoples of the Andes. He was not impressed by the Quechuas he met, despite their having descended from the populace of the once-great Inca empire. After watching a "poor, half clad Indian" submit meekly to a savage whipping from an army officer, Bingham concluded that "there is no doubt about the Quechuas being a backward race . . . bred to look upon subjection as their natural lives, they bear it as the dispensation of Providence." The Indians' reliance on chewing mildly narcotic coca leaves, he wrote, had left them "stupid, willing to submit to any injury" and, what must have been a high crime to Bingham, "lacking in all ambition." Even worse were their neighbors the Aymaras, who in addition to possessing all the faults of the Quechuas were "insolent and unruly." Bolivia's oligarchic government was an absolute necessity in Bingham's eyes, "the only possible outcome of an attempt to simulate the forms of the Republic in a country whose inhabitants are so deficient both mentally and morally."

After attending the Pan-American Scientific Congress, Bingham entered Peru for the first time in January 1909. He had picked up a new companion in Santiago, swapping Coot Smith for another well-connected young man, Clarence Hay, the son of a former U.S. secretary of state. The two men rode the train to Cusco. The city that had once been the gold-plated nexus of the vast Inca kingdom, the royal seat of one of the largest empires on earth, was now a seedy provincial capital notorious for what Bingham called its "unspeakably filthy" streets.

Hardly had the explorer disembarked from his train, however, than he began to fall under Cusco's spell. Approaching along the bank of the Huatanay River, he caught his first glimpse of the Roman Catholic monastery of Santo Domingo, constructed atop the convex Inca walls of the Koricancha, the ancient Temple of the Sun. He was mesmerized by the city's "long walls of beautifully cut stone, laid without cement, and fitted together with the patience of expert stone cutters"—walls whose perfection he would remember two years later when he came upon Machu Picchu. The palaces of the Incas—for that was the title of the supreme ruler, the Sapa Inca, or more commonly just the Inca— had once ringed the square. Conquistadors had constructed new homes atop their royal foundations.

The stone buidings of the Incas, Machu Picchu in particular, are the empire's most easily recognizable legacy. The most important ones, constructed for religious purposes or for members of the royal family, are famous for their jigsaw-puzzle masonry; the stones are held together without mortar, wedged so tightly that it is impossble to insert a knife blade between them. (It is equally impossible for a visitor to take a guided tour of Cusco during which this fact is not demonstrated.) How the Incas, who possessed no iron tools, no draft animals and no wheeled vehicles, carved and transported these stones is still something of a mystery.[3] The likeliest explanation is that the Incas had an enormous, well-organized work force that employed different methods from those that developed in Europe. Where an artisan in Florence might have taken a chisel to a chunk of marble, his counterpart in Cusco chipped off bits of granite with an especially dense

---

3   The explorer Percy Fawcett, of City of Z fame, reported erroneously that the secret was a solvent obtained from plants, which softened rock long enough that it could be shaped like clay.

hammer stone until he achieved the exact shape he wanted. The inter-locking stonework serves an engineering purpose in addition to an artistic one. During earthquakes, mortar crumbles, causing walls to topple. The interlocking stones in an Inca wall are said to "dance" dur-ing seismic turbulence before falling back into place. When a huge earthquake struck Cusco in 1950, many Spanish buildings collapsed, revealing intact Inca walls underneath.

Shortly after arriving, Bingham learned that word had been sent out from Lima that the American *delegado* to the scientific conference—a doctor from a prestigious institution—was to receive the warmest hospitality from local officials. This included a guided tour of Sacsa-huaman, the extraordinary stone edifice that overlooks Cusco.

It's safe to say that if it still looked as it did in the sixteenth century, Sacsahuaman, and not Machu Picchu, would be the most famous ar-chaeological site in the Western Hemisphere. At its peak, historian John Hemming has suggested, the quarter-mile-long structure—a massive, three-tiered citadel with three towers at the center, con-structed in the imperial-quality stonework that the Incas reserved for their most important buildings—would have resembled a gigantic granite battleship. Huge, perfectly carved boulders remain fixed in the original zigzag walls. One has been estimated to measure twenty-eight feet in height and to weigh more than three hundred tons. The blocks seem even more incredible in that when the Incas wanted to move something big, they pulled it themselves. Even after generations of local builders had carried off any stones not too large to budge, Bingham was stupefied by what he saw. "There are few sights in the world more impressive than these Cyclopean walls," he wrote. "What remains is the most impressive spectacle of man's handiwork that I have ever seen in America." When I visited with Alex a hundred years later, it was hard to disagree.

Continuing with his itinerary, Bingham departed Cusco for Aya-cucho, the site of Bolívar's final crushing defeat of the Spanish forces in 1824. The road he followed had once been a major Inca thorough-fare; Francisco Pizarro, the wily Spanish conqueror of Peru, had endured its roller-coaster climbs and descents on his way to the Inca empire's capital. As it often does near Cusco, the topography transformed almost immediately. "The trail, a rocky stairway not unlike the bed of a mountain torrent, led us rapidly into a warm tropical region whose dense foliage and tangled vines were grateful enough after the bleak mountain plateau," Bingham wrote. "Parti-colored lantanas ran riot through a maze of agaves and hungry creepers. We had entered a new world."

Four days out of Cusco, Bingham's party was given an enthusiastic welcome in the town of Abancay. The local prefect, J. J. Nuñez, buttonholed the visitor and begged him to make a detour to Choquequirao —an old Inca fortress that clung to a steep ridge more than a mile above the roaring Apurimac River, a glacier-fed source of the mighty Amazon. The name Choquequirao means "cradle of gold" in Quechua. Nuñez had raised thousands of dollars to blaze a trail to the nearly inaccessible ruins and take part in what was—and still remains—one of the great Peruvian pastimes: searching for treasures left behind by the Incas.[4] It was from Nuñez that Bingham first heard a legend that had grown around Choquequirao: that it was the final refuge of the Incas, thousands of whom were thought to have escaped to this hidden citadel in the clouds when the Spaniards invaded in 1532. With them, according to the tale, the Incas had carried the most spectacular treasures of the empire, "instead of letting it fall into the hands of Pizarro," Bingham wrote. Supposedly, when the last Incas had died out in their mountain sanctuary, the secret location of this ancient loot was forgotten as the buildings of Choquequirao were enveloped by the mountain's fast-growing vegetation.

Bingham was unconvinced by either the story or Nuñez's pleas until the prefect played two aces: first, he claimed that Choquequirao

---

4 Non-Peruvians have been at least as eager as the natives to find this hidden loot. Even the French oceanographer Jacques Cousteau once spent eight weeks trolling Lake Titicaca in a miniature submarine, searching in vain for a two-ton gold chain that, according to legend, had been taken from the Koricancha and dumped in the lake to keep the Spaniards from discovering it.

had never been visited by a white man. ("A statement that I later found to be incorrect," Bingham subsequently grumbled.) Second, Nuñez stressed that Peruvian president Augusto Leguia had personally requested that all excavation work at Choquequirao be put on hold until the esteemed Dr. Bingham from the scientific congress could have a look and give his opinion of the site's archaeological worth.

Bingham and Hay left Cusco on February 1, at the peak of the rainy season in the Peruvian Andes. (Crazy weather is an annual feature of Peru's austral summer. Storms near the end of January in 2010 washed away the train line to Machu Picchu; the Inca Trail is closed altogether every February.) This particular rainy season was the heaviest in twenty-five years, and the group encountered "well-nigh impassible bogs, swollen torrents" and "avalanches of boulders and trees." Within hours of departing Abancay, they could hear the Apurimac River roaring thousands of feet below them. The route down to their riverside campsite corkscrewed back and forth, each segment about twenty feet long. After sunset the group continued on "the tortuous trail" in complete darkness.

About three hundred feet from the bottom, the mule Bingham was riding pulled up abruptly at a small waterfall that sliced through the path. The scientific delegate got off and weighed his options. "As I could not see the other side of the chasm, I did not dare to jump alone, but remounted my mule, held my breath, and gave him both spurs at once."

It was a leap of faith that would set him on the road to Machu Picchu.

Beware of Fat-Suckers

Lima, Peru

Peru is a wonderful place. It is also wonderfully weird. The first time I visited, in 1997, several people I met in Lima warned me to take extra care when driving, because local thieves had perfected an ingenious new robbery technique. Near isolated intersections, street urchins heated discarded spark plugs over fifty-five-gallon drum fires. When a car stopped at a traffic light, the young thieves pressed a white-hot plug against its passenger-side window, causing it to shatter. Before the driver realized what was happening, a live rat was tossed into his or her lap. During the ensuing wrestling match with the (presumably agitated) rodent, the thief helped himself to handbags or anything else that looked inviting. If the driver understandably chose to exit the vehicle, the thief hopped in and drove off with his bewhiskered accomplice.

Peruvians have an insatiable appetite for such stories. The autumn that I arrived in Cusco, exactly a hundred years after Hiram Bingham first heard the legend of the Cradle of Gold, the news was dominated by reports that police had busted a ring of killers. The criminals had murdered sixty people and siphoned out their fat in order to sell it by the liter to shadowy international cosmetics manufacturers. A couple of frantic weeks passed before the police realized that no one had actually been reported missing in the area where the homicides had supposedly taken place. It sounded like something out of a Mario Vargas

Llosa novel. Actually, it *was* something out of a Vargas Llosa novel. In *Death in the Andes*, Indian villagers blame *pishtacos*, a breed of adipose tissue–sucking vampires, for three mysterious disappearances.

Peru's political history, too, reads like something that might have flowed from the pen of a Nobel laureate, and not just because Vargas Llosa nearly won the presidency not long ago. Let's just look at the last quarter-century, a period of relative stability in Peru. Alan Garcia, a young, handsome Kennedyesque liberal, was elected to lead the nation when he was just thirty-six. It's difficult to pinpoint which dubious achievement Garcia was subsequently most loathed for: allowing the inflation rate to soar to over 20,000 percent annually; failing to halt the growth of the Shining Path terrorist movement; or turning a blind eye toward corruption, the most public example of which was the $300 million spent on his Train to Nowhere, an elevated railway project whose ghostly concrete pillars still haunt the medians of some of Lima's nicest avenues. Everyone assumed that the dashing Vargas Llosa would be elected in 1990. He lost out to Alberto Fujimori, the nerdy son of Japanese immigrants. Fujimori essentially declared himself dictator and crushed both the Shining Path and inflation by whatever violent methods worked. (Aurita remembers watching an announcement on Peruvian television that effective immediately, gasoline prices were increasing twentyfold; the next morning, in place of the swirling pandemonium of Lima traffic, one could hear the sound of birds singing and children playing in the empty streets.) When the head of the national intelligence service was found to have videotaped thousands of politicians, judges and journalists accepting bribes, Fujimori escaped to Japan, where he faxed in his resignation. He's now back in Peru—in prison.

Alejandro Toledo, a former shoeshine boy and Peru's first indigenous president, was elected in 2001 as an anticorruption candidate despite reports that he had been spotted with prostitutes and had tested positive for cocaine. (He had an unassailable defense: he'd been kidnapped and drugged by Fujimori's henchmen.) Meanwhile, Toledo's French wife, Eliane Karp-Toledo, almost single-handedly blew up an agreement that Yale had reached with Peru's government to return artifacts that Bingham had taken to New Haven. The most recent election, in 2006, came down to a two-man race: a retired army officer, under investigation for murder, who vowed to nationalize foreign businesses, versus a reasonable-sounding elder statesman, back from a long trip abroad with at least one hundred extra *pishtaco*-tempting pounds packed onto his frame. Alan Garcia was back, running on a platform that boiled down to "I was an idiot last time." Garcia won. A few years later, he announced new plans to build an elevated train system in Lima.

It's possible that all this craziness is just geography as destiny. Peru's borders contain some of the world's most varied topography and climate. Measured in square miles, the country is not especially large. On a globe it looks like a swollen California. Within that space, though, are twenty-thousand-foot peaks, the world's deepest canyon (twice as deep as the Grand Canyon), unmapped Amazon jungle and the driest desert on earth. Peru is an equatorial country that depends on glaciers for drinking water. It's one of the world's hot spots for seismic and volcanic activity. (Both Lima and Cusco have been leveled by earthquakes; the country's second-largest city, Arequipa, sits beneath a smoking peak that could blow its top at any time.) Scientists have calculated that there are thirty-four types of climatic zones on the face of the earth. Peru has twenty of them. "In Inca Land one may pass from glaciers to tree ferns within a few hours," Bingham wrote, still astonished years after arriving. I was about to see for myself.

TEN

Peruvian Standard Time

Cusco

Six weeks after my first meeting with John Leivers, I was sitting in the Cusco offices of the adventure outfitter Amazonas Explorer, drinking my fourth cup of instant coffee and waiting for Juvenal Cobos to arrive. One of the things about Peru that I'd found it hardest to adjust to—even more so than the popularity of Nescafé in a country that grows some of the finest coffee beans in the world—was *la hora peruana*, Peruvian Time. This is the code, indecipherable to North Americans, by which Peruvians determine the latest possible moment that it is acceptable to arrive for an appointment. The statement "I'll be right back" can mean just that, or it can mean that the speaker is about to depart via steamship for Cairo. The habit drove Bingham bananas and hasn't improved over time, despite a widespread government campaign to combat tardiness a few years back. By one estimate, each Peruvian arrives a total of 107 hours late each year, a number that is shocking only because it seems so low. My friend Esteban, an Ivy League–trained businessman living in Lima, needed to lie to his own mother to get her to his wedding on time. He told her the ceremony began at noon when it actually started at 4 P.M. She arrived at ten minutes to four, red-faced and puffing.

Even after ninety minutes of gritty coffee and idle chitchat, I wasn't too upset, though, because we were waiting for a legend. In terms of exploring in the Andes, getting Juvenal Cobos to lead my team of mules was the equivalent of pasting a flyer up at the local Guitar Center inviting people to a jam session and having Eric Clapton show up in my basement. The Cobos family had worked on virtually every important expedition in the region we were heading to since the 1950s, including two famous attempts to follow up on Bingham's 1911 search for the Lost City of the Incas. Juvenal was also, John told me gravely, famous for padding the bill with extra mules.

I had noticed three things about John. One, he never removed his hat. Ever. Two, he was a bit of a misanthrope. He often spoke wistfully about a volcanic explosion that had happened 73,000 years earlier, almost wiping humanity off the face of the earth. John thought that Peru was destroying itself through population growth that could be reversed only by a huge flu pandemic, that the long march of civilization had peaked a few years earlier, and that the world had entered a deep, probably irreversible decline. "In some places, I wouldn't be surprised if we went back to the Dark Ages soon," he told me. I wondered if the guides who led luxury mystical excursions to Machu Picchu started their tours by scaring the bejeezus out of their clients.

The third thing I'd gathered about John was that he was a little tight with his money. It wasn't that he was cheap, really, just that his sense of fair play was offended when he felt that something was overpriced, which was often. When I returned to Cusco, we'd eaten lunch in a restaurant that had once been the finest house in Peru, an Inca palace so large, the chronicler Garcilaso de la Vega recalled, that sixteen men on horseback could joust inside it. I couldn't stop staring at the gem-cut stone walls. John gawked at the menu, fixated on the price of a bowl of soup. "Really, what's in there? Noodles, broth cubes, maybe a little egg. Fifty cents of ingredients sold for five dollars! That's immoral."

We sat in the Amazonas Explorer office a few minutes longer, until John finally got impatient. He stood up and started yanking the contents of what appeared to be a mobile field hospital out of two gigantic bombproof suitcases and spread them over the floor.

"Take a seat over here, Mark, you'll need to know where these things are in case anything happens. Our policy is we avoid *all* problems. Now, this is for broken bones," he said, holding up some sort of bendable stiff material that evidently wrapped around a fracture. "Satellite phone—fifty dollars just for the phone card, and that only lasts an hour and expires in a month. Epi pen. God, these things are expensive. They can save your life, though. You have any serious allergies?

"Now we'll get into the serious stuff. Let's see. I don't think we'll need *this* many bandages. Metallic blanket for hypothermia. Bronchodilator. You have bronchial problems at altitude, and *whew*, that's trouble. Any blood pressure problems?" I assured him that I'd been working out like a madman, which was true. I'd found fear of failure and death to be excellent motivators.

Maria, the assistant office manager at Amazonas Explorer, approached carrying two oxygen tanks. Did we want the large one or the small one?

"Let's think about that for a second," John said, looking at me. "We'll take the . . . small one."

Juvenal Cobos entered the room, two hours late, shook hands all around and eased himself into a chair. He was seventy-four years old, a great-grandfather. He took one look at the pile of stuff on the floor and exhaled loudly. "We're going to need more mules," he said. Juvenal and John argued for about ten minutes in Spanish with Juvenal repeatedly hinting *ciertas cosas*—certain things—needed to be considered in the final price. John insisted that *teniamos un acuerdo*, we had an agreement. I finally figured out that they were haggling over the muleteers' daily wage. Juvenal was angling for an extra seventy cents a day per man.

"If it'll help keep the peace, I'm happy to pay the difference," I told John. "Four mules, five mules—let's just get off on the right foot."

"It's your money," John said. "I just want what's fair and reasonable."

Mule business settled, we walked over to the kitchen to meet Justo, our cook. The Quechua are a small people. Children in Aurita's extended family have long looked forward to the day that they stand taller than Nati, a rite of passage that in Alex's case occurred just after his tenth birthday. Skeletons that Bingham's team found showed that the average height for workers at Machu Picchu was about five feet, a measurement that hasn't budged over the five intervening centuries. But Justo was short even by Andean standards, about four feet six. He looked like an anime version of Ricardo Montalban, if the star of *Fantasy Island* had capped his front teeth with gold and been left in the clothes dryer on high heat for a couple of years. John called him "Hummingbird," because Justo was constantly in motion and talked nonstop.

"Nice to meet you Señor Mark nice to see you Señor John could you pass me that ketchup thank you do you like yogurt we've got yogurt have some tea."

"He averages about fifteen thousand words a day," John said as Justo fluttered around the kitchen opening and closing drawers and cabinets, his chatter never pausing. "I've counted."

ELEVEN

On the Road

Westbound on the Capac Ñan

J usto was still talking the next morning as he and I made the rounds at a market outside of Cusco, plotting to commit a Class B felony. As the paying client, I was obligated to provide the Peruvian team members with as much coca as they could chew. The bulging plastic sack that we purchased—roughly the dimensions of a family-size bag of Doritos—would earn me a mandatory five years to life in the States for possession with intent to distribute. In the highlands it was just the final item on the shopping list. Tea brewed with coca leaves is served everywhere in Peru—it's supposed to mitigate the symptoms of *soroche*, or altitude sickness. I'd sampled it on a few occasions without ever feeling the urge to dance the night away.

There were five of us in the Land Cruiser: John, me, Justo, Juvenal and Edgar, our driver. We followed the route of the old Capac Ñan, the great Inca highway. In the glory days of the Inca empire, which lasted less than a century, this system of roads was one of the marvels of the pre-Columbian world. Stretching more than ten thousand miles in length, the Royal Road, as the Spaniards dubbed it, was the nervous system of the empire.

Peru is diligent about protecting its most famous archaeological treasures. There's an entire branch of the government, the Instituto Nacional de Cultura, or INC, charged with overseeing the maintenance of places like Sacsahuaman. With the exception of the Inca Trail to Machu Picchu, though, the old Capac Ñan is disappearing beneath asphalt like the road we were driving on. The loss is doubly sad because the trails were built to last forever, over some of the most diverse terrain in the world. "The INC says that there are twenty miles of original Inca trails left in this area," John said from the backseat. I had assumed that there was only the one Inca Trail (capital *T*) in Peru, but as John explained, there were actually many Inca trails (small *t*) crisscrossing the former empire. "I know of at least a hundred and fifty miles' worth, some of which you're going to see. They're *fantastic*. Of course there'll be twenty miles left by the time the INC's done protecting them."

The road system is believed to be the work of the greatest Inca of all, Pachacutec. The name means "he who shakes the earth." If the Incas were the Romans of the Western Hemisphere, then Pachacutec was one part Julius Caesar and one part Romulus—a more or less historical figure who expanded a modest state near Cusco into Tawantinsuyu. Separating fact from fiction in Inca history is impossible, because virtually all the sources available are Spanish accounts of stories that had already been vetted by the Inca emperors to highlight their own heroic roles. Imagine a history of modern Iraq written by Dick Cheney and based on authorized biographies of Saddam Hussein published in Arabic, and you'll get some idea of the problem historians face.

Using Pachacutec's roads, fleet-footed messengers called *chasquis* could relay a message from Quito to Cusco—a thousand mountainous miles—in twelve days. For comparison's sake, that was about half the average speed of the Pony Express—though the *chasquis* were running through terrain more rugged than the Rockies (and a *lot* more rugged than Kansas). According to some accounts, the *chasquis* carried fish from the Pacific to Cusco, three hundred miles away, where it arrived fresh enough to serve to the Inca.

Near sundown, having left the asphalt behind hours earlier, the Land Cruiser bounced through the tiny town of Cachora. At the very end of the road, we pulled up at the farm of a fellow named Octavio. We'd expected to be met by one muleteer who would assist Juvenal.

We were greeted by two. Mateo was the older of the pair, about fifty. He wore unlaced rubber boots and a wool cap and had a profile that belonged on a medieval coin. Julián, who was in his late thirties, had youthful features that were not dimmed by his Boy Scout–style shirt and wispy beard. He was the special surprise guest, necessary because Juvenal had decided to provide us with six mules instead of the agreed-upon five. "Don't worry, don't worry, Julián will work just for tips," Juvenal said when John asked what was going on. This appeared to be news to Julián.

I asked John how I might help in setting up camp. He seemed to think it was a better idea for me to stay out of the muleteers' way. "These guys only have two speeds—absolute idleness and complete chaos," he told me. Our four-man team shifted into second gear as they got to work, pumping water, passing propane tanks and erecting the gigantic orange cook tent shaped like a circus big top, inside which Justo set to work peeling and chopping. Edgar climbed atop the Land Cruiser and threw my big bag to Juvenal, who caught it and ran up the hillside. Mateo and Julián set up tents for John and me. John crawled into his and spent about fifteen minutes dragging things around, grunting as if he were trying to subdue an intruder. I unrolled my virgin sleeping bag, stared at it for a moment, then stepped outside, uncertain what to do with myself. The view looking north was astonishing—a panorama of jagged peaks converging in the snowcapped Mount Padreyoc, nineteen thousand feet high. Two kids ran past down the dirt road, barefoot, pushing an old wheel with a stick.

A story in *The Economist* a few years back cited Peruvian cuisine as one of the world's finest. The secret ingredient—what butter is to classic French gastronomy—is corn oil. (When Nati makes *aji de gallina*, a rich, velvety chicken stew, a quart of Mazola vanishes into the pot, along with an entire loaf of de-crusted Wonder bread. My sister, a professional chef, says it may be the most delicious thing she has ever eaten.) Justo presented a homemade pumpkin soup, followed by beef cutlets in tomato sauce and bananas flambé. Rain had begun to fall and we dined by candlelight. Justo piled our plates high and appeared

with his steaming pot and ladle the moment we finished our first serving, asking, *"Más? Más?"*

"Better have seconds, Mark," John said. "Eat plenty of meat. The
last thing you want is to lose weight out there. Makes you weak."

John was a lifelong student of fitness, and for someone with such a
hearty appetite, he kept himself in amazing shape. When he'd taken
his shirt off that afternoon to wash I'd noticed that he had thickly
knotted arms and those ropes of muscle around his pelvic bones that
you see on Olympic swimmers.

"When I led trips across Asia and Africa, there'd always be one
person who insisted he was a vegetarian," John said, holding up a fork-
ful of beef. "We'd go to ten different shops to get all the amino acids
they need. Then a week later you'd see them sneaking meat. They
craved it."

"I guess the menu could get a little monotonous in the Sahara, huh?"

"You've probably read about chocolate as a substitute for sex. When
we'd get to Morocco some women would see a chocolate shop and
make me stop the truck. Remember, we've been driving for months.
Some of them ate chocolate until they vomited."

We stood up from the table Thanksgiving stuffed. It was only seven-
thirty, but complete darkness had descended. There really wasn't anything else to do but go to bed.

"Um, anything in particular I need to know about camping out in
Peru?" I asked, stifling a belch.

"I'd meant to ask you—when was the last time you slept in a tent?"

"It's been a little while," I admitted. "Maybe even longer than that."

Growing up in Illinois, I had skied on slopes with less incline than
the one we were camped on. John gave me some pointers about stuff-
ing things under my air mattress when trying to sleep on a hillside. "And roll up your fleece to use as a pillow," he said. I asked a few
awkward questions about where one might relieve oneself without
offending our host or his livestock, and we said good night. A few pages
of Bingham's *Across South America* put me out within minutes.

About 1 a.m. I awoke with a start, my arms pinned to my sides. I had rolled down into the corner of my tent. I untangled myself and stepped out into the blue light of an impossibly large full moon, bright enough to read by. Flickering around it like luminescent moths were things I hadn't seen since New York had experienced a power blackout years before—millions and millions of stars.

TWELVE

Off on the Wrong Foot

En Route to Choquequirao

"I t's important that you know a few things about traveling with mules, Mark."

It was about 6:30 A.M. and we were ready to depart. The day had gotten off to a bumpy start. Justo, deputized to wake us at 5:30, instead roused us at 4:15. Things could've been worse—when I checked his wristwatch, it was off by three and a half hours. John went through a quick equipment check after breakfast and was shocked to learn that I'd only brought a single water bottle. "That's all you've got for the hike to Choquequirao?" he asked. I offered to run the ten minutes back to Cachora to grab a few extras, but John dismissed the idea as an unnecessary waste of time and money. Juvenal must have guessed what we were talking about, because he walked over to Octavio's trash bin and plucked out three almost empty bottles of Inca Kola, the neon yellow, bubblegum-sweet soda that is Peru's national soft drink. John rinsed them out with iodine. These would meet my hydration needs until Machu Picchu. The muleteers didn't carry any water at all. To them, drinking water was a sign of weakness.

"Usually we have the right-of-way," John explained, pointing at one of the mules Mateo and Julián were loading up with Justo's conga drum–shaped food containers. "But if the mules do get in front, let them go because they're stupid and they do stupid things. Of course you know not to stand within"—here he spread his arms wide—"of a mule. I saw a kid a few weeks ago with a hole kicked in the side of his head. He'll probably get better because he's a kid. I've seen adults with dented skulls that are never going to heal."

We would need the better part of two days to reach Choquequirao. John said that we were a little less than six miles as the crow flies from the ruins, but we had more than twenty miles of ground to cover on foot. The map I consulted at breakfast made clear that this would be a very long and winding road; the trail zigzagged like it had been blazed with an oscilloscope. And that was just the horizontal part—the easy part.

"Today, we've got about five hundred feet up, then three quarters of a mile down to the river by lunchtime," John said as we waved good-bye to Octavio. "Then we'll cross the Apurimac River and start the climb to Choquequirao." That climb would be another vertical mile up. A Peruvian archaeologist with whom I'd lunched in Cusco, who had spent months working at Choquequirao, couldn't believe that I planned to walk there voluntarily. "You've got to hire a horse, Mark," he pleaded. "I can make some phone calls. It's not too late." Bingham had had a similar experience; at a dinner party the night before his departure from Cusco, a fellow guest told him that the walk had "nearly killed him."

John insisted that the hiking would get easier as we went on, because my body would adapt. "There's a general law in life," he said. "The body and mind only get stronger when they're traumatized."

It occurred to me, not for the last time, that this was probably not the sort of thing one heard a lot on the Inca Trail.

We quickly fell into what became our daily rhythm. We hiked for a couple hours, until we'd sweated through our shirts. Mid-morning, we stopped to consume some of the fifteen hundred calories' worth of snacks that Justo packed for us in brown paper bags each morning (mostly fruit, cookies and candy), then soldiered on until lunch. The muleteers stayed behind to finish packing up camp, then passed us on the trail around snack time. Justo usually led the mule parade, carrying a huge pack and a transistor radio, the tinny Andean tunes making him seem even more like a windup toy. Juvenal and Julián followed in succession. Mateo brought up the rear, yelling, "Moo-lah! Moo-lah! Moo-lah!" (He was saying "mule" in Spanish, but he sounded like the slightly unhinged TV pitchman for a state lottery.) By the time John and I caught up to them, Justo had lunch ready and a table set for two. Each of the four men greeted me differently. Justo called me Señor Mark, or Don Marco, the title "Don" in Peru being roughly equivalent to "Mister" in the old South. Mateo greeted me as Papi, or Pops. Juvenal, who had probably done a thousand of these trips in his life, just called me *usted*, the formal Spanish version of "you." Julián hid whenever he saw me.

Walking downhill was more complicated, and taxing, than I'd imagined. It takes a lot of energy to stop oneself from sliding down a dusty path littered with rocks the size and shape of marbles. I had to plant my foot and cut hard in the opposite direction at each switchback, like a ball carrier trying to slip past the free safety. The altimeter watch I'd purchased indicated that we were dropping a hundred feet with every turn. The dirt changed color as we descended, from brown to black to red. High sierra scrub gave way to dry, subtropical vegetation, dominated by Seussian cacti shaped like gigantic asparagus stalks. We passed ravines like the one Bingham had jumped across, spanned by packed-dirt bridges. Each one had a single wobbly handrail and a bilingual sign that warned NO SE APOYA/DO NOT LEAN. Most of the signs and railings had tumbled down the hillside.

The Peruvian tourist board has been pushing Choquequirao as "The Other Machu Picchu" for a few years. Part of their strategy is to divert some of the throngs who crowd the more famous ruins. I'd heard reports from a couple of adventure travel snobs that the path to Choquequirao had become "infested" by overflow crowds from Machu Picchu. On our two-day walk to the site, the only other people we saw were a pair of sisters marching to school in their matching uniforms, a farmer heading toward civilization with two mule loads of bananas and coffee beans (and who, recognizing Juvenal, handed him a letter and asked him to post it whenever he got to the next town), and a German guy whose head had been roasted fuchsia by the sun.

When we sat down for lunch, the temperature was ninety degrees in the shade. I'd guzzled a half gallon of water on the way down. We filled our bottles in the mornings with boiled water, so each warm sip contained doubly unhealthy echoes of plastic and Inca Kola. None of the mule team had drunk a drop, and they all looked queasy. Justo in particular wore the facial expression of a man who'd eaten some bad shellfish, and the others were having a laugh at his expense. John called everyone together and demanded that each man drink a bottle of water into which he mixed an electrolyte powder. The packets looked like something the Red Cross might hand out in Africa; their label said that the elixir had been formulated for babies suffering from cholera.

Even if my chances of running into anyone I knew on the trail to Choquequirao were pretty low, I was feeling a little self-conscious. Have you ever seen Mr. Travel Guy? He's the fellow who strides through international airports dressed like he's flying off to hunt wildebeests—shirt with dozens of pockets, drip-dry pants that zip off into shorts, floppy hat with a cord pulled tight under the chin in case a twister blows through the baggage claim area. All of this describes exactly what I was wearing. Between my microfiber bwana costume and the bags of candy that Justo kept foisting on me, I could have been trick-or-treating as Hemingway. John wore the same set of clothes every single day: a Bolivian park ranger shirt with one button missing; hand-me-down blue Adidas hiking pants that a film producer from Munich had given him years ago; and a pair of Merrell boots that looked like they'd turned up after a sandstorm in the Sahara. No matter the weather, the only flesh he exposed was his face, beneath the wide brim of his bush hat, and the tips of his fingers, which protruded from gloves cut off at the second knuckle.

My own boots were the only part of my ensemble that I knew wasn't ridiculous. I'd spent a month picking out the perfect pair for this trip—I e-mailed *Adventure*'s equipment guru so many times that he finally stopped responding—and walked around in them for two weeks before departing for Cusco. Unfortunately, amid all my research, I hadn't come across the Wear Two Pairs of Socks Rule. This is evidently one of those dictums like "Don't Keep a Moody Two-Hundred-Pound Male Chimpanzee in Your Home," a principle that seems so obvious that no one bothers to mention it until something has gone horribly wrong.

"You wore *one* pair of socks on the walk down from Cachora?" John asked, when I mentioned that my feet had begun to hurt. "Well, *that's* your problem."

When I pulled off my boots at camp late that afternoon, John was flabbergasted. The big toes on each foot were swollen on two sides. The middle toes were rubbed raw. My little toes looked like the sort of meat that ends up in hot dogs. Each had a chickpea-sized blister that, when punctured, squirted like a Super Soaker.

"These the first blisters of your life, Mark?" John asked as he sterilized a needle with iodine.

"Don't be ridiculous," I said. "Trust me, I've had much worse than these." This was true, though I declined to mention that the cause of my previous torment had been a tight pair of patent leather shoes that I'd worn with a tuxedo to the FiFi Awards—which are, of course, the Oscars of the fragrance industry—several years earlier while working at a men's fashion magazine.

For the next two weeks, I wrapped my six aching toes in electrical tape each morning, which gave them the look of piano keys. Then I slathered them with Vaseline and pulled on the only two pairs of thin socks that I'd brought. "You'll want to splay your feet when walking downhill, to ease the pressure on your toes," John told me. Now I was Mr. Travel Guy Who Walks Like a Duck.

Because Bingham has been accused of exaggerating the details of his expeditions, I'd been a little suspicious when I read his description of the climb from the Apurimac to Choquequirao. "At times the trail was so steep that it was easier to go on all fours than to attempt to maintain an erect attitude," he'd written. That one checked out.

"Occasionally we crossed streams in front of waterfalls on slippery logs or treacherous little foot bridges." Ditto. He recalled having to stop and rest approximately every thirty feet. I would have gladly taken that option had I not been so fixated on keeping up with John's slow-but-steady pace. During one rest stop, he caught me pressing my fingers against my neck, checking my pulse.

"What's your heart rate, Mark?"

"About . . . one thirty," I said, subtracting ten beats.

"You're *joking*."

"Why? What's yours?"

He touched his wrist. "About eighty."

Probably the nicest thing I can say about the second day's walk is that because it was the exact opposite of downhill, my toes were spared further damage. That's all I can remember because every time I opened my notebook to jot something down, so much sweat dripped off the end of my nose that it blotted out whatever I'd written. (There has been talk of building a cable-car track up the far side of the Apurimac valley, to facilitate tourism at Choquequirao. I wish them the best of luck.) With each view backward, I saw the roaring river shrink farther until it was a slim white ribbon.

At the top of the ridge, the ground flattened out enough for some enterprising family to have carved out a tiny farm. Here, the mule team stopped to order some *chicha*, the sour home-brewed corn beer of the Andes. A bowlegged señora waddled out of the house, outfitted in the customary attire of the mountains: stovepipe Stetson, billowing skirt and a hand-made cardigan woven in colors that could stun a deer. She carried a plastic pitcher with a creamy-looking liquid in it. Before anyone could take the first sip, Justo grabbed the vessel and poured out a dribble onto the ground, "for the Pachamama!"—a salute to the Earth Mother.

I declined Justo's offer of a swig and showed my respect for the Pachamama by lying down in the dirt and embracing her with every traumatized cell in my body.

THIRTEEN

Cradle of Gold

At Choquequirao

A t the start of the twentieth century, the relatively new science of archaeology had men pondering the ancient wonders that might lie in the earth beneath their feet. No archaeological discovery was more romantic—or more likely to grab the public's attention—than a lost city. The unearthing of Troy in 1868 and Knossos in 1900 had been inspired by ancient Greek tales. At the moment Bingham staggered into the abandoned citadel of Choquequirao, excavations were under way at the Mayan site of Chichen Itza and in Egypt's Valley of the Kings that were expected to reveal some of the greatest treasures of antiquity. A front-page story published in *The New York Times* in January 1911, six months before Bingham arrived at Machu Picchu, reflects the mania for vanished civilizations: GERMAN DISCOVERS ATLANTIS IN AFRICA.

The few explorers who had the fortitude to reach Choquequirao during the nineteenth century were driven less by dreams of finding what had come to be known as the Lost City of the Incas than they were by a desire to cash in on a potential mountaintop El Dorado—the legendary city of gold that the conquistadors had sought in vain. The Frenchman Léonce Angrand described hearing that "immense treasures were buried among the ruins when the last survivors of the race of the sun retired to this savage asylum." J. J. Nuñez, the prefect who had pleaded with Bingham to visit the site, was hunting the treasure assumed to be hiding in the "cradle of gold," buried beneath the vegetation high above the Apurimac River. The idea that ancient ruins constituted part of Peru's proud *patrimonio*, or heritage, was still a few years off. When Bingham arrived, Nuñez's men were setting off dynamite charges, blasting Inca buildings in search of hidden Inca loot.

One of Bingham's great strengths as a historian was compiling evidence. At Choquequirao he closely followed the protocol laid out in the Royal Geographical Society's handbook *Hints to Travellers*, which served as a sort of *Exploring for Dummies* for two generations of novice globe-trotters. ("In one of the chapters I found out what should be done when one is confronted by a prehistoric site," Bingham wrote. "Take careful measurements and plenty of photographs and describe as accurately as possible all finds.") His four busy days on the hillside above the Apurimac were a dress rehearsal for the discoveries he would make at Machu Picchu two years later. Bingham was also honing his skills as a self-promoter. Within days of his departure from Choquequirao, a short notice appeared in *The New York Tribune*: "Professor Hiram Bingham, of Yale University, who is in Southern Peru on a trip of historical research, writes that he has made discoveries of Inca remains near Abancay of the greatest importance."

What Bingham couldn't have known at the time he arrived was how much Choquequirao resembles Machu Picchu. Like its cousin, Choquequirao is built on a ridge far above a sacred river, with extraordinary mountain views in almost all directions. It was situated to look out onto three skyscraping peaks—important *apus*, or mountain gods, in Inca cosmology—much like the sacred summits visible from Machu Picchu. Both sites have distinct upper and lower levels, were built around a central plaza and were designed with an elevated viewing platform at one end. Both are surrounded by stone-walled terraces that served as places to plant crops and as engineering supports to buttress a precarious building site. Neither one was, or is, especially easy to get to. And each seems to fuse almost seamlessly with its rocky location, hammered onto its mountaintop like a crown on a cracked molar.

At both sites, the nice views were important for aesthetic and religious reasons. The Incas were pantheists who worshipped nature, and the sun god, Inti, was near the top of the divine pecking order. The Sapa Inca's right to rule over his theocracy, of course, stemmed from his putative status as the son of the sun. The benevolent Pachamama was (and still is) revered as the goddess of fertility. The largest *apus* were believed to possess various powers and, in some cases, individual personalities. An Inca priest would have had no shortage of *apus* to choose from at Choquequirao.

"It's said that the Spaniards never found Machu Picchu, but I disagree," John said as we looked up at the ruins. "It's *this* place that they never found. The cloud forest here"—thick, misty, high-altitude foliage—"grows over in about three years and can get up to forty feet high." Indeed, what had looked from afar like grassy, rolling hills fit for a picnic were actually steep slopes crammed with lush, jungly vegetation. Some archaeologists think Choquequirao may be larger than Machu Picchu, though we won't be sure for a while, since only 20 to 30 percent of Choquequirao has been uncovered. "When this is all cleared, it'll be one of the most spectacular archaeological sites in the world," John said.

As is, it's pretty impressive. The masonry at Choquequirao is not as jaw-dropping as at some Inca sites; the softer stone available in the area required the use of clay as mortar, so the igloo-like precision of the buildings at Cusco and Machu Picchu was impossible to replicate. As an example of location scouting and landscape architecture, though, Choquequirao is a masterpiece. I spent a few hours hobbling up and down the site behind John. Twice, we made the long hike up to the giant hilltop *usnu* platform that marks the western edge of Choquequirao. *Usnus* were used to conduct religious rituals. They were also a special interest of John's. We were followed to this one by a stray puppy that either had a bad paw or was doing a pretty good impression of my Chaplinesque walk.

"Notice how the *usnu* bisects those two peaks," John said as he paced back and forth, GPS in hand, taking measurements. "Right down the middle, that's the winter solstice line." This particular *usnu* was also famous as the spot where former first lady Eliane Karp-Toledo's helicopter landed on her visits to the site, which was a pet project of hers. (Though her husband was out of office and she had moved on to teach at Stanford, Karp-Toledo was still a favorite subject of wild rumors in Peru. One I heard repeatedly at Choquequirao was that she and "the French" were plotting to build a five-star hotel there.) There were perhaps five other visitors at the site, and guests were outnumbered at least two-to-one by the eager young workers from the INC.

John had something of a love-hate relationship with the INC. In Cusco, he had ranted about how they politicized everything, lost important artifacts and allowed developers to destroy Inca ruins in the name of progress. By stringing together John's various complaints, I was able to deduce that he had offered to share his research with the INC on more than one occasion, and that these offers had not been appreciated—or worse, hadn't been acknowledged. At Choquequirao, he griped about how the INC had clumsily reconstructed some buildings. He had a point. While Inca engineers were far ahead of the rest of the world in many respects, it is safe to assume that they did not install the poured-concrete lintels that now held up a few doorways. In the most recently rebuilt section of the site, the stonework bore a striking resemblance to my grandmother's flagstone fireplace.

Still, each of the dozen or so times I saw John interact with an INC employee out in the field, the same thing happened. The INC worker would approach asking to check our ticket stubs, and within five minutes was asking John questions and staring at his photos, which he kept in a small plastic album with Snoopy on the cover. Inside were pictures of some of the wonders John had seen during his years of rambling: pre-Inca settlements, lost trails, sacred rock formations. He'd stashed several boxes of his little blue notebooks, each crammed with firsthand observations, measurements and GPS readings, along with more than one hundred thousand photographs and four hundred hours of videotape in a storage room he rented outside of Cusco. (He kept the rest of his collection at his mum's house in Australia.) John had read virtually everything that had been published on the Incas and had formulated his own theories, seasoned with years of firsthand observations. These he freely shared.

"Don't you ever worry that someone's going to steal your ideas?" I asked him.

"I only do it so that maybe they'll do something to save these Inca sites."

Word about John tended to spread quickly. Which is why, on our second day at Choquequirao, we were visited in our cook tent by Julio, the assistant chief archaeologist at the site. "Would you care to join me on a visit to the llamas?" he asked.

The llama is the unofficial mascot of Peru, a camel-like fuzzball with a reputation for spitting and kicking. For the Incas, llamas were a one-stop shop, a source of wool as well as pack animals that could easily negotiate the vertical Andean terrain. Their dung was burned as fuel, and they were sacrificed in religious ceremonies. By one estimate, 95 percent of the meat consumed at Machu Picchu came from llamas or their close relative, the alpaca. All of which explains why llamas are a common theme in Inca artifacts. But no homage can equal the one found at Choquequirao in 2005. On the far side of the mountain ridge on which the ruins sit are row after row of agricultural terraces, staircasing hundreds of feet down toward the Yanama River like the side of a Babylonian ziggurat. Bricked into their gray stone faces are huge decorative mosaics of more than two dozen white llamas, most taller than a man. No one knows if more are hiding; the terraces are nowhere close to being fully excavated. I'd always assumed that nothing worth discovering remained hidden on the face of the earth. The llamas changed my mind.

"See how all the llamas face north," Julio pointed out as we walked down the hundreds of stairs that led to the terraces and out to a viewing platform that appeared to have been constructed from very old popsicle sticks. "We think that signifies the Inca conquest of the Antisuyu, the jungle."

"I'm not so sure about that," John mumbled to me. John believed that Inca sites like Choquequirao and Machu Picchu weren't so much separate entities as parts of a vast Inca network. To illustrate his point, he dragged me and my aching feet up to a viewing spot at the very top of the ruins, at the crest of the ridge. As I sat down on a rock to rest, I instantly recognized it as the place where Bingham had experienced an epiphany in 1909. The view seemed to take in all of creation— mountains and glaciers and rivers and deep green valleys branching off forever to the distant horizon. It was the most beautiful thing I had ever seen.

"That's big, big country out there," John said, pointing his bamboo walking stick like a field marshal. "Very few people have ever set foot on most of those peaks. But do you see how it's all interconnected? This *usnu* links up with that trail. You've got *apus* there, and there, and there. Rivers below on both sides." He seemed to be explaining why the Incas had chosen this impractical spot to build on, but all I saw was the postcard panorama.

Bingham had been equally enchanted by what he saw from this spot. "The whole range of the White Mountains or the Great Smokies of Tennessee and North Carolina could have been placed on the floor of this great valley and not come much more that halfway to the top," he wrote in *Lost City of the Incas*. Looking into the immensity before him, Bingham was reminded of the most famous lines from Rudyard Kipling's poem "The Explorer":

> *Something hidden. Go and find it.*
> *Go and look behind the Ranges—*
> *Something lost behind the Ranges.*
> *Lost and waiting for you. Go!*

FOURTEEN

Kicking and Screaming

At Choquequirao, continued

U sually, when we arrived at camp at day's end, Justo greeted us in his ankle-length apron with a shout: *"Los aventure-ros!"* This time, he was pacing back and forth outside the cook tent with his hands behind his back.

"Tenemos un pequeño problema," he said. We had a little problem. "Julián was kicked by a mule."

Juvenal, who'd witnessed his share of such injuries over the years, said he'd had a look at Julián's knee and didn't like what he saw. John and I walked over to where Julián was sprawled out on the grass flat on his back. His face was the color of pea soup. He tried to roll his pant leg up for us to see what had happened, but his knee was swollen to the size of a cantaloupe and he couldn't raise his ragged cuff over the hump. His lower leg was shiny and black from the patella down; he looked like he had frostbite of the shin.

An hour later, John weighed our options over dinner. "That knee looks bad," he said. "I'm worried that Julián will try to prove how tough he is by walking all the way to Huancacalle and end up with permanent damage."

A female voice rang out of the dark. *"Tranquilo!* I am doctor!"

While John and I had gone off to have a glacial meltwater shower (the water so cold that every person who stepped under the spray screamed in shock—"GAHHH!"—and then moaned—

"huhuhuhuhuh"—through chattering teeth), Juvenal had canvassed the campsite and found Ana, a doctor visiting from Barcelona. She and John held a brief conversation in which Ana insisted on speaking imperfect English and he insisted on responding in imperfect Spanish. She went off to have a look at Julián's knee.

Ten minutes later she returned. "I give the man the treatment. I think he will be having the recovery but he cannot walk on that leg, or he may be losing it. This is very, very important. I will return for the morning to see how goes the curing."

I couldn't sleep much that night. When morning came, I dragged myself into the cook tent around four-thirty. Juvenal and Justo were already up (they kept country hours and usually rose before four), jabbering in Quechua. My Spanish wasn't great, but after ten years of on-and-off Spanish lessons, I could more or less make myself understood. Quechua, however, is a guttural tongue, like Russian, and sounded completely alien to my ears. (How alien? The makers of *Star Wars* chose Quechua when they needed a language for Greedo, the character who speaks gobbledygook before Han Solo blasts him in the cantina.) Quechua relies heavily on a "K" sound that bears more resemblance to the sound of a cracking walnut than to any English or Spanish consonant, which is one reason why place names in the Andes have so many spellings. Choquequirao also goes by Chokekiraw and a half dozen other variants; Cusco (formerly Cuzco) may soon be known officially as Q'osqo.

Justo placed a red plastic mug in front of me and handed me the can of Nescafé powder. "*Buenos días*, Señor Mark. You don't look like you slept well. Of course nobody did, because of Mateo's snoring."

"The *avioneta*," Juvenal said, rubbing his temples. The little airplane. The four men slept together in the cook tent at night, on top of sheepskins.

I was going to explain that the chickens wandering the campsite and the occasional bloodcurdling scream from the showers had been more of a problem, but before I could speak, a homeless dog stuck its nose into the tent and Justo changed the subject.

"Did you know that they eat dogs in Lima, Señor Mark?" He leaned out of the tent to toss some fruit peelings to the beggar and, without pausing to inhale, continued, "I never learned to read. Never got around to it. There was a Swiss lady once, she promised to teach me, but she went away and never came back. How about granola for breakfast?"

Shortly after sunrise, Doctor Ana came by to look at Julián's leg. "I used a combination of the traditional and the modern therapies," she said, unwrapping his bandages. A minty smell rose from his knee. She had enveloped his wounded leg in coca leaves and Flexall cream. The swelling had completely vanished. Julián stood up and limped over to the cook tent, where Justo poured him his usual bowl of morning coffee, which he took with twelve spoonfuls of sugar.

"But what about all the black stuff below Julián's knee?" I asked Justo. "Can he really walk on that?"

"That black stripe? That's a scar from when he was a kid. Probably played too close to a fire. I've got six kids of my own, all healthy, all working good jobs, thanks be to God." He folded his hands, raised his eyes to heaven and picked up his knife. "Señor Mark, did you know that on the Inca Trail, Brazilian women just strip naked wherever they want?"

FIFTEEN

A Deal with the Devil

New Haven, CT, and Cajamarca, Peru

When Bingham returned to Yale, he had already decided that contrary to what anyone in Peru thought, Choquequirao was not the last refuge of the Incas. Even if they blew the place sky-high with dynamite, no one was ever going to find treasure on its grounds. The notion of the Incas escaping to a final refuge intrigued him, though. And the more hours he spent in the university library researching the final days of the Inca empire, the more convinced he became that their lost city really did exist—except that it was called Vilcabamba.

As for where one might start searching for Vilcabamba, Bingham thought back to the vast land "behind the Ranges" that he'd seen while looking north from the top of Choquequirao. "The clouds would occasionally break away and give us tantalizing glimpses of snow-covered mountains," he recalled. "There seemed to be an unknown region . . . which might contain great possibilities. Our guides could tell us nothing about it. Little was to be found in books." Perhaps the mysterious Inca capital "was hidden there."

Before 1532, the thought that Inca royalty could be chased into hiding would have been unfathomable. In one of history's little scheduling ironies, the earth-shaking Pachacutec's grandson Huayna Capac took charge of the empire at almost the same moment Christopher Columbus landed at what is now the Bahamas aboard the Santa Maria.

(Colonialism fun fact: after Columbus returned home to report his discovery, Pope Alexander VI briefly set aside fathering children with his various mistresses to issue a papal bull dividing the New World between Spain and Portugal—which is one reason that most South Americans speak Spanish, but Brazilians speak Portuguese.) By 1513, Vasco Núñez de Balboa was crossing the Panamanian isthmus in search of gold when he spotted whitecaps instead, thus becoming famous as the first European to see the Pacific Ocean. Six years later, Hernán Cortés landed on the east coast of what is now Mexico. Within two years he had subdued the Aztec empire and its king, Montezuma, making himself impossibly rich in the process.

Francisco Pizarro had served as a senior officer on Balboa's expedition, a role that would have allowed a less ambitious man to live comfortably ever after in Panama as a landowner. Pizarro was illiterate and a bastard (in the genealogical sense, though he was no dream date as far as the Incas were concerned, either), a man who burned to overcome his humble beginnings. Like his ruthless role models Balboa and Cortés, he was a product of the Iberian peninsula's Extremadura province, a harsh land that produced some of the Age of Discovery's toughest explorers. After a 1522 expedition returned from what is now the southern coast of Colombia, a land believed to be called Birú (or Virú or Pirú), with reports of great riches, Pizarro formed a syndicate with two other men to explore the area. First and foremost they were entrepreneurs. Their business plan was to find the land of Birú—soon to be altered to Perú—and suck out its riches, just as Balboa and Cortés had done in Mexico.

A first expedition failed miserably, but two later voyages turned up hints of an advanced civilization. In 1528, Pizarro landed at Tumbez in the northernmost part of Peru. He was greeted warmly at this impressive settlement by an Inca magistrate, who was as fascinated by the odd visitors' chickens, pigs and shiny armor as the Spaniard was taken by the exquisite pottery, woven goods, and gold and silver objects that the Incas possessed. Pizarro returned to Spain and received permission to conquer this promising new land in the name of the crown.

Pizarro sailed into Tumbez again in 1532. The city that he had visited a few years prior now lay in ruins. The cause of the destruction was a civil war that had broken out when the reigning Inca, Pachacutec's grandson Huayna Capac, had died unexpectedly of a disease, possibly smallpox, introduced to the New World by early Spanish explorers, that had swept through the kingdom. His son Huascar, who had a reputation as a playboy, assumed the title of Inca in Cusco. The Incas did not have a tradition of easy successions, however; a new emperor's right to rule was often challenged by one or more of his brothers. In this instance the fierce Atahualpa, who led the empire's strongest armies from a base in modern-day Ecuador, declared war on his half brother Huascar. A brutal campaign dragged on for a few years, decimating the empire and culminating in the capture of Huascar just days before Pizarro's group of 168 Spaniards arrived at the Inca city of Cajamarca. There, Atahualpa was camped with his battle-hardened army of at least forty thousand soldiers.

Pizarro had learned from the capture of Montezuma in Mexico that seizing the emperor would put him in a very advantageous bargaining position. To the Incas, Atahualpa was a god, the divine son of the sun. Though the Spaniards were grossly outnumbered, Pizarro did have a huge technological edge. His men had brought horses (which the Incas had never seen), harquebuses (an early form of long-barreled firearm more useful for noisy intimidation than sharpshooting) and, most importantly, swords forged from Toledo steel. The most feared army on the South American continent fought primarily with slingshots and clubs, literally using sticks and stones to break foes' bones.

Thanks to his *chasqui* messengers, Atahualpa had known the Spaniards were approaching almost from the moment they landed on his coast. Preoccupied with having finally triumphed over his brother, the Inca had failed to recognize the bearded strangers as a serious threat. He'd already made plans for his guests, he said, to "take and breed their horses" and "sacrifice some of the Spaniards to the sun and castrate others for service in his household and in guarding his women."

Seated in the golden litter that carried him everywhere, Atahualpa arrived in the town square at Cajamarca for a meeting with Pizarro. Atahualpa's thousands of attendants were unarmed. The Spaniards fired four cannons and launched a surprise attack. In the violence that followed, Pizarro pulled Atahualpa from his gilded chair and took him hostage. Hundreds, possibly thousands, of Incas were slaughtered like sheep, Atahualpa's nephew later said. The Spaniards suffered no losses.

Atahualpa quickly figured out what the Spaniards wanted and made Pizarro one of the most extraordinary offers in history. In return for his freedom, the Inca told his captor, he would fill a twenty-two-by-seventeen-foot room with treasure three times to a height of more than eight feet—once with gold and twice again with silver. When word of Atahualpa's deal with Pizarro went out to his subjects, precious metals poured in from all over the kingdom. The capital of Cusco and the sacred Koricancha were stripped of their gold ornamentation. More than six tons of twenty-two-and-a-half-carat gold were melted down over the following months. Double that amount of silver was shipped out of Peru during that time.

To show his thanks, Pizarro reneged on his promise and ordered Atahualpa garroted in the Cajamarca town square. When the new ruler of Peru rode his horse into the royal city of Cusco for the first time, he took for himself the finest palace. It's now a restaurant loathed by John Leivers because it sells five-dollar bowls of chicken soup.

Bingham wasn't especially interested in the story of Pizarro and Atahualpa, which had been told many times before, most famously in William Prescott's *History of the Conquest of Peru*. Much more interesting to the explorer was the puppet ruler whom Pizarro installed to help keep peace with the natives.

When Pizarro arrived in Peru, Manco Inca Yupanqui was just shy of twenty years old, the kid brother of Atahualpa and Huascar. (One of the many job benefits of being Sapa Inca was the right to take as many wives, and father as many children, as one wished.) Today, perhaps because Machu Picchu is so popular among the spiritually inclined, the Incas are sometimes portrayed as a peaceful race who graciously invited neighboring tribes to join their thriving territorial conglomerate. In reality, they could be as brutal as the conquistadors. Atahualpa in particular was not someone who'd make a good long-term house-guest. He often drank from a ceremonial cup crafted from the skull of a former enemy, and he ordered his army to find and slaughter the male members of his family who had opposed him in the civil war. Atahualpa's men had been searching for Manco. Had he been found, he surely would have been killed in some unpleasant fashion.

Francisco Pizarro named Manco the new Sapa Inca in 1533. The traditional boozy monthlong coronation ceremony in Cusco followed, at which the mummies of previous emperors were paraded around the square. Deceased Sapa Incas were not only treated as immortals; their mummies continued to live in their palaces with all of their worldly goods and a large staff of servants and advisors, who channeled the wishes of the former emperors when their advice was sought. So much *chicha* was guzzled during Manco's investiture, one witness recorded, that the drains of the city "ran with urine throughout the day . . . as abundantly as if they were flowing springs." Imagine a presidential inauguration held during Mardi Gras, at which the taxidermied re-mains of Thomas Jefferson and Dwight Eisenhower were incorpo-rated into float themes, and you'll get some idea of the horrified reaction the Spaniards had to this spectacle.

The good times rolled only briefly for Manco. The Spaniards who occupied Cusco—including Francisco Pizarro's three younger brothers—treated his home like an ATM and demanded continuously that he bring them more treasure. The most hotheaded of the Pizar-ros, Gonzalo, seized Manco's favorite wife, who also happened to be his half sister. (Like bigamy, incest wasn't frowned upon by the Incas.) Spies overheard Manco giving a fiery speech at a secret meeting of Inca elders, and when he was caught trying to leave Cusco, he was chained around the neck and feet, struck repeatedly in the face and used as a urinal by his captors. Shortly thereafter, Manco convinced another Pizarro brother that if the Spaniard would just let him loose for a few days, he would bring back a life-sized gold statue of his father as a token of his gratitude. Instead, Manco was about to take command of a massive native army that had quietly assembled in the hills surrounding the city.

The following months would see some of the most extraordinary battles in South American history. Manco's army set Cusco afire, driving the occupying Spanish forces into just two buildings, which miraculously refused to burn. The Incas took control of Sacsahuaman, but were driven out by a daring Spanish attack. Bingham dispensed with all of this in his best-known book, *Lost City of the Incas*, in a single sentence, catapulting the story forward to the point where it attracted his interest: "In 1536, after several bloody encounters, Manco's troops were routed and fled with him from the vicinity of Cusco down into the Urubamba Valley." The Urubamba Valley was exactly where Bingham was headed next.

SIXTEEN

Distress Signals

Somewhere in the Andes

"We've got quite a walk today," John told me at breakfast. To limber up we'd ascend about fifteen hundred feet just to cross the ridge on which Choquequirao sits, then plunge five thousand feet to the Yanama River for lunch, then up another four thousand feet to our campsite at the farm of a man named Valentin. It was like walking to the top of the Empire State Building and back four times in one day. The big payoff for our day's effort was that we'd get to sleep in a barnyard. I had always assumed, based on Saturday morning cartoons, that roosters crowed at sunrise. I had learned from the birds strutting around the campsites at Octavio's farm and Choquequirao that roosters were perfectly happy to belt one out at midnight, 3 A.M.—whenever the hell they felt like it. To make matters worse, Justo informed us, we would have to pass a man-eating devil goat that guarded the entrance to Valentin's farm like a ruminant Cerberus.

"He's got giant horns like Satan!" Justo explained as he poured a quarter inch of corn oil into his skillet to scramble four eggs. "He'll eat us alive! He's already killed three men!"

"Who told you all this?" John asked.

"Don Juvenal! He's seen it with his own eyes!"

"I thought so," John said to me, stirring his tea. "For whatever reason, Juvenal doesn't want to camp at Valentin's house. Must be bad blood between them. Of course it'd be far too easy to just come out and say it."

Outside the tent, Juvenal and Mateo were securing our bags to the mules with rawhide nets that looked like they'd been left over from one of Bingham's expeditions. If Juvenal was the general, Mateo was his chief of staff. Juvenal checked and double-checked everything like an airplane mechanic, then wordlessly signaled to Mateo to go over everything one more time. Bearing loads is serious business in the Andes. According to the fascinating book *The Languages of the Andes*, Quechua includes a vast number of words to denote the act "to carry." Distinct verbs have evolved to express carrying in the arms, holding in the lap, carrying with both hands, carrying on the back, holding in the mouth, carrying in a skirt, carrying among four people and so on. When he finished his inspection, Mateo adjusted his wool cap, smacked the lead mule on the haunches with a stick and yelled, *"Vamanos!"*

Julián's knee seemed to have almost completely healed. He was the quietest of the group, possibly because he was obviously the poorest. His clothes were dirty and torn, and his sandaled feet were coated in a thick layer of grime. Anytime I tried talk to him, he winced and mumbled, *"bien, bien,"* and hurried away. Today, Justo had told me, Julián's teeth were bothering him, so he employed an old Andean folk remedy of gargling with his own urine.

"Studies have shown that it actually works," John said.

He wasn't joking. John wasn't much for irony, I'd learned. Nor did he have more than the most tangential grasp of popular culture. Combined with my lack of knowledge about archaeology, rugby and mountaineering techniques, this rather limited our topics of conversation on the trail. At times, even the different dialects of American English and Australian English caused confusion. An hour or so out of camp, John paused and unslung his daypack.

"I'm going to take a wee break here," he said. I plopped down next to him and cracked open a bottle of water, delighted that John was already feeling tired, too.

"Do you mind if I wee in privacy?" he said, reaching for his fly.

Desperate for something to talk about during our twelve or more hours spent each day in each other's company—including three face-to-face meals—I flipped through my mental Rolodex for topics before hitting on the canon of adventure literature. But even here we seemed to speak two different languages. I'd read stacks of entertaining man-versus-wild tales for my work; John read them like instruction manuals. My favorites were classics like *Wind, Sand and Stars*, a dreamy existential memoir of piloting an open-cockpit plane over deserts and mountains, written by the author of *The Little Prince*. John was partial to books such as *The Long Walk*, in which an escapee from a Soviet prison camp wanders from Siberia to India, scavenging food and facing down death as he crosses the Gobi Desert and the Himalayas.

"When I was driving across Africa, I was always calculating—time, water, diesel, daylight," he told me at one snack break. "I knew that if something went wrong I had to fix it or I'd die. You always have to be ready for a survival situation. Always have your headlamp. Your poncho for shelter. A little bit of food and water."

Sometimes, to keep the conversational ball rolling, I slipped into reporter mode and asked rhetorical follow-up questions. John tended to stop, plant his bamboo pole, turn to look at me and then pause for about fifteen seconds, as if my query was so inane that he couldn't walk and formulate a response to it at the same time. Eventually, he'd say, "Actually . . . no." Then he'd wait a few more uncomfortable seconds before answering.

"If you ran out of food, couldn't you survive out here on edible plants?" I asked. I was fairly certain that I'd read something about this in one of the many "How to Survive Anything" stories I'd read. One thousand one, one thousand two . . .

"Actually . . . no. Survival is a matter of self-discipline, Mark. There was a girl in a plane crash a few years ago, in the Amazon. She had lived in the jungle with her family, so she *knew*—you *always* follow the water and you *never* eat anything. And if you *have* to eat something, put a little on your arm and wait a couple hours for a reaction. If nothing happens, put some on your lips. Only then can you try to eat a tiny bit."

"What about drinking water?"

"I learned a little survival trick when I was mountain climbing with some Russians. If you have no clean water, take some dirty water and filter out all the bits with one of your socks. Leave the bottle out in the sun for six hours, and the UV rays will kill all the bugs. I've used that one a couple of times."

Everywhere we walked in the mountains of Peru, we were surrounded by cold, running water—rivers and streams and springs and cascades. Almost none of it was safe to drink, thanks to the habit of livestock at all altitudes to use these picturesque sources as latrines. As we made the final climb to Valentin's farm, I could feel some serious intestinal discomfort building, presumably a case of Atahualpa's revenge. Every traveler to Cusco is warned not to drink the tap water or eat uncooked vegetables, and John, who had suffered from epic stomach troubles due to his travels, had even stricter regulations. *"Always* make sure you wash after shaking hands with Mateo," he had told me sternly.

When the sun goes down in the Andes, the temperature plummets. Afternoon was just sliding into evening when we arrived, soaked with sweat, at Valentin's farm in the clouds. Valentin's wife and daughter invited John and me to dry off inside their toasty home. *"Mi papá no está,"* the daughter explained—Valentin was away, working. The daughter served us each a gigantic tin mug of fresh-brewed *café con canchitas,* strong, sweet black coffee with roasted corn kernels floating on top. The house was built with mud-brick adobe and was a marvel of compactness and efficiency. It had two rooms, each about eight by ten. There were niches in the walls for storage, like those the Incas built into their walls to display idols.

"There's where you store your food," John said, pointing over our heads. Removable bamboo ceiling panels allowed access to the space beneath the straw roof, which had been waterproofed by grease from the cooking fire. Guinea pigs—*cuys*—scurried about underfoot, eating any scraps that fell to the ground. ("Had I not been very hungry, I might never have known how delicious a roast guinea pig can be," Bingham wrote of his introduction to this Andean delicacy. "The meat is not unlike squab.") A cat curled up next to the wood fire, in what was evidently its regular spot. We sat in the warmth of the orange glow, smiling at Valentin's wife, who spoke only Quechua. She sat at the doorway with stick in hand, swatting at chickens that tried to enter every couple of minutes.

On our way back out into the chilly night, we crossed paths with the killer devil goat, who was about the size of a Labrador. Juvenal was guilty of exaggerating, not lying. "Give him a wide berth," Valentin's daughter explained. "He's a little aggressive around strangers."

The coffee, unfortunately, had its usual peristaltic effects, and the contents of my abdomen churned like an industrial mixer from the moment I lay down. After staring at the ceiling of my tent for hours, I went out around midnight, opened the wooden gate that I had been told led to the designated zone for doing one's business, and tiptoed along a mountainside trail in the dark. My headlamp revealed no discernible hole in the ground, so I finally dropped my pants and unburdened myself in what seemed to be an inconspicuous nook in the rock face. Directly in front of me was a one-thousand-foot drop. Miles off in the distance, the lights of the nearest town with electric power twinkled proudly like fireflies beneath the cloudless sky. It was a lovely view, and I was to appreciate it several times before dawn.

At daybreak, it became obvious that I had been squatting not in some hidden crevice, but in the exact middle of the only trail that led north out of the farm—the direction in which we were departing after breakfast. Had I employed a compass and sextant, I doubt I could have calculated a more conspicuous spot. Small fistfuls of blindingly white toilet paper that I had tossed, imagining them drifting into the chasm, were arranged festively in the branches of a bush.

Over breakfast tea—it seemed a good day to pass on the coffee—I told John about my trouble. He was immediately interested. He thought my problem was probably giardia that I'd picked up in Cusco.

John had once suffered from a super strain of the parasite, and the episode appeared to have scarred him. "It's *highly* contagious. Have your family tested when you get home." He pulled out the medical kit and began removing various packets of pills.

It was nice to have something in common.

When we said good-bye at the wooden gate and settled the bill for camping, I slipped Valentin's daughter an extra couple dollars and thanked her profusely for her warm hospitality. When she turned her back, I ran away.

SEVENTEEN

No Small Plans

New Haven

The Mitchells built a thirty-room Mediterranean-style mansion for their daughter on New Haven's tony Prospect Street. Annie Mitchell, furious with what she saw as Hiram's mismanagement of Alfreda's money—he'd lost a bundle investing in the stock market—kept title to the house and insisted on approving its final plans. Her son-in-law was able to set aside a study as his sanctuary. The walls were lined with bookshelves, over which hung roll-up maps of South America. A portrait of Alfreda gazed down from above the fireplace, flanked by a Peruvian pot and a Gilbertese idol. This private lair contained a hidden bathroom, entered through a hinged bookcase, and was accessed via a ladderlike staircase that led from Hiram's bedroom.

When the 1910–11 edition of *Who's Who* came out, Hiram Bingham's name was listed for the first time. He chose to be identified as "Bingham, Hiram: Explorer."

Bingham's elevated interest in adventure was no accident. The years preceding World War I have often been described as the Heroic Age of Exploration, and for young men seeking glory at the ends of the earth, it was a wonderful time to be plying one's trade. The seaman Joshua Slocum completed the first one-man circumnavigation of the globe in 1898, and earned fame and fortune through his book *Sailing Alone Around the World*. A few years later the Norwegian Roald Amund-

sen made the first crossing of the frozen Northwest Passage, successfully navigating the arctic waters linking the Atlantic and Pacific
oceans, a sea route that mariners had sought since the fifteenth century. Mountaineers were taking aim at the world's highest summits.
In the first years of the new century, English teams that included the
future occultist (and Led Zeppelin muse) Aleister Crowley reached
unprecedented heights on the Himalayan peaks K2 and Kanchen-
junga, the second and third tallest in the world. (Mount Everest would
not be seriously attempted until the 1920s, because Nepal and Tibet
refused access to foreign climbers.) Dr. Frederick Cook became a
household name in 1906 after he reported having climbed Alaska's
Mount McKinley, the highest spot in the United States, though the
claim was later disproved.

Most celebrated of all were the polar explorers. Dr. Cook competed
against naval officer Robert Peary to plant the first flag at the North
Pole. Within a week of Peary's sending the cable trumpeting his triumph in April 1909, the dashing (and doomed) Robert Falcon Scott
announced a new expedition to grab the South Pole for Britain.

The impetus behind Scott's charge—and much of the exploration
happening around the globe—was a muttonchopped septuagenarian
living in London. Sir Clements Markham was the former president of
the Royal Geographical Society. Coincidentally, he was also the En-
glish-speaking world's reigning expert on the history of the Incas. In
1910, he published *The Incas of Peru*, a new chronicle of the Spanish Conquest. *Incas* was the first major work to examine the years following the
puppet king Manco's escape from Cusco, and it had a huge impact on
Bingham's thinking. So did Markham's translations of newly discovered
sixteenth-century works by a Dominican friar and a Spanish army officer. Both writers had traveled to a secluded Inca settlement called Vilcabamba. Bingham had singled out Vilcabamba as the true Lost City of
the Incas, where Manco had established his rebel capital. Buried within
Markham's translations were hints to Vilcabamba's location.

Then a new clue surfaced, one that initially seemed to confuse matters. A researcher at the national library in Lima, combing through an

account left behind by another Spanish friar, had come across a passage that indicated that Manco had fled to a *different* city. In this version, the Inca capital was called Vitcos.

In the spring and summer of 1910, as Bingham sat in New Haven sifting through the evidence about Vilcabamba (or was it Vitcos?), the newly self-described explorer would have found it almost impossible to pick up a newspaper without reading about one expedition or another. Cook and Peary were feuding publicly over who had reached the North Pole first. Norway's Amundsen sent England's Scott a telegram announcing that he planned to beat him to the South Pole. And a group of amateur "sourdoughs" shocked the mountaineering world with their claim to have climbed the north summit of Mount McKinley, fueled by doughnuts and hot chocolate.

The world seemed to be running out of potential discoveries. The writer Arthur Conan Doyle, who was drafting a novel about four explorers in deepest South America—a book soon to become the adventure classic *The Lost World*—teased Robert Peary at a London luncheon held to honor the polar pioneer. "There had been a time when the world was full of blank spaces," he told the attendees. "But owing to the ill-directed energy of [our] guest and other gentlemen of similar tendencies these spaces [are] being rapidly filled up."

Around this time, Bingham received a copy of the historian Adolph Bandelier's *The Islands of Titicaca and Koati* to review. Buried in a footnote was the interesting fact that Mount Coropuna in southern Peru, estimated to top out at twenty-three thousand feet, "is likely (unless some higher peak be found yet in northern Peru) . . . the culminating point of the continent." In other words, the tallest mountain in the Western Hemisphere—which had never been climbed—was probably in Peru, not far from where any search for Vilcabamba would take place. Bingham was intrigued by the opportunity "to enjoy the satisfaction, which all Alpinists feel, of conquering a 'virgin peak.'" He surely had more than personal gratification in mind. When he arrived in Lima for the first time in 1909, the city was still buzzing about the achievements of Annie S. Peck. This American mountaineer had just received a gold medal from Peru's President Augusto Leguia (and barrels of newspaper ink in the United States) for the achievement of climbing Mount Huascaran, which *she* claimed was the highest peak in the hemisphere. Peck had recently conceded that perhaps Coropuna held that honor, and she was planning a high-profile assault on the mountain in 1911.

When a former Yale classmate expressed interest in funding the first topographical survey of Peru's seventy-third meridian (a latitudinal line that circles the globe near Machu Picchu and also happens to pass within a few miles of New Haven), Bingham sketched out an audacious plan. The official prospectus written up by the soon-to-be director of the Yale Peruvian Expedition of 1911 made clear that Bingham's primary objective was to earn immortality as an explorer, one way or another. In the span of about six months, he would sail to Peru, search for Vilcabamba (or maybe Vitcos—he'd sort that out when he got to Peru), summit Mount Coropuna (with any luck, Annie Peck would fail in her attempt), oversee the seventy-third meridian survey *and* measure the depth of the remote Lake Parinacochas. This last objective seems to have been an attempt to curry favor with Sir Clements Markham, whom Bingham pestered frequently for advice through the early part of 1911. Then he'd sail back to New York. He budgeted that he'd need six men and about $12,000.

Bingham scrambled to cover his trip expenses. As a matter of pride, he hoped not to have to dip into Alfreda's savings as he had for prior excursions. In the end, he sold four prospective magazine articles about the voyage to *Harper's* and put up for sale a plot of land in Honolulu that his father, recently deceased, had promised to his church. In the timeless tradition of explorers everywhere, he reached out to every potential corporate sponsor he could think of—obtaining photographic equipment from George Eastman of Eastman Kodak and securing a discount on gear from Ezra Fitch of Abercrombie and Fitch. When time ran short, he asked Alfreda for money to hire a team doctor.

By late spring, Bingham had assembled his team. The Yale Peruvian Expedition would depart as soon as spring classes ended.

EIGHTEEN

Far Out

Yanama, Peru

"Here, Mark, take a pinch of this," John said. He pulled out a Baggie of coca and invited me to grab a wad. "Chew it until it's almost a mush, then stick it between your cheek and gum."

I hadn't tried anything like this since my hero Carlton Fisk suggested during NBC's *Game of the Week* that kids like me ought to sample a tin of Copenhagen chewing tobacco. Chewing coca, I was delighted to learn, had almost nothing in common with dipping snuff. Instead of tasting like a Marlboro unraveled in your mouth, it had the flavor of green tea with a hint of bay leaf. Unlike my vertigo-inducing initiation into the nicotine club, I felt no head rush the first time I sampled coca. I didn't feel anything at all. And there was no spitting.

It would be no exaggeration to say that the Andes have, for thousands of years, run on coca. When the Spaniards arrived, only the Inca royalty were allowed to chew this sacred plant, which acts as a mild narcotic—suppressing hunger, boosting energy, and alleviating the effects of *soroche*. Although very illegal in the United States, coca leaves have about the same relationship to cocaine that Sudafed cold tablets have to crystal meth. Each member of our team happily received his ration every morning, and the few strangers we encountered along the way, once we left Choquequirao, invariably tried to beg a pinch off the muleteers. Twice I saw Juvenal holding a fan of three coca leaves before his lips, as if making an offering to the *apus*. I was too intimidated to ask what he was doing.

Bingham was not a huge fan of coca. "The Indians of the highlands have now for so many generations been neglected by their rulers and brutalized by being allowed to drink all the alcohol they can purchase and to assimilate all the cocaine they can secure, through the constant chewing of coca leaves, that they have lost much if not all of their racial self-respect," he wrote.

Our next destination was Yanama, the only speck of civilization on the four-day walk between Choquequirao and Juvenal's hometown of Huancacalle. The route we were following was genuine Inca-built trail, laid down half a millennium ago. The smooth roadwork, intended to bear the soft feet of humans and llamas, had been ground to bits by mules and iron-shod horses. For mile after mile, baseball-sized rocks littered the path, each step reminding me of my tender toes. Every time we crested a ridge, another canyon lay before us. To an observer from above we would have looked like a small army of ants marching across the world's largest salad bar, one gigantic bowl at a time.

John approached the act of walking like a craftsman. "Every step, every second, I'm thinking, concentrating," he told me. "I remember every trail I've ever been on. I can remember where I made wee stops in India in 1987." Occasionally, he'd bark out a bit of advice over his shoulder. "You'll want to stay as close to the edge as you can, Mark, to catch the breezes from below on the updraft. Just watch your footing."

I was not concentrating especially hard. As I walked hour after hour with little to focus on but John's dusty boots in front of me and a deep chasm off to one side, random thoughts and buried memories began to percolate into my brain. *Does Juvenal dislike me? I don't think he's called me by name once in the entire week we've been out here. . . . Remember that time in first grade when you forgot your lunch? And Sister Teresa took you over to the convent where all those super-old nuns dressed like penguins ate roast beef and made you drink a mug of Sanka with Sweet'n Low because it was so cold out? . . . Oh, we'll all have chicken and dumplings/*

When she comes. . . . What could John be hiding under that hat? Is he bald? Does he have one of those Gorbachev wine stains? . . . Whatever happened to that long-legged girl in your Victorian poetry class who invited you over to make fondue and watch The Unbearable Lightness of Being? *Didn't you stay out until 4 A.M. the night before and cancel on her because you were so hungover? It never occurred to you until this very moment, in the middle of the goddamned Andes, that she might have had more in mind than bread and cheese, did it?*

The path narrowed around a rock ledge to just two feet wide, and I held my breath and forced myself to focus for the sixty seconds I needed to pass through it. Curiosity got the best of me midway. I tensed every muscle in the lower half of my body and tilted my neck for a peek into the abyss. A wall of sand-colored rock dropped straight down. There seemed to be no bottom.

When we reached the far side, John looked back and said, with some disappointment, "I think they've widened it. Someone must've lost a mule and complained."

As the day grew hotter, the distant rumbles of rock slides punctuated the quiet. At a spot where stones spilled across the trail, John paused to listen for any further avalanches on the way. "It's not so bad up high where we are, but down there," he said, nodding into the chasm to our left, "the rocks will be coming at a hundred miles an hour or more. Once you hear them it's too late to react." The sun was blinding. Every surface was coated with flecks of mica, which gave the impression that some crazed fairy had tossed glitter over the entire valley.

We were headed toward the ruins of Vitcos. I was especially excited about this because Vitcos happened to sit in a crucial location—near a hostel owned and run by Juvenal's family. This meant a bed for three nights. The muleteers were excited, too—the stop meant two days off from the trail. John was excited—by his standards, anyway—because to get to Vitcos we would have to hike through some serious Inca country.

"There are fewer people walking this route now than there were fifteen years ago, and there weren't many then, either," he said. Less than fifty miles to the east, a couple thousand people were walking the Inca Trail to Machu Picchu.

"It's usually just the hard-core types you see out here?" I asked.

"Oh, I doubt we'll see anyone on the trail until we get to Juvenal's house"—two days away. The last foreigners we'd seen were a French couple who shadowed us for a few hours on the hike out of Choque-quirao: they wore matching eyeglasses with nickel-sized lenses and hiked with a walking pole in each hand, as if working out on his-and-hers NordicTracks. Our last sight of them they were setting up camp by what looked to be a charming riverbank. "They'll change their minds when the bugs come out," John said, with a final glance back.

The town of Yanama consisted of a one-room school, a shop selling rice and Inca Kola, and a few small houses. We camped at a farm by the side of a stream. After two straight days of walking until my clothes were drenched with sweat, then passing through clouds of dust and mica flakes, drying off in the hot sun during lunch and repeating the entire process in the afternoon, both I and my Travel Guy attire had crusted over. I stripped down to a pair of shorts, a bit of immodesty that made the señora of the house shriek "Ay!" and hide her face behind the brim of her hat when she saw me. Her two boys, ages eight and nine, watched me from the hillside.

At the bottom of the hill, a hand pump drew water from the river, and I chatted with Mateo while he hurriedly filled a bucket for cooking. The late afternoon sun warmed my bare back. Mateo was a laconic and sociable fellow—he chuckled when he pointed to my ankles, which had two-inch stripes of dirt like Samoan warrior tattoos—so I was surprised that he seemed to be agitated about something he called "poo-moo-blah-blah-blah" (at least that's what it sounded like) and bolted up the hill the moment his bucket was full. Of all the times he could have chosen not to shake my hand repeatedly, I wondered, why did it have to be when I was carrying a bar of soap?

A friend who had gone off to work in the Peace Corps in the Amazon basin once wrote me a letter that began: "At a certain point, you resign yourself to the fact that there are at least three bugs on you at any time, and that one of them is going to bite you." I had noticed, both in Cusco and at Choquequirao, that many of the travelers I met had constellations of welts on their lower legs. How was it possible to get bitten so many times on one spot? I wondered. Had they never heard of insect repellent? Or slapping? Was this some variety of hives, an allergic reaction to too much cooking oil? I began lathering my hands in the frigid water, and the answer came to me almost immediately.

First, I felt a couple of painful pinches around my ankles. Then a few more on my hands, and back, and neck. In the span of perhaps five seconds, I was completely swarmed by a fog of tiny, black biting insects the size of pinheads. I was bitten in places I hadn't imagined bugs knew existed: they got me inside my ears, on the palms of my hands, in crevices where the sun hadn't shined since Nixon was president. I swatted at myself like I was on fire, rinsed off what soap and bugs I could under cold water and ran up the hill to my tent, passing Mateo en route. "Poo-moo-blah-blah-blah!" he yelled after me, raising one water bucket in salute. In my tent I started to survey the damage but gave up after counting sixty bites. Each welt was like a little bull's-eye, with a red circle surrounding a white one and a black dot in the middle.

After several minutes of fruitless scratching, I got dressed and walked to the cook tent. Juvenal was sitting outside the flap with the two boys, quizzing them about something in Quechua. In his yellow Polo button-down shirt, V-neck sweater and striped wool pants, he could've been someone's grandpa who'd just spent twenty minutes finding the perfect parking spot for his Buick, except that the town of Yanama had never seen a motorized vehicle.

He saw me scratching the backs of my hands and motioned for me to come over so he could have a look. "*Puma wakachi*," he said, pointing to his tear duct. "The bug that makes the puma cry. Put cold water on them." Then he turned back to the boys to finish his lesson.

Quechua kids are famously adorable, because they have coal-black eyes and perpetually rosy cheeks, and these two were no exception. The boys didn't have much to do. Their teacher, who taught all the children in the area, had gone off for the week to a festival up the valley somewhere. Fortuitously, a promising source of entertainment had wandered into their yard—me. After about an hour of stalking me from a distance as I laid out my laundry to dry in the waning sunlight and clawed at my ankles, the older boy screwed up the courage to ask a question.

"Where do you come from?"

"I'm from New York."

I might as well have said I was from the planet Zebulon.

"Have you heard of New York?" I asked.

"No."

"Have you heard of the United States?"

"No." His brother shook his head dubiously in support.

"Have you heard of Machu Picchu?"

"Yes, of course." Big smiles.

"Well, I live north of Machu Picchu."

This seemed to satisfy them. Then the younger one thought of another question.

"Is it true that Michael Jackson is dead?"

I tried, and failed, to come up with the Spanish words to say, "The King of Pop will live forever in our hearts." So I just nodded yes and tried to look sad.

At dinnertime I ducked into the cook tent and showed my bug bites to John.

"Ah, I figured they'd get you sooner or later. I know you won't let it happen again."

As we sat down for dinner, the boys squatted about twenty feet from the open tent flap, watching us as they would a particularly engrossing cartoon. I wondered what my sons, whose daily schedules were so regimented, would do if I moved them to a place like this. Probably report me to child services. I asked John what it had been like to grow up in Western Australia in the fifties and sixties.

"Australia was a pretty austere place after the war, up until the midsixties. Every Sunday night for a treat we had beans on toast. I was one of the last generation that could live in a big town like Perth, on an acre of land, and walk to school through the bush, with the birds and snakes. I could go and pick fruit, build cubby houses."

"Sounds like studying might not have been your first priority."

"I didn't like school. The educational system was flawed. They didn't teach you how to live." John had been a sickly child. In his early teens, he suffered from hay fever and asthma so severe that in order to breathe he had to get up every night around one o'clock to take ephedrine. His eczema was so bad that his mother wrapped his limbs in cloths before bed so he wouldn't tear into his skin. "I'd wake up in the middle of the night stuck to the sheets from blood," John said.

One night John took a walk around the house after his ephedrine dose and noticed that he felt better than usual. "The next night I took less medicine and went for a walk outside. Then I tried a little jogging with the walking. Eventually, after several weeks, I found that after twenty minutes of sweaty exercise, the asthma would be gone." Almost everything that John had learned in life since, he'd picked up on his own. He'd walked out of the only Spanish class he'd ever taken, years ago—"we kept talking about pillows—how's that supposed to help me get through customs?"—and then practiced the language by talking to people and translating the newspaper. When I used a word that he liked, he wrote it down in his blue notebook.

Juvenal had invented some menial task for the boys to do, so that John and I could eat without feeling like we were onstage. With their crouched little bodies no longer blocking the view, we could watch the mules drinking from the rocky stream rolling down the hillside.

"You never told me how you got into guiding," I said.

"Well, that's sort of a long story we can get into later. I had a lot of jobs before that. I told you how I was an engineer, overseeing multimillion-dollar projects. I worked as a gardener. I was a beach inspector for seven years."

This sounded like the sort of job that only existed on novelty T-shirts. "What's a beach inspector?"

"It's what you would call a lifeguard." Justo set bowls of quinoa soup in front of us, along with a freshly made peppery *aji* sauce that was hot enough to clear our sinuses. John dumped several spoonfuls in his bowl, then passed it to me. "How's your stomach?" he asked.

Sniffing the *aji* made my mouth water and my intestines rumble. I reluctantly passed it back toward John. "Let's just say that tomorrow might not be a great day to attend a chili cook-off," I said.

John blew on his spoonful of soup and reached for his pen. "What's a chili cook-off?"

NINETEEN

Up, Up and Away

Choquetacarpo Pass

Yanama sat at almost twelve thousand feet, and most of our hiking the next day was uphill. Each time we crested a ridge, the terrain edged a few degrees further from green to brown. Streams appeared from nowhere, and we crossed them via a few logs laid above their gurgling current. We hadn't seen rain since starting out at Cachora, and water levels were low. Most of the paths we'd followed thus far had been dusty mule trails. Today's route was so far off the map that the Inca stonework was in near-mint condition. "Just think, Pachacutec and Manco probably came along this trail on their way from Vitcos to Choquequirao," John said.

Our objective for the day was to stop just short of Choquetacarpo Pass. This was one of the many fifteen-thousand-feet-high breaches in the Andes that had brought the Spaniards to their knees with *soroche* when they tried to pursue the Incas. The Quechua people have long known that coca helps the body adapt to the lower levels of oxygen in the thin air of the Andes. They also have biological advantages over lowlanders like me. Their hearts and lungs are larger, which is why so many Andeans have barrel chests like stevedores; they also have blood richer in red cells than a person raised at sea level. These don't seem to be genetic adaptations, but rather physiological advantages that one earns by growing up at altitude. This made me feel a little better each time Juvenal sprinted uphill past me on a trail pitched like the roof of an A-frame.

In midafternoon we crossed into a moonscape, a long valley with steep craggy sides capped by jagged black rocks that blocked out most of the sun's rays. The blue-light effect was not unlike walking through the canyons of midtown Manhattan on a cloudy winter day. The ground was covered with moss and sickly scrub grass. Boulders the size of large cars and small houses were strewn about. At the far end of the gorge a blinding white glacier seemed to seal off any exit at the spot where John had said Choquetacarpo Pass would be. A shaggy wild mule wandered out of a cave, looking for food. Finding none, he disappeared into another cave. Where he'd come from originally I couldn't begin to guess. There were no homes here, no farms, not even a rooster, just us and the rocks and Pachacutec's trail. Two hours earlier we'd been sweating through Southern California; now we were freezing in northern Scotland.

The only colorful spot in this landlocked fjord was our orange cook tent, dwarfed by rocks on three sides. As John and I approached, a tiny red dot also came into view—I half expected it to be the beacon of a UFO or Doctor Who's phone booth, but it was Justo bundled up against the chill in an ancient maraschino-cherry skiwear ensemble that Jean-Claude Killy might have worn as a boy. "Look out, Señor Mark, that guy is watching you," he said when I arrived for tea, pointing up toward a rock formation directly above us. It was shaped exactly like a giant Easter Island head.

I woke up in the dark the next morning. It was four-thirty. Frost covered the ground under my tent.

"Got to get going early today," John said. Once humidity from the jungle crept up the valley—we watched a cloud of mist drift slowly toward our camp like a puff of cigar smoke—and hit Choquetacarpo Pass at mid-morning, the collision of hot and cold air could dump enough snow to cancel school in Buffalo. "I've seen it get ten feet deep up there," John said. We all grabbed an extra ration of coca and were off by five-thirty.

"I've got a small suggestion, Mark," John said. "This time, chew your coca thoroughly for a few minutes and then give it another chew occasionally. It's supposed to dissolve in your mouth."

Well, *hey*. The day before, the coca had kept *soroche* at bay. Today it gave me a small buzz, a slight tingling in the mouth followed by a lovely clearheadedness. Approaching fifteen thousand feet, I felt like I'd had a nap and downed a double espresso.

"*This* may be the finest stretch of original Inca trail left in all Peru," John said as we crossed a small rise, looking down onto a path that snaked ahead of us like a miniature Great Wall of China. The road was beautifully engineered. The surface was elevated and paved with white stones. Masoned retaining walls on both sides protected the causeway from flooding. In the few spots where the trail had worn through, the deep and intricate foundation work laid down five centuries ago was evident. We were walking on a work of art.

Choquetacarpo is two miles higher than the famed Khyber Pass, taller than the Space Needle stacked on top of Mount Rainier. When it became obvious that we wouldn't be hit by any snowstorms—there was hardly a cloud in the sky—we slackened to a strenuous stroll. Fifteen-thousand feet was almost certainly the highest I would ever stand on earth, and I wanted to savor it.

The canyon we'd walked through was beautifully desolate, a brown badlands hemmed in by two sets of sharp, rocky incisors. The top of the pass was crowded with dozens of *apachetas*, towers of rocks stacked on top of each other. Nati had explained these to me once. Local people who come through a mountain pass create a new *apacheta* or add a stone to an old one, asking for a favor from the *apus* or hoping for good luck on a journey. The piles reminded me of the votive candles my mother used to light in church. John checked his watch. "Two and a half hours to the top, not bad," he said.

We sat down to dig into our bags of snacks. "Did Bingham ever write about the scenery?" John asked. I assured him that Bingham had referred to the green basin into which we were about to descend as "a veritable American Switzerland."

"That's right! The valley down below here is *beautiful*. Almost perfectly intact. We're right on the dividing line of the watershed. Everything behind us drains into the Apurimac River. Everything ahead goes into the Urubamba"—the river that winds around Machu Picchu.

John was too excited to remain seated. He pulled an armful of gadgets out of his daypack and waded into the field of *apachetas* as if stepping onto a giant chessboard, taking photographs and video from all possible angles.

"How many times have you been through here?" I asked.

"Don't know precisely. Eight, ten?" He held his yellow GPS in front of him like the handle of a fishing pole and scribbled notes furiously in his blue notebook, reeling in secrets.

The tiny oranges that Justo had packed seemed to have skins of Kevlar. I struggled with mine like it was a Rubik's Cube. I finally hacked away enough peel to get to the edible center. Having massacred the fruit, I shoved the entire thing in my mouth, seeds and all, as juice ran down my face. I stacked my tiny bits of peel into an *apacheta* and made a wish of my own, begging the *apus* to spare my toes on the descent ahead.

Sure enough, within a few minutes we rounded a bend and entered *Sound of Music* country, snowy peaks framing deep green bowls. "Look how the valley has been perfectly rounded by glaciers," John said, tracing the curve with the flat of his hand. "You go ahead, Mark, I'm going to take some more video." Each time I looked back, John was raising and lowering his Handycam, gazing around at the panorama. "God, this is just a beautiful place, isn't it?" he said when he caught up to me.

The rest of that afternoon we descended an Inca staircase, thirty-five hundred tall stone steps dropping almost a mile in elevation down toward Vitcos. With each long step down, the air seemed to warm a little more, and the alpine briskness gave way to Amazonian humidity. The ground off the trail was like a wet green washcloth, permanently soaked from the river that wound through the valley. John pointed out a pair of white birds. "Andean geese. Very territorial, one pair per valley. They mate for life. People eat almost any animal around here, but very few geese, out of respect."

Signs of civilization slowly began to reappear. A small house. A *campesino* plowing his potato fields on a distant hill, bent over pushing a big stick. A log fence that some enterprising farmer had built across the trail, to keep people out of his crops. ("God, some of these farmers are assholes," John muttered as we scrambled across.) Stone walls started to divide the small plots of land into a quilt of green and yellow rectangles. A motorcycle roared in the distance. Electrical wires materialized overhead. Stray dogs came out to give us a sniff. Finally, when we had walked through four seasons in one day, the trail ended abruptly. We'd arrived in Huancacalle.

TWENTY

Hunting for Clues

Cusco

The expedition that would make Hiram Bingham famous was nearly canceled at the last minute. In April, two months before his departure date, his father-in-law, Alfred Mitchell, fell gravely ill. Bingham accompanied Alfreda on the six-day sea journey to her father's bedside at his estate in Jamaica. Alfred rebounded briefly. Bingham returned to New York. Alfred died and Bingham returned to Jamaica once more, for his father-in-law's funeral. Alfreda joyfully scribbled "Plan given up!" in her diary. Her premature relief suggests she'd forgotten her husband's love of solving logistical problems. Bingham again returned to New York, settled his hysterically grieving mother-in-law in a hospital and bid good-bye to his wife and sons. When the steamship *Marta* left New York Harbor on June 8, the expedition director was aboard.

Bingham kept track of an impressive number of particulars while preparing the 1911 expedition: begging friends for money, interrogating experts on the Incas about minor details, inspecting swatches of material from which tents were to be sewn. (Some one-hundred-year-old canvas samples were still in his files at Yale.) Bingham took immense pride in such control freakery. Just six paragraphs into *Inca Land*, the book that should have been a riveting account of the discoveries he made in 1911, Bingham stopped the narrative cold to lecture his readers about the exquisite care that he and the expedition's naturalist, Harry Foote, had put into selecting provisions for the trip. By the time he got around to explaining that "we had to eliminate foods that contained a large amount of water, like French peas, baked beans, and canned fruits," even an army quartermaster would have dozed off.

Such diligence carried over into Bingham's search for Vilcabamba. His first weeks in Peru were largely devoted to shoe-leather detective work. Within twenty-four hours of arriving in Lima, Bingham went to the National Library to meet with Carlos Romero, the historian whose archival research had raised the prospect that Vitcos, not Vilcabamba, was the Lost City of the Incas. ("He seems to be rather deaf and somewhat cross, but quite a scholar," Bingham noted.) Bingham spent much of his brief time in Lima talking with Romero and copying passages out of one of the important new sources the scholar had found buried in the library's collection, Father Antonio de la Calancha's *Coronica Moralizada*, a "pious account of the missionary activities in Peru," published in 1639. According to the historian Christopher Heaney, when Bingham asked Romero which had been the last Inca redoubt—Vitcos or Vilcabamba—Romero explained the reason for the confusion. Vilcabamba was the name of the *province* that the rebel Incas controlled. Vitcos was the name of the *capital*.

It was an elegant solution with one serious flaw: Romero was only half right, as Bingham discovered when he read further into Calancha's text. Manco had indeed established a new, remote capital at Vitcos after escaping from Cusco. But he had also constructed *another* capital, deeper in the jungle, when even Vitcos became unsafe. Suddenly, Heaney writes, "Bingham wasn't searching for one lost city; he was searching for two."

Bingham continued his fact-finding, obtaining copies of maps from the Lima Geographical Society, including one made by the famous nineteenth-century geographer Antonio Raimondi, whom Bingham considered the "greatest of Peruvian explorers." He added these to his copies of the Royal Geographical Society's latest maps of southern Peru, believed to be definitive. He also had in his possession what may have been his secret weapon: a hand-drawn map he'd been given by a friend, the Harvard anthropologist William Farabee.

In his final and best-known book, *Lost City of the Incas*, Bingham claimed that finding Vilcabamba and/or Vitcos was his only concrete objective as he advanced down the valley of the Urubamba. He arrived on the now-famous ridge at Machu Picchu, he wrote, "without the slightest expectation of finding anything more interesting than the ruins of two or three stone houses." In an interview that Bingham gave to *The New York Sun* just before departing, however, which ran under the headline WILL SEEK LOST CITIES, he told a reporter: "There are current in the country many reports of the existence of ruined cities along the Urubamba River, which reports we hope to run down. Indians frequently bring these reports. Dr. Farabee, who was in charge of the Harvard expedition of four years ago, told me of a rumor, pretty well authenticated, which he had got from Indians, of a big city hidden away on the mountainside above the Urubamba Valley." Machu Picchu was (and to the present still is) the only major "ruined city" ever found in the Urubamba Valley. "The map I sent you," Farabee wrote to Bingham in early 1911, "is a composite of many more or less inexact and some fairly exact elements." Were those elements exact enough to lead Bingham to Machu Picchu? It's impossible to know.

As Bingham approached Cusco by train, he was met outside the city by Albert Giesecke, the Philadelphia-born rector of the University of Cusco. Like the historian Romero, Giesecke is one of several essential supporting figures in the discovery of Machu Picchu. According to an interview Giesecke gave in 1962, he told Bingham that he'd recently traveled up the Urubamba Valley, along Bingham's proposed route. At a place called Mandor Pampa, Giesecke said, he met a farmer named Melchor Arteaga, who operated a small tavern. Arteaga had spoken of some impressive ruins that sat on the mountain ridge above the trail and offered to take Giesecke to see them sometime. Because it was January, the rainy season, a quick trip up was out of the question.

Bingham continued his sleuthing in Cusco. A businessman he'd

befriended on his previous visit introduced the explorer to the owners of several nearby haciendas, the enormous farms that dominated
the Peruvian countryside. One invited Bingham to stay at his family's
estate near Mandor Pampa, the spot where Albert Giesecke had suggested that Bingham stop. Another landowner, named Jose Pancorbo,
assured Bingham that he would find significant ruins near a town
called Puquiura. This news grabbed Bingham's attention, for Puquiura
was the name of the town that Father Calancha had mentioned in his
Coronica as being a short distance from Vitcos.

Later, a chatty old prospector informed Bingham that he had seen
ruins "finer than Choquequirau" at a place called Huayna Picchu. This
name echoed one that Bingham had read in the famous French explorer Charles Wiener's book *Perou et Bolivie*; Wiener had been told
several decades earlier "that there were fine ruins down the Urubamba
Valley at a place called 'Huaina-Picchu or Matcho-Picchu,'" Bingham
recalled.

Bingham's departure from Cusco was briefly sidetracked when he
and team geographer Isaiah Bowman stumbled across a human femur
jutting out from a recently cut road outside of the city. Bowman convinced Bingham that the bones he found there were, in fact, evidence
of "a man of the glacial epoch . . . probably 30,000 years old." The discovery would have rocked the world of anthropology by pushing back
the estimated arrival of *Homo sapiens* in the Western Hemisphere
by thousands of years. Such a find would have instantly made the expedition's leader as well known as Othniel Charles Marsh, a professor
during Bingham's undergraduate years who was described upon his
death in 1899 as "probably Yale's most famous scholar." Marsh cata-
pulted to world renown as one of the founding fathers of paleontol-
ogy (triceratops and stegosaurus were but two of the eighty dinosaur
species he found and named). Bingham could barely contain his excite-
ment. "You can easily imagine how pleased I am to have actually
discovered the bones myself," he wrote to Alfreda.

By the time he finally left Cusco on July 19, Bingham had cobbled
together solid leads on three sets of Inca ruins, any one of which would

be a major discovery. Multiple sources had suggested that there was something worth seeing on a ridge above Mandor Pampa, at a place that might be called Huaina-Picchu or Matcho-Picchu. He was confident that there were ruins close to the town of Puquiura—quite possibly those of Vitcos. Calancha's *Coronica* had provided yet another tantalizing clue: "close to Vitcos . . . is a House of the Sun, and in it a white rock over a spring of water." If Bingham could locate ruins that were near both Puquiura and this white rock, he would have solid proof of Manco's capital in exile.

The location of Bingham's third objective, the lost city of Vilcabamba, final sanctuary of the Incas, was somewhat murkier. Spanish chronicles indicated that it was situated northwest of Cusco and that the first checkpoint on the road to Vilcabamba was the ancient fort of Ollantaytambo, about forty winding miles from Cusco. On muleback, Bingham was able to reach the site in two days.

Ollantaytambo is one of the masterpieces of Inca architecture. Seventeen imposing terraces (which an awestruck Bingham wrote "will stand for ages to come as monuments to the energy and skill of a bygone race") lead up to a fortress where six enormous rectangular granite slabs stand watch over the Urubamba River valley, like the world's largest royal flush. Unlike Machu Picchu, about which next to nothing is known for certain, Ollantaytambo appears prominently in histories written by both the Incas and the Spaniards, for it was the scene of the greatest victory that the native Peruvians ever enjoyed against their invaders. During Manco's siege of Cusco, during which the former puppet Inca came close to ejecting the conquistadors from his capital, the fortress of Ollantaytambo served as the rebel headquarters. Early one morning, one of the Pizarro brothers led a sneak attack, hoping to end the revolt by carrying off the Inca as prisoner.

The Spaniards were dumbfounded by what they saw when the sun rose: Manco Inca, holding a spear and issuing commands to his troops as he rode a stolen horse atop Ollantaytambo's highest terrace. In an instant, the historian William Prescott wrote, "the air was darkened with innumerable missiles, stones, javelins and arrows, which fell like a hurricane on the troops, and the mountains rang to the wild war-whoop of the enemy."

Anyone who's hiked the Inca Trail also knows Ollantaytambo as a place where one can hop off the train to reach the starting point of the four- or five-day trek. Whether one continues west on foot or by rail, it's impossible not to be struck by how quickly the landscape changes. The desolate, mountainous terrain that has held steady since Cusco segues rapidly into tropical forest dotted with orchids—the beginnings of the Amazon basin. Virtually every explorer who came before Bingham had been required, at this point, to choose between two grueling mountain passes—both "higher than the top of Pikes Peak," Bingham noted—to move farther west beyond the well-mapped environs of the Sacred Valley near Cusco. Luckily for Bingham, a new mule road had been blasted out along the riverbank in 1895, to allow plantation owners an easier route for transporting their goods. Bingham was exaggerating only slightly when he claimed the new road allowed him access to a "mountainous wilderness" between the two routes that "had been inaccessible for almost four centuries."

Bingham continued down the riverside, accompanied by two expedition members and a soldier known only as Sergeant Carrasco. His services had been provided on the orders of President Leguia, and Carrasco's ability to speak Quechua would prove invaluable. On July 23, three Yale men dressed like Connecticut deer hunters, with a military escort in his brass-buttoned uniform and a few anonymous Andean muleteers and porters, arrived at a small hut known as La Maquina. It had been named after a large piece of machinery, rusted beyond recognition, that sat nearby. Bingham guessed that the iron wheels had once been intended for a sugar farm down the valley.

The road began to narrow, so the men found a place to camp along the riverbank. "Opposite us, beyond the huge granite boulders which interfered with the progress of the surging stream, was a steep mountain clothed with thick jungle," Bingham later recalled. He had arrived at Mandor Pampa. The group was soon sought out by Melchor Arteaga, the man whom Albert Giesecke said had told him about the possible ruins. Bingham explained through Sergeant Carrasco what they had come searching for. Arteaga replied that "there were some very good ruins in this vicinity," according to Bingham, "in fact, some excellent ones on top of the opposite mountain, called Huayna Picchu, and also on a ridge called Machu Picchu."

This sounded promising. They made a plan to take a look in the morning.

In his books recounting the story of Machu Picchu, Bingham paused the action here and addressed readers directly. "Suffice it to say that the ruins he showed me were not near a 'great white rock over a spring of water' and that there was no evidence that this was Vitcos, Manco's capital for which we were looking," Bingham wrote. Instead of chronicling what happened next on July 24, he skipped ahead a couple days, fast-forwarding past the most important twenty-four hours of his life, a narrative trick that allowed him to save the juiciest part of his tale for the end.

John and I were following Bingham by the book. Which is why we, too, were about to encounter Vitcos.

TWENTY ONE

Sixpac Manco

Huancacalle, Peru

Two towns sit below the ruins of Vitcos: Puquiura and Huancacalle. Remember those bucolic little burgs that courier companies used to feature in their commercials to demonstrate how willing they were to deliver packages to the ends of the earth? ("Look, my grandson in America spent the equivalent of three oxen to send me this handmade birthday card!") Puquiura looked like that. Compared to Huancacalle—where we were staying—Puquiura was like Vegas. Huancacalle had two streets and a few dozen houses, almost all jerry-built of mud brick. None of them seemed a wise place to be visiting when one of Peru's infamous earthquakes struck.

Far and away the nicest thing going in Huancacalle was the Sixpac Manco, the hostelry run by the Cobos family. If there is a finer place in the universe to stay for $5 a night, I have yet to encounter it. The second part of the hotel's name was taken from the rebel Inca. The Sixpac part refers to the preferred beverage of the explorer Vincent Lee, a Cobos family friend who helped bankroll the operation.

John and I wandered into the Sixpac courtyard with the mules and unloaded our gear. The muleteers lined up to be paid for the first part of the journey, and I handed each his tip with a handshake and a *"muchisimas gracias."* Julián, by far the least experienced of the crew, was the most excited to get paid. (Probably because I pretended to have forgotten Juvenal's earlier suggestion that Julián would work for tips.) He was also the only muleteer who gave the traditional soft Quechua handshake. Bingham had been so unnerved by this "extremely fishy" grip that he had a group of men hooked up to a dynamometer and found the average squeeze strength to be "only about half of that found among American white adults of sedentary habits." The soft handclasps I received along the trail seemed more like acts of gentleness than failures of manliness; each time I met a stranger, I felt like I was being handed a baby bird.

Mateo and Julián marched off to their nearby farms to spend a few days with their families. Juvenal walked up the hill to see his wife. Justo unpacked his gear in the Sixpac Manco kitchen. John disappeared into his room and threw his stuff around noisily for a few minutes. I had nothing to do except attend to my filthy clothes, which I washed out in the garden with a bar of soap and a scrub brush. My two shirts and two pairs of pants took half an hour to get passably clean. When I finished, I peeled the electrical tape off my toes and took a luxurious lukewarm shower in the open-air bathroom. The water was supposed to be heated by an electric contraption attached to the shower head that had all sorts of wires sticking out of it; this in turn was connected directly to the town's main power cable. "Electrocuted while bathing" seemed a rather pathetic cause of death. So I let the tepid water run over me and tried to think of what I might be doing in New York at that hour. Then I realized that I didn't even know what day it was.

Huancacalle was a lot less isolated than it had been just a few years ago. The Cobos family had a telephone that could make calls within Peru, though service was dependent on the positions of satellites and could be disrupted by things like high winds, clouds and sun spots. Juvenal's daughter Rosa said that it was possible to make international calls at a shop just up the hill, the one with the parabolic antenna outside. I wasn't sure exactly how many days it had been since I'd spoken with Aurita, but I did know it was the longest stretch since we'd collided on that New York street sixteen years earlier. Rosa giggled and shooed me toward the door when I explained why I needed to find a phone, but John seemed baffled by my desire to call home.

"I call my family back in Australia once a year, and they're fine with it," he said. He had spoken with his eighty-nine-year-old mum not long before we'd departed. "If she gets a call she knows something's gone wrong."

"I'm beginning to understand why you've never been married," I said.

Walking up to the general store, I felt like a gunslinger strolling through Dodge City. The road was dirt, the buildings were dusty, and the only people visible were peering out at me from dark windows and doorways. Only one thing felt off: I was marching up a crazily steep hill. The sheriff in a Huancacalle gunfight would need to aim his pistol as if he were shooting skeet.

I found the store and stepped over the wooden dog gate in the doorway. The proprietress, a young mother in her twenties, stood behind a glass case filled with candy, toiletries and matches. It smelled like dried soup mix and disinfectant inside the store, like it does sometimes in old people's houses.

"Good day, it would please me to make an international call to the Estados Unidos," I said in carefully measured Spanish.

From behind me a loud voice interjected. "Well, someone wants to make a call to THE EH-STAH-DOS OO-NEE-DOS." I hadn't noticed that the shoplady's husband was sitting at a table in the corner, picking apart a chicken carcass and drinking (judging from the impressive collection of empty Cusqueña bottles) his eleventh beer of the afternoon.

"Um, yes, that is correct. It is possible?"

"Yes, sir," the woman said. "Let me find the code for the United States."

"EH-STAH-DOS OO-NEE-DOS!" shouted the husband, pointing at me with a drumstick bone. It was hard to tell if he was angry, or mocking my pronunciation, or practicing his geography.

I dialed, but no one answered. I dialed again. Then I did a quick calculation and remembered—of course, no one was home because it was Columbus Day in the United States. The arrival of Europeans in the New World was not a major cause for celebration in the Andes.

"It seems to me that no one is in the house," I said to the woman. "I am going to call another time later."

"Call the EH-STAH-DOS OO-NEE-DOS," her husband added. He had a look in his eye that any American who has spent time around non-American drunks may recognize, the leer that precedes either projectile vomiting or a lecture about the CIA. Sometimes both. I hopped the dog gate in the doorway and hurried downhill.

Back at the Sixpac Manco, Justo had prepared a feast of stuffed potatoes with breaded chicken cutlets, choclo (Peruvian corn with huge white kernels), and rice pudding for dessert. I had read somewhere that chewing coca helped the body break down carbohydrates, but I'd begun to wonder if the Spaniards had banished green vegetables along with the Incas' pagan rituals. Justo dug deep into one of his conga drums and produced a box of red wine. John poured out mugs for Rosa, Juvenal, Justo and the two of us. Justo and Juvenal stood and lifted their drinks overhead, shouted "Salud!," tossed the wine back in a single gulp, sat back down and resumed the conversation they were having in Quechua. John pulled out his maps of Vitcos and tried to explain how one of the most important sites in the Inca empire could be forgotten for centuries even though it was located a short walk from two towns.

Part of the obfuscation may have arisen from popularity of the name Vilcabamba. In the region to the west of Machu Picchu, Vilcabamba is about as common a name as Peachtree is in Atlanta. On John's maps, I could see a Vilcabamba region, which spread across hundreds of square miles; a Vilcabamba River, which flowed west of the Urubamba; the Cordillera Vilcabamba, a mountain range that included the apu Salcantay and Machu Picchu; a town called Vilcabamba the New, founded by the Spanish; and the archaeological site of Vilcabamba the Old, also known as Espiritu Pampa, where we'd be heading in a few days. During Manco's reign, the entire rebel state was known as Vilcabamba.

An hour later, my head numb with dancing Vilcabambas, Quechua gossip and Chilean merlot, I walked back to my room, climbed beneath clean sheets and thick wool blankets and slept the sleep of the dead.

TWENTY-TWO

The More Things Change

Lost in Puquiura

Andean folk are my kind of people—early risers. At five-thirty in the morning at Sixpac Manco the kitchen was full. Florencia Cobos, Juvenal's wife, was collecting scraps for their guinea pigs; she wrapped the fruit peelings and moldy bread in a large *manta*, a hand-woven cloth. She dressed traditionally, with layered skirts, a long braid and a tall hat that John Smith might have worn on a date with Pocahontas. Her daughter Rosa wore a Polartec fleece pullover and jeans. She fed twigs into the wood-burning stove and told me she was stressed out because her son, who was attending school in Cusco, needed a laptop and it had been a slow year for tourism. Justo prepared breakfast—twenty tiny trout that he had pulled out of the river, God knows when—and listened to his radio, which was blaring pop songs sung in Quechua. The tune sounded awfully familiar. Or familiarly awful.

"Justo, I feel like I know this song. What's he singing?"

"Oh, this song, Señor Mark? This is a great one. It goes: *"Es el ojo del tigre . . ."* Translation: It's the eye of the tiger. "I'm going over to Puquiura today to buy some chicken. You can't get anything in Huancacalle on Tuesdays. You want to visit the hospital to get some cream for those bug bites?"

What became an epic search for a tube of anti-itch cream later reminded me of a couple of major beefs that Bingham had with the

Andean people. One was that it was nearly impossible to get anyone started on a project. His writings are loaded with crabby memories of cooling his heels while some Indian muleteer took half the morning to get the animals loaded and ready to move.

His second big complaint was that Peruvians would tell him whatever they thought he wanted to hear, just to make him happy. A foreman at one hacienda near Huancacalle told Bingham that he had seen spectacular ruins at a spot with a name that sounded like Yurak Rumi—Quechua for White Rock, one of the key clues to finding Vitcos. After waiting several days for a trail to be cleared, Bingham marched for several hours, only to find that this Yurak Rumi "consisted of the ruins of a single little rectangular Inca storehouse." A decade later, Bingham was still piqued at the incident. "In this country one never can tell whether such a report is worthy of credence," he wrote. "'He may have been lying' is a good footnote to affix to all hearsay evidence." I had been advised that when traveling outside of Lima, I should get a second and third opinion even if I was just asking the time.

The only driver available in Huancacalle twice refused to take Justo and me to Puquiura; at first, he said, because he was finishing a very important bottle of soda, and then because it wasn't worth his while to take only a single fare. After about half an hour sitting on the hood of his car, listening to Justo hold forth about the culinary preferences of past clients for whom he had cooked ("Italians—all they want is pasta, even at breakfast; with Spaniards, it's ham, ham, ham"), the driver capitulated and drove us the two miles in about seven minutes.

Puquiura was a town of maybe a thousand inhabitants, with a central square and main street lined with brightly painted buildings. It also had a military checkpoint with a gate, manned by an armed soldier—presumably a holdover from Peru's antiterrorism campaigns of the late eighties. Justo marched through with a mock salute to the guard. We asked an old woman where the hospital was.

"Go down to the river, you can't miss it," she said with a smile. We went down to the river. No hospital.

"It's up on the hill," said a man carrying a bucket of water. We went up the hill. No hospital.

"You need to go back to the center," said a shopkeeper at the end of the road. We knew this couldn't be right because we'd already done two laps of the middle of town.

Finally, a guy in a shirt that said (in English): NEW JERSEY, SINCE 1956, pointed at a building with a large cross painted on it. I bought some bug cream from the well-stocked hospital pharmacy—because of my language limitations, the pharmacist initially brought me a box of hemorrhoidal suppositories that contained cocaine as their active ingredient—and we walked back through town, on a futile search for poultry. An entire fleet of taxis extended down the main street, but the dispatching system allowed the first driver in line to wait as long as he wished for a promising fare. Taking us back to Huancacalle didn't qualify. No other driver was allowed to jump the line. Justo and I bought a bag of popcorn and some *chicha morada* (the nonalcoholic purple version of the corn drink) and sat on a bench for forty-five minutes, watching the dozen or so drivers smoke and pick their noses as they waited for some big spender to show up and ask for a ride to Mexico City. Finally, we walked back. It had taken me four hours to buy a tube of bug cream. I was beginning to sympathize a bit with Bingham.

Back in town, I stopped by the empty general store and tried my call again. To my surprise, Nati answered. *"Hola, señor explorador!"* she said. "Have you seen any of my cousins?"

"You have cousins around here?"

"No, my cousins the Incas!" She laughed and handed the phone to Aurita.

"Hi, honey, where are you? We got your message that you were in a place called Huancacalle, but it doesn't show up on Google Maps."

"That doesn't really surprise me," I said, looking over my shoulder out the doorway. Every word I spoke was echoed back to me on a two-second delay, as if I were shouting into the bottom of a well. "We're sort of in the middle of nowhere. How's everything there?"

"Let's see. Of course everybody misses you. Alex took third place at his cross-country meet. Lucas and Magnus are fighting over the medal. Yesterday a cat came into the clinic with a tumor the size of a tennis ball."

I was just warming up to the sounds of normal familial contentment—rarely has a description of one's stack of waiting mail sounded so inviting—when I noticed a digital timer on the phone, very rapidly counting down the few seconds I had left on my prepaid phone card. "Um, I'm sorry, baby, but we're about to get cut off. I love you and . . ." Click. I walked downhill through the deserted town.

I used to think that the musicians who play Andean pan-flute music in subways around the globe—those guys are probably Peru's third-largest export, after precious metals and Machu Picchu souvenirs—were just annoying. Bingham would have agreed; he described llama herders playing "weird, monotonous airs" of "simple strains . . . varied with high, screechy notes." But as I walked back through Huancacalle after my abbreviated phone call, it occurred to me that living in the chilly shadow of the Andes, you probably acclimate to melancholy just like you do to the altitude. It's no wonder pan-flute virtuosos can make a rendition of "Walking on Sunshine" (which I later heard at the Cusco airport) sound like a funeral dirge. The Andes are a lonely place.

Juvenal had invited everyone over to his home for lunch. The house was a carbon copy of Valentin's: two rooms, mud brick, thatch roof. This was evidently a semiformal occasion, for Mateo had not only removed his wool hat but combed his hair and put on a clean soccer jersey. John was wearing his nicest baseball cap. Rosa, Mateo and the Señora Cobos ate next to the fire in the cooking area. I sat at the table in the other room with John, Juvenal and Justo. The menu was roast chicken with seven or eight varieties of potato, offered in a palette of colors straight out of the J.Crew fall catalog, from ecru and rust to cinnamon and grape. We ate with our hands. The chicken was lean and gamy—even the breast meat tasted like a cross between duck and the drumsticks I knew at home. I asked Justo where he'd found it. His mouth full, he jerked his thumb over his shoulder out the open door toward the garden, where a small flock of poultry was pecking the ground.

"Juvenal found this one out there an hour ago. He's quieter in here." He patted his flat belly.

After the meal, we drank an herbal infusion made from greens picked in the Cobos's garden, which magically dissolved the lump of meat and potatoes in my gullet. Juvenal, who was usually too busy performing his twin roles as *jefe* and mule whisperer to chat, was relaxed at the head of the table and seemed open to answering some random questions. I asked how expeditions through this area had changed since Hiram Bingham's time.

"Well, the mules are easier to work with," he said. "Back then the mules were much more wild and forceful. Now they've been bred to behave."

I asked about a trick Bingham had boasted of using in this region—slipping a coin into the hand of Quechua farmers, which by custom required them to drop everything to work for his expedition, no matter how much they pleaded to be left behind and tend to their crops.

"You mean the *obligatorio*," Juvenal said. "Oh yes, that was definitely true. It was the tradition that if someone gave you money, then you had to do what they asked."

"It was a holdover from the Inca practice of *mit'a*," John said. "You were obligated to give a certain number of weeks each year to the state—farming, or weaving, or fighting in the army—and in turn the state would make sure everyone was always clothed and fed. Of course the Spaniards exploited it."

"Do you recall when you first started hearing about Machu Picchu?" I asked Juvenal.

"I think it was around 1940. My grandfather mentioned it around that time and it seemed like people had started talking about it. I visited Machu Picchu with my school in the early 1950s on what we called a 'promotion,' which was a group outing. What was it like? More or less the same as it is now, but more dangerous. There were no fences or anything back then, just straight drops two thousand feet down to the river. Guides used to tell stories all the time about people who took one step too far and—*adios!*"

"Bingham mentioned visiting a town called Tincochaca on his way to Vitcos. Any idea where that might have been?"

"We're in Tincochaca now. It's the same place as Huancacalle, just with a different name."

"Really? In that case, have you ever heard of a Spanish ore-crushing mill?" Bingham saw one about five feet in diameter and took that as a sign he was nearing Puquiura—and therefore the White Rock. It seemed like the sort of thing that might have been big enough to stick around for a century. "Any guesses where it might have been?"

"I don't know where it was then, but right now it's in my cousin Jose's backyard. Just knock on his door and tell him I sent you."

I stopped by Jose's house that afternoon, hoping to touch the stone that Bingham had, but no one was home. A neighbor assured me that he'd be back any minute, but I'd had enough waiting for one day. Rosa told me later that he wasn't expected to return for another week.

TWENTY-THREE

The Haunted Hacienda

Huadquiña, Peru

The day after his mountaintop excursion with Melchor Arteaga, Bingham continued down the Urubamba Valley. He knew that he'd seen something spectacular on that ridge; he just wasn't sure *what* he'd seen. It didn't match the geographic descriptions he had for either Vitcos or Vilcabamba, and he had no time for a second look, since he was expected at the Huadquiña hacienda, a half day's walk from Machu Picchu. On July 25, 1911, the day after Bingham made the discovery that would catapult his name into the pantheon of great explorers, the South Pole teams led by Amundsen and Scott were huddled in Antarctica, waiting out the austral winter's months of darkness and monotony. ("This journey has beggared our language," one of the survivors of Scott's expedition later wrote. "No words could express its horror.") Hiram Bingham was seated at the dining room table of "the finest sugar plantation and cattle ranch in this part of the valley," sipping red wine and enjoying a dinner cooked especially for him.

Huadquiña was a two-hundred-square-mile plantation and "a splendid example of the ancient patriarchal system," according to Bingham. The haciendas were holdovers from the earliest days of the Conquest, when Pizarro handed out large land holdings to his loyal supporters. When I'd asked Juvenal at lunch what he knew about the old estates in the area, he shrugged his broad shoulders and said,

"There isn't much left to see." Bingham's beloved hacienda system had lingered until the late sixties, when a leftist dictator ordered Peru's largest agricultural landholdings seized and redistributed to farmers, many of whom had been working under near-feudal conditions for generations. During one trip in the Land Cruiser, we passed near Huadquiña and I asked if we could stop and have a look.

I was glad that Bingham had taken a photo of the place in its prime, because the buildings I saw had decayed beyond recognition. The elaborate front gate was still standing, but the walls around the property had crumbled. Waist-high weeds thrived in cracks between paving stones. Much of the main Spanish-style house had collapsed, and its tile roof was covered in corrugated steel sheets. Hand-carved wooden balconies, where Bingham may have sat and gone over his notes as he puzzled over what he'd found at Machu Picchu, were slowly disintegrating. All the doors were padlocked.

"I understand why the land reforms happened, but how could the farmers around here just let this place fall apart?" I asked John as we tried, and failed, to find a path down to what had been Huadquiña's spectacular riverfront gardens. Comparing what I saw to the photograph Bingham had taken, the only recognizable feature was the campanile, which still held its two bronze bells. "Couldn't they find a use for it?"

"'Hacienda' is still a dirty word in these parts," John said.

Through a wrought-iron gate, we looked into what had likely been the dining room. The interior had been stripped clean except for some built-in shelves that held stacks of yellowed papers. It was probably the room in which Bingham had shown off his first freshly developed photographs of what he had seen at Machu Picchu. "They were struck dumb with wonder and astonishment," he remembered of his hosts' reactions. "They could not understand how it was possible that they should have passed so close to Machu Picchu every year of their lives since the river road was opened without knowing what was there."

From Huadquiña, Bingham continued on to another hacienda, Santa Ana. The owner introduced him to a friend, "a crusty old fellow" named Evaristo Mogrovejo, the lieutenant governor of a nearby town. Bingham offered Mogrovejo a silver dollar for each Inca ruin that he could show him. Mogrovejo accepted the proposal. One place Mogrovejo strongly urged him to visit was called Rosaspata, a name that mixes Spanish and Quechua to mean "hill of roses." It stood on a hill above the towns of Tincochaca—the modern Huancacalle—and Puquiura. If this was the same Puquiura that Calancha had described, Bingham knew, "Vitcos must be nearby."

TWENTY-FOUR

The White Rock

At Vitcos

L ike Bingham, the rebel king Manco Inca had thought long and hard about the location of Vitcos. In the middle of 1537, he realized that with Spanish reinforcements constantly pouring into the former Inca empire, he couldn't hold out for long at the fortress of Ollantaytambo. He called his chiefs together and delivered a rousing thank-you speech, concluding with what sounded like the imperial equivalent of resigning to spend more time with one's family. Manco informed his audience that he would be departing Ollantaytambo for an extended visit to the Antis, a jungle tribe that had been conquered by his great-grandfather, Pachacutec. The Antis lived in the Antisuyu, the easternmost of the four quarters of Tawantinsuyu. The land of the Antis was where the mountains collided with the Amazon jungle—the Spaniards are believed to have begun using the name Andes based on the name of the tribe.

On its well-fortified mountaintop, Vitcos was a good choice for a new headquarters. The move must have been planned as a permanent one. Manco brought along the mummies of his father, grandfather and great-grandfather. He was joined by his queen and favorite wife, Cura Ocllo, who had escaped from her captivity in Cusco. As they withdrew, Inca soldiers attempted to destroy the trails behind them, as if to slam the door on any Spaniards who came sniffing around. Manco's respite was a short one, however. Just weeks after the Inca left Ollantaytambo, a Spaniard named Rodrigo Orgoñez led a team of three hundred men toward the Antisuyu. The army stampeded into Vitcos, where one of the Incas' heavy drinking festivals was under way. The conquistadors found riches worthy of a king: glittering housewares forged from gold and silver; a golden sun idol; jewels; fine cloths; thousands of llamas and alpacas; several suits of stolen Spanish armor. Orgoñez even captured Manco's five-year-old son and the mummies of his royal predecessors. Mesmerized by these treasures, the Spaniards didn't notice Manco escaping with Cura Ocllo.

When Bingham followed Mogrovejo to the top of the ridge at Rosaspata, he took note of the mountain panorama, which seemed to match one Spaniard's description of views that encompassed "a great part of the province of Vilcabamba." On the far end of the bluff he spied the remains of an enormous building, which also squared with written accounts he'd read. The lintels of its doors were "beautifully finished," as would befit a royal residence, and the stonework was of a higher quality than he had seen at Choquequirao. Between the masonry and the site's proximity to Puquiura, Bingham was almost certain that he'd found a match. "If only we could find in this vicinity that Temple of the Sun which Calancha said was 'near' Vitcos," he knew, "all doubts would be at an end."

Once you've reached Huancacalle, it's a bit easier to find Vitcos these days. John and I walked there in under an hour from Sixpac Manco. We entered along a narrow crest that widens into a main plaza, like the stem of a wineglass expanding into the bowl. Row upon row of mountains unfolded in all directions, like the pews in an enormous natural cathedral. Crossing over to the plaza reminded me of my days as an altar boy, waiting nervously in the church vestibule for the organist to begin playing. Justo had tried to explain the *apus* to me while we sat in Puquiura munching popcorn. "They're sort of like God, Señor Mark. They watch over things. But it's like faith—you have to believe in them. If you don't believe in them, they don't exist."

"You'll notice that Vitcos, Choquequirao and Machu Picchu are all at the junction of rivers or have rivers winding around them," John

said, tracing his gloved hand in a semicircle. "That's no coincidence.
Nor is it a coincidence that Machu Picchu and Espiritu Pampa"—the
modern name for Bingham's Vilcabamba—"are almost equidistant
from this exact spot."

John pulled out a notebook and sketched a diagram of the trails that
led from Vitcos in Manco's time. It looked like a child's drawing of
the sun, with lines shooting out in all directions. "Everything had to
be interconnected for the Incas. Vitcos is a hub of the Inca trail system.
There were four major trails to Vitcos, branching into maybe twenty
others, which branched off into others. It all connected, like it was,
er, Minneapolis." He paused to let his unexpected analogy sink in.
"You could have walked from the south of Colombia to the center of
Chile. Look over there—that's the trail that Bingham took to Espiritu
Pampa."

The main building at Vitcos was enormous, much larger than anything at Machu Picchu—like a Walmart built with stone. When Bingham saw it, it was largely in ruins, torn apart by Spanish religious
fanatics infuriated by Inca paganism and generations of Andean treasure seekers looking for Inca gold. (Harvard's Farabee had warned
him: "Any good find ought to be thoroughly explored before leaving
it or it will be destroyed by the natives.") Vitcos has since been rebuilt
by the INC, but even as rubble a hundred years ago, its suitability for
the Sapa Inca must have been obvious. "It is 245 feet by 43 feet," Bingham wrote, awestruck by the dimensions. "There were no windows,
but it was lighted by thirty doorways, fifteen in front and the same in
back. It contained ten large rooms, plus three hallways running from
front to rear. . . . The principal entrances, namely, those leading to
each hall, are particularly well made."

"Here, try this," John said. He walked over to the perfectly rhomboid central doorway of the main building, walked through, turned
around and came back. "Now you try."

I tried. The portal narrowed as I entered. Then it narrowed as I
exited. Wait a second, wasn't that physically impossible? "How did they
do that?" I asked.

"The Incas were big on special effects," he said.

John and I ascended to the upper level of the site. Except for one young woman from the INC—Vitcos is so far off the main tourist trail that they don't even bother charging admission—we had the entire place to ourselves. John whipped out his GPS and began to take readings.

On my first trip to Cusco, John had taken me to a bookstore and loaded my arms with reading material. Then we waited ninety minutes for the proprietor to return from "right next door" with one final volume. (At one point he called the shop to pass along the message that he was "in a taxi, two minutes away.") The delay was worth it, for that book was Johan Reinhard's *Machu Picchu: Exploring an Ancient Sacred Center*. In it, Reinhard suggests that trying to understand places like Machu Picchu and Vitcos as individual, self-contained sites misses a larger point. These monuments were built in relation to the sun, the stars, the mountains—and to one another. Trying to wrap my head around such an idea, sitting in the middle of Manhattan, was like trying to understand what the color red looks like based on its dictionary definition. Standing center stage at Vitcos, though, the Sacred Center theory started to make sense. Kind of.

"See that small fort on the hilltop ahead?" John said. "A straight line leads from that fort through the middle of the site here to"—he turned around—"Inca Tambo, a very important peak, which is almost exactly due north of here. The walls of the building up here are perfectly north-south east-west, but the main building below us is a slightly different angle. I'm wondering if . . ." He waited for his GPS readings to update. "Look at that. *That* building has perfect alignment to Choquequirao. Amazing. How did they do that?"

Bingham had his own puzzle to solve while standing up here. He needed to find Yurak Rumi, the White Rock. Calancha's *Coronica* had pinpointed the White Rock's location through the story of two Spanish friars, Marcos and Diego. This pair, having heard that Indians were communicating with Satan up at a gigantic rock on the other side of Vitcos, decided to put a stop to the diabolical practice. They collected some converts and firewood and marched up from Puquiura. Bingham, having spent his childhood watching firsthand the effects of uninvited missionaries cramming their beliefs down the throats of natives, must have found a tale of dogmatic Christian proselytizers butting heads with the Incas irresistible.

Next to the White Rock was a large and important sun temple; beneath the boulder was a spring of water in which the Devil himself had been reported to have appeared. Having decided that a full exorcism was in order, the friars raised a cross, piled the kindling around the rock and its adjacent buildings, "recited their orisions," as Bingham put it, and torched the whole thing. Only the charred boulder remained intact. Calancha proudly recorded that "the cruel Devil never more returned to the rock nor to this district." Nor, most likely, did the friars, since the Incas were not amused by an act that, had the roles been reversed, could have been equated with blowing up St. Paul's Cathedral.

John and I followed a route down from Vitcos that wound around the mountain, dotted with the ruins of small Inca outbuildings. Most had deep holes burrowed in each corner. "Of course some of the *huaqueros* dug those," John said. "There's looted tombs everywhere here. They think it's where the Incas would have buried some gold."

We had seen almost nothing but blue skies since leaving Cachora, but today it was overcast gray with thick cottony clouds. "I think we'll have a big rain tomorrow or the next day," John said. The gray above contrasted with the lush green meadow we came to at the bottom of the trail. This field is known as the Andenes, Spanish for "terraces." The Incas landscaped the gentle slope into tiers, like the gardens of an English duke's country home. Scattered about were rounded granite boulders of various sizes. Several had geometric shapes carved into their faces; others had been cut into sofa-like banquettes. Many had flattened tops as smooth as if they'd been power-sanded. At least one rock had been chiseled into a perfect scale model of the hill right behind it. None that I could see, however, seemed to fit the description that Bingham had taken from Calancha.

"Did I miss something?" I asked John. He pointed ahead and to the right.

"This way."

Moments later, we came around the hill, and there it was—a gigantic boulder, fifty feet long and twenty-five feet high, a giant abstract sculpture that, when I squinted, looked like a large tugboat had been dropped into the middle of the Andes.

Once completely white, the rock was now coated with gray lichen. A wide horizontal stripe was carved into the side facing us, from which cube-shaped pegs protruded. ("It is significant that these stones are on the northeast face of the rock, where they are exposed to the rising sun and cause striking shadows at sunrise," Bingham wrote.) The spring beneath the rock had long ago dried up. Underneath, though, were some beautifully carved niches, possibly seats of some sort. John bent underneath for a closer look.

"I think that's where the princesses—the *ñustas*—sat," he said. "The top of the rock was for llama sacrifices." Bingham shared this opinion and noted that a small channel ran down from the flat top, possibly a gutter that carried away the blood from sacrifices. One spot was still white, a splotch at the very top of the rock. It looked familiar. I opened one of Bingham's books and compared the photo he had taken. "Look at this," I said to John. "The spot hasn't changed in a hundred years."

"There might be something in llama blood, or even some chemical they added to it, that prevents the lichen from growing," John said.[5]

We circled the rock. On the opposite side was a series of steps—whether they were altars, sacrificial platforms, or just an uncomfortable set of bleachers, we'll probably never know. This was the side adjacent to the sun temple that the friars had burned. In his book *For-*

---

5 There's one other possible explanation. Like many Inca sites, the White Rock has multiple names, one of which is Ñusta Ispanan, or "the Place Where the Princess Urinates." On a follow-up trip in 1912, Bingham noted: "Yesterday a little girl acting on her Indian mother's orders went and sat and urinated where the Inca princess is said to have done it years before. My examination of the rock today seemed to show that this custom was fairly common."

gotten Vilcabamba the explorer and architect Vincent Lee has a fascinating drawing depicting what he thinks this spot looked like in Manco's
day. If it's accurate, the Spanish priests had plenty to worry about. The
White Rock was the center of a large religious complex.

"That was a major temple entrance, what's left of it," John said,
pointing to the remains of what had once been a very impressive stone
door frame. Nearby was an enigmatic torpedo-shaped rock with a hole
drilled into it.

"This rock looks important," I said. "Must have been part of a ceremony."

"Actually . . . no. I call that the penis rock, on account of the shape.
Because everyone thinks there's gold inside these rocks, someone
drilled a hole into this one to stick in a piece of dynamite. Instead of
blowing up the rock, the dynamite flew out like a rocket."

As usual, proximity to Inca ruins had charged John's batteries, so
instead of retracing our steps back up and around on the INC-approved
path, he suggested that we return to Huancacalle by going *over* the
thousand-foot-high hill, which was covered by thick vegetation.
"Come on, Mark, let's do a bit of Bingham work," he said, a reminder
that regardless of how nice the sleeping accommodations might have
been on the 1911 expedition, Bingham wasn't afraid to cut his own
path when he suspected there was something good hiding in the vegetation. John led us up the steep slope through vines and brambles,
whacking branches out of the way with his bamboo pole. We couldn't
see more than a few feet ahead.

We emerged at the top an hour later, scratched and filthy. At the
summit stood the remains of an Inca structure with jagged ten-foot
walls like those at Sacsahuaman. A variety of plants sprouted from
every crevice, making it look like the Lost Chia Pet of the Incas. I
guessed that no one had visited the hilltop in a long, long time.

"Bingham was here," John said softly as he gazed out over the valley. Watching him scribble down notes as he prowled the tops of the
fortress ramparts, it wasn't difficult to imagine that I was seeing another omnivorous explorer doing the same thing a hundred years ago.

TWENTY-FIVE

The Road to Vilcabamba

Somewhere in the Peruvian Rain Forest

Back at the Sixpac Manco, Juvenal and Rosa were sitting around a table, laughing and sharing a liter of beer. They may have been celebrating Juvenal's success in convincing John and me that even though we'd used up most of our food and had dumped some empty gas canisters, we still needed six mules to get us to Espiritu Pampa. I was hoping they'd invite me to join the festivities when the garden gate swung open and in walked a caravan of mules and several weary-looking *arrieros*, bearing gear for a dozen Swedish trekkers. In minutes, our quiet oasis was thronged with chatty Scandinavians unpacking their bags and making bottoms-up hand gestures as they pointed at the half-empty bottle of beer. Checkout time.

The next morning, we were back on an old Inca trail, the very route Manco had used to flee from Vitcos. "Can't you just see Manco running over these stones, the conquistadors in pursuit?" John said.

After sneaking away from Vitcos as the Spaniards looted, Manco spent months trying to rebuild his rebel army. Painfully aware that he would never be able to defeat the occupying Spanish forces in traditional combat, he settled for guerilla warfare. His followers began to attack merchants who traversed the road from Lima to Cusco. The sixteenth-century Spanish conquistador and traveler Cieza de León recalled that those who were killed after being robbed were considered lucky. As for the unfortunate survivors, Manco's insurgents allegedly "tortured them in the presence of their women, avenging themselves for the injuries they had suffered, by impaling them with sharp stakes forced into their victims' lower parts until they emerged from their mouths." A thriving bodyguard business soon sprang up.

Manco decided to make his new home at a remote Inca trading settlement called Vilcabamba. The capital that he ordered hastily built sat about one hundred miles from the old one at Cusco, which had been established at a dry eleven thousand feet. Vilcabamba was constructed in rain forest below five thousand feet. "The difference in climate" between the two cities, Bingham noted, was "as great as that between Scotland and Egypt, or New York and Havana."

Manco used Vilcabamba much as Yasir Arafat employed his headquarters in Gaza: to rule his shadow kingdom and plot attacks on his enemy. One ambush killed twenty-eight Spanish soldiers who'd come to capture him. In April of 1539, the furious governor Francisco Pizarro dispatched "three hundred of the most distinguished captains and fighting men" in his army to take revenge, led by a man Manco despised—the youngest and nastiest Pizarro brother, Gonzalo. This was the same man who in Cusco had stolen Manco's favorite wife, Cura Ocllo, and then ordered Manco to be put in chains.

The search party paused at the deserted settlement at Vitcos, then marched through the windy, desolate Kolpacasa Pass. As they descended into the tropics, the vegetation became almost impenetrable. Horsemen in full armor were forced to abandon their mounts and proceed on foot, often single file and sometimes on all fours. Within this jungle labyrinth, the Incas had constructed diversionary bridges to funnel the Spaniards into a narrow defile. There, three dozen invaders were crushed by boulders that Manco's troops rolled from the tops of the surrounding hills.

The Incas had constructed a rock barrier that blocked the path to Vilcabamba. Rather than lay siege to this stronghold, Gonzalo Pizarro ordered some of his men to conduct a decoy attack while the rest of his troops circled around. Manco's defenders soon found themselves pinned down under harquebus and crossbow fire from above. Three quick-thinking Indians swept up their king and carried him to the river, where he swam across. From the far bank he shouted, defiantly, *"I am Manco Inca! I am Manco Inca!"* He declared that he had killed two thousand Spaniards and would kill the rest, too. Then he escaped once more into the jungle.

Their path cleared, the Spaniards descended the winding stone staircase into Vilcabamba. Here they found a new Inca capital hidden in the jungle—hundreds of stone dwellings, temples and even a massive White Rock to match the one at Vitcos. The city was all but deserted. The troops tore apart Vilcabamba, searching for treasure. Manco's wife Cura Ocllo was bound and taken prisoner.

Governor Francisco Pizarro received word in Cusco that Manco might now lay down his arms and enter negotiations toward his surrender. Delighted, Pizarro dispatched three attendants to the Inca, bearing exquisite gifts and a pony. Manco had the envoys put to death and killed the pony for good measure.

Pizarro channeled his fury at Cura Ocllo. The governor commanded that the Inca queen be stripped, beaten and tied to a post. A team of Cañari Indians, enemies of the Incas, shot her with arrows. Horrified Spaniards looked on as their leader ordered the queen's body dumped into a basket and dropped into the river, so that it would float downstream toward Manco's army. Several high-ranking Incas who were imprisoned in Cusco protested their queen's murder. They were burned alive in the central plaza.

When Manco's men retrieved Cura Ocllo's body from the river and reported the news to their ruler, the Inca wept uncontrollably.

TWENTY-SIX

Off the Map

Crossing Kolpacasa Pass

The Spaniards who ventured into the jungles of the Vilcabamba region in pursuit of Manco were entering terra almost entirely incognita. Reports claimed that the Antis were not merely cannibals but would slice pieces of flesh off their prey like sashimi, allowing the victim to witness himself being eaten alive. The tales were false, but as I'd learned from the devil goat episode at Valentin's house, the mischievous twins of Superstition and Legend tended to thrive in the Andes. Bingham got a taste of this after two local residents reviewed the passages from Calancha that referred to Vilcabamba. They guessed that the Lost City might actually be a place called Concevidayoc. This obscure settlement could be reached from Vitcos by following the Inca trail that ran west alongside the Pampaconas River—the same trail that Gonzalo Pizarro had used.

When Jose Pancorbo, the rubber baron who told Bingham about the ruins near Puquiura, heard that Bingham was planning to descend the trail to Concevidayoc, he asked the American to desist. Concevidayoc, Pancorbo said, was ruled by a fellow named Saavedra, "a very powerful man having many Indians under his control and living in grand state, with fifty servants, and not at all desirous of being visited by anybody." The Indians, he warned, were "very wild and extremely savage. They use poisoned arrows and are very hostile to strangers." Bingham and his naturalist, Harry Foote, tallied the pros and cons.

Their supplies had begun to run low. The two men were tired and would need to press-gang a new team of porters using the old silver-dollar *obligatorio* trick. On the other hand, Pancorbo's warnings were likely motivated by his own fears of being caught exploiting the local natives; rubber barons were despised by their Indian laborers, who were often beaten, tortured and treated as slaves when they weren't being worked to death. And the magical city of Vilcabamba might be just a few days away. Bingham and Foote decided to forge ahead.

John and I headed northwest with the mule team, passing beneath the tiny town of Vilcabamba the New. Bingham had stopped there to ask if anyone might point him toward the original Vilcabamba. One Indian told him that he might need to look beyond Concevidayoc to a place called Espiritu Pampa, or the Plain of Ghosts. Bingham was about to step off the map of the known world. "Would the ruins turn out to be ghosts?" he wondered. "Would they vanish on the arrival of white men with cameras and measuring tapes?"

The farther we traveled from Cusco, the more closely our movements mirrored Bingham's hundred-year-old travelogue. "We crossed the flat, marshy bottom of an old glaciated valley," he wrote, exactly describing our progress. "Fording the Vilcabamba River, which here is only a tiny brook, we climbed out of the valley and turned westward." John and I walked uphill to the Kolpacasa Pass, where a gale-force wind whipped our sweaty shirts like flags. "This is the gateway to the jungle," John shouted. I could barely hear him because my teeth were chattering so hard. John clambered atop a former *usnu*. I turned to look at the ground we'd covered that day. Far off in the distance we could see a row of snowy peaks, which turned out to be the Pumasillo Range. I could scarcely believe that this was the backside of one of the mountains that I'd seen from the top of the ruins at Choquequirao.

"There's a whole series of platforms like this leading all the way down to Espiritu Pampa," John shouted through the wind. "I'm sure Manco came up here and did his bit." John believed that *usnus* like this one may have been plated with gold or silver, so that when the sun shone on them, a chain of brilliant explosions linked the countless valleys of the Inca empire, like a game of telephone. "Can you imagine the impact something like that would have on the subjects? They must have been completely awed." His GPS readings showed that we were directly on the solstice line from Espiritu Pampa; on certain important days of the year, the *usnus* lined up directly with the point on the horizon where the sun rose—as well as with several important Inca sites, including the one to which we were headed. "It just blows my mind," John said.

According to Bingham's maps, when he reached the top of the Kolpacasa Pass, he should have been standing in the middle of the Apurimac River, the same one that flows beneath Choquequirao. In fact, the Apurimac is about twenty miles south of Kolpacasa. His later surveys showed that Bingham had entered "an unexplored region, 1,500 miles in extent, whose very existence had not been guessed before 1911." It was as if the ghost of Manco Inca had whispered the words, "Open sesame."

As John and I descended, the arid land became greener and haze clung to the hills. We stopped for lunch in an empty, marshy valley, where Justo and Juvenal were having a heated argument over what had been the largest fish ever spotted in a nearby river. Juvenal, as he always did with Justo, got the last word when he said, "One time I saw a fish bite a dog's head off."

The next day we entered the cloud forest, misty, mountainous terrain like that which surrounds Machu Picchu. We reached a suspension bridge, the kind that wobbles like Jell-O when you walk on it. The trick, John told me, was to move quickly rather than tiptoe across—a steady pace limited the shaking. "Once we cross this bridge, it'll be out of the fridge and into the oven," he said as we walked above the river. Bingham said essentially the same thing; he called the drop ahead of us "4,000 feet through the clouds by a very steep, zigzag path, to a hot tropical valley."

On the far side of the river we were startled by the first person we'd seen in hours. He was an old campesino, so withered that his hands and feet curled like claws. He asked us the same two questions everyone around there did, and received an affirmative response to both: Yes, we knew Juvenal, and yes, he could have a pinch of our coca. As he reached into John's plastic Baggie, I noticed that the farmer had raccoon circles around his eyes, which on closer inspection turned out to be coca leaves pasted around his sockets. "My eyes are in very bad shape," he told us, before bowing his head in thanks and trudging across the bridge and into the mist.

When I mentioned the stranger with the bad eyes to Justo later, after we'd suffered some serious bad luck, he was amazed that I hadn't recognized a bad omen when it stared me in the face. "The eyes, Señor Mark," he said, shaking his head. "The eyes never lie."

TWENTY-SEVEN

Trouble

Approaching Vista Alegre

After seven years of hideous fortune, Manco finally caught a break. The Spaniards who had chased him from Vilcabamba received word of bigger problems in Cusco and abruptly abandoned their pursuit. Manco returned to his jungle capital in exile and entered his first period of relative calm since he'd fled Cusco. He was able to split his time between Vilcabamba and Vitcos undisturbed. Attacks on Spanish travelers resumed with surprising ease.

In Cusco, a civil war had broken out between the Pizarro brothers and Diego de Almagro, one of Francisco Pizarro's two original business partners in the conquest of Peru. Almagro had arrived late to the bloodbath at Cajamarca and received only a small fraction of the bonanza from Atahualpa's ransom; he also deeply resented the title that the king of Spain had bestowed upon his partner. In revenge, Almagro seized control of Cusco. The Pizarro brothers overran Almagro's army in a battle outside of the city, after which Almagro was captured and executed in the Plaza de Armas. A group of surviving *Almagristas* retaliated by bursting into a dinner party at Francisco Pizarro's house in Lima and chasing down the sixty-three-year-old conqueror of Peru. Pizarro killed two of his attackers before his own throat was cut. His last act, William Prescott wrote, was "tracing a cross with his finger on the bloody floor," which he was bending over to kiss as he received a blow to the head that ended his life.

In an early example of the country's magical realist politics, seven of Pizarro's murderers sought asylum with Manco. The Inca allowed them to live in comfort at Vitcos, and in return they instructed their hosts in horsemanship, European weaponry and recreational games. While playing horseshoes in 1544, one of Manco's guests pulled out a dagger and stabbed the emperor from behind. The Spaniards, who had plotted the regicide in the hope of ingratiating themselves with the new post-Pizarro regime in Cusco, crowded around the Inca and knifed him repeatedly. They mounted their horses and fled, but Manco's men discovered them hiding in a thatched hut, which was set afire. The assassins were shot with arrows and clubbed to death as they attempted to flee. Three days after the attack, the great rebel Inca died at Vitcos of his wounds.

For the next two decades, Manco's sons Sayri Tupac and Titu Cusi played political cat-and-mouse with the Spaniards, who in a radical strategic shift, tried to co-opt the native leaders rather than exterminate them. Sayri Tupac eventually accepted a Spanish offer to leave Vilcabamba in return for a grand estate; he later converted to Roman Catholicism. Titu Cusi took his interest in the conquerors' religion further. He allowed priests to establish a church near Vitcos; when they burned down the White Rock temple, they left behind the clues—via their hagiographer Father Calancha—that ultimately started Bingham on his search for the Lost City of Incas.

The independent Inca state remained alive until Titu Cusi's sudden death in 1571, when the title of Inca passed to a third son of Manco, named Tupac Amaru. The new Spanish viceroy in Cusco noted a chill in diplomatic relations with Vilcabamba and decided to resolve the ambiguous political situation. On the Sunday before Easter 1572, he declared a "war of fire and blood" against the rebel Inca state.

At a newly constructed fort called Huayna Pucará, built along the road that John and I were following to Espiritu Pampa, the natives again plotted to drop boulders on their enemies. This time, the Spaniards seized the high ground immediately. Tupac Amaru fled deeper into the jungle, to what was now the last city of the Incas.

"This is a trail almost like Bingham would have seen," John said as we approached the onetime fort at Huayna Pucará. The cloud forest we walked through was thick with creatures: birds, lizards and lots of very big spiders with webs like hammocks. The path was just wide enough for two mules to pass each other. "Of course, Bingham would have had about half the clearance we've got. Imagine how daunting that was. To come into the forest and the clouds and the mist and think, *Oh shit—where are we going?*"

Walking briefly in the lead, I spotted a red snake with black and yellow stripes. I froze and quickly ran through the serpent-identification ditty that I'd learned researching a how-not-to-die-in-the-woods story a few years earlier:

> *If red touches black/You're okay, Jack*
> *If red touches yellow/You're a dead fellow*

"S'dead, Mark," said John. He walked up and flipped the stiffening body with his bamboo stick. "Looks like a false coral snake. Completely harmless."

The trail was a roller coaster; long, steep downhills broken up by sudden inclines. Bingham had raved about what wonderful agricultural country this was—he saw eighteen-foot stalks of corn—and I had equated that in my mind with the farms surrounding the land-grant universities of the Midwest. "I had sort of hoped things would level off by now," I confessed to John.

"You'd think the terrain would flatten as you get lower," he said. "Actually, the opposite is true."

We stopped outside the gate of a farm owned by the Condore family. The father sent for his son Samuel, who he said could lead us up to the top of Huayna Pucará. John had been here years ago and seen piles of boulders exactly as the Incas had left them before fleeing under fire from the Spaniards. "They're like cannonballs, lined up along the ridge!" he told me excitedly. Personally, I'd have preferred to skip another thousand-foot climb and descent to see some rocks that Bingham hadn't even known existed, but John kept staring up at the ridge in anticipation, so I kept quiet. As sweat seeped down to my knees, another Condore son stood close enough to us that I could feel his breath and told John four times, in a voice that I wouldn't describe as friendly, how much he liked his watch and wanted to buy it.

Samuel arrived and led us up a hill with a near-vertical slope. The ridge had recently been cleared by fire, and the soil was the blackest I'd ever seen, with the crumbly consistency of coffee grounds. Irregular rows of corn were being weeded by hand; most of the weeds were ferns. I struggled on all fours, grabbing any available tree or, more often, burned-out tree stump, as Samuel raced ahead in his unfastened galoshes.

After what seemed to me the sort of climb that should end with a champagne toast, we reached the top. No boulders. John suggested we move over to a higher peak, where he was certain he'd seen heaps of rocks the last time he was here. Reading manuscripts at my desk in New York, I had often puzzled over the term "knife-edge ridge." Now I could see clearly that it was the crest of a very, very steep hill where one had to walk as if on a balance beam. We ascended to the higher peak, but there was nothing there, either. "It looks like some kids pushed the rocks off," John said, gazing over the edge. "They're all gone."

For a moment, he looked like a child who'd dropped his ice cream cone. "Well, I tell you what. Let's have a bit of fun on the way down."

We gave Samuel a tip and asked if there was a route down that would let us keep moving forward toward the main trail rather than doubling back past his farm.

"Well, it's *possible*," he said, glancing sideways at the thick brush. Visibility down the hillside was about eighteen inches. "But it's a lot easier and probably faster if I just lead you back."

"Don't worry about us, we'll take care of ourselves," John said.

Samuel, obviously relieved, waved good-bye, turned and vanished before we could change our minds.

"It's about time you had a go at this, Mark," John said. He reached behind his shoulder, unsheathed his machete from its leather holster and held it up like Excalibur. *Yes!* I'd been begging him for a machete tutorial since we left Cusco. "All right, then. Make sure you strike the target at thirty degrees." Here he unleashed a series of samurai strokes that sliced easily through inch-thick branches and vines. In seconds, a pile of vegetation lay at his feet.

"You're going to lead for a while. Remember to cut with short, sharp strokes. And watch your feet—always make sure you're on solid ground. When in doubt, follow the higher trail."

Any trail that existed was invisible to me, but John, who saw corridors where most people would see impenetrable walls of bush, patiently nudged me in the right direction each time I got stumped. It will perhaps not come as a complete shock that I was not a natural with the machete. Mostly, I hacked branches four or five times before the sticks finally snapped under their own weight. Those times that I did hit the branch squarely, though, the feeling was electric—like hitting a perfect tee shot.

For about ten minutes we advanced a few feet at a time, Luke and Yoda slicing through the wilds of Dagobah. We reached a point where the trail seemed to fork higher in two directions. I chose left, stepped confidently onto what I quickly realized was not earth but three feet of grass-covered air, and did a perfect banana-peel pratfall onto my butt. The machete spun upward like a juggler's bowling pin and landed about six inches from my thigh.

"Well done, Mark," John said, holding my shoulder firmly with one gloved hand and retrieving his machete with the other. "Think I'll take over now."

The foliage thickened as we moved lower. The grass was waist high and ferns towered a foot over my head. Bamboo had crept into every free inch of ground space. Vines reached out and grabbed me around the neck and ankles. After falling down for the eighth time, I stopped counting. Solid ground was still difficult to recognize, and I had to poke the earth with my walking stick ahead of each step. John stopped every few seconds to cut trail, switching hands with the machete occasionally. "Otherwise your arm gets tired," he said.

Visibility may have been limited, but the cloud forest *smelled* wonderful. Herbal odors drifted through the air: wild mint, sage and thyme. At a brief clearing, John pointed out a waterfall across the valley, a thin stripe of white water cascading hundreds of feet down a hillside crammed with what looked like a million heads of broccoli. I wondered where all that water could possibly come fr—

Thwack.

"AIIHHGHHH!"

Uh-oh.

John dropped his machete, covered one eye with his hand and rocked back and forth, moaning. He'd sliced through a skinny branch that whiplashed back at him. Between deep breaths he exhaled two words: "Sloppy work."

John turned and brought his face close to mine, one eye clamped shut. His other eye had welled up with tears, and clear mucus was pouring out of his nose; he looked like he'd just been teargassed. He tilted his head back slightly and pried his eyelid open with two fingers. "How does it look? Any bleeding?"

The gash looked like the kind a kid gets on his elbow when he falls hard on the sidewalk, and then runs to his mother, who turns white and wonders if her son needs stitches. Like that—except it was in John's eye. Just looking at it, a nauseating Swiss-cheese taste crept up the back of my throat.

"Well, it's definitely scratched," I said, gulping. "There's some blood."

"Shit."

Had it been me who had walked into the branch—which two minutes earlier would have seemed to both of us an infinitely more likely scenario—I suspect that I'd have been forcibly immobilized like a papoose and given an injection of morphine that William Burroughs might have waved off as too risky. John removed his backpack and rooted around for a moment. He pulled out a vintage black Guns N' Roses bandanna and wrapped it over one eye, pirate-style.

For the first time on our trip, I considered the precariousness of the venture. We were still at least five hundred feet above the road, which was who knew how many miles—twenty? forty?—of hard walking from the nearest town in either direction. The trail down was steep and, from my perspective, utterly impenetrable. Dark clouds were rolling in. And John now had no depth perception.

Without a word, he shouldered his pack and started slicing anew with the machete.

An hour later, we reached the trail and continued onward to a log bridge. We stopped for a drink of water. John's one visible eye was clenched shut.

"That was a mistake," he said. It sounded like an apology, though whether to me or to himself I couldn't tell.

"You know, we can go back to the hospital at Puquiura if you need to."

"No, no, as long as the wound is clean we should be fine. Just pour a little water in it, would you?" He lay back, and I knelt behind him and dripped water from my bottle into his eye. I couldn't help but notice we'd almost assumed the position of Michelangelo's Pieta, with yours truly in the Virgin Mary role. John's nose was still running from the pain. He winced as the water splashed into his eyeball, tilted his head up and blinked hard, then let his neck drop.

"That's a . . . torrent duck . . . over there in the water," he said, pointing into the white water below us as I tilted the bottle again. "Swims in the rapids."

I nodded in agreement.

"I think . . . I think we may stop for camp early tonight."

We walked on to our lunch rendezvous. Juvenal began to approach with his usual toothy grin but took one look at John, spun around and started to unpack the medical kit. John wanted the eyedrops, and I

pulled out dozens of tiny boxes labeled in various languages searching
for them. One was marked GOTAS OTICAS. *Gotas*, I knew from listening
to bad Latin love songs in New York, were drops or tears. I remembered from my days working at a men's fashion magazine that *ottica*
was the Italian word for an eyewear shop. Italian and Spanish, as any
professor of Romance languages can tell you, are pretty similar. Getting to my feet, I marveled at the human brain's ability to pull together
such disparate knowledge in moments of crisis.

"Make sure the bottle says 'optica,' not 'otica,'" John said from his
chair. "Gotas oticas are eardrops."

I resumed the search.

We consumed our enormous lunch slowly. The four team members,
who usually wandered off as we ate, sat nearby in a tight group, watching us as they would a Ping-Pong match: John, Mark, John, Mark. They
were trying to decide if Señor John was still up to leading the expedition, because if he wasn't, Señor Mark was in charge by default. No one
was very excited about that possibility.

"Well, at least the rain never came, right?" I said as we sipped our
scorching hot tea in the midday sun.

"Sky was too clear this morning," John said. "Too much heat too
soon means rain. Should be a big one."

Around one-thirty, the clouds that had bounced around the corners
of the sky most of the day congealed and swelled. We put on our waterproof jackets and pack covers and waited for the deluge. It didn't
take long.

If I had to choose one word to describe the cloud forest in a rainstorm, it would be *slippery*. Dusty dirt trails swell into gooey mud-
slides. Rocks take on boot-repellant properties. Pretty log bridges over
gurgling streams are transformed into menacing frictionless cylin-
ders, plotting to hurl careless walkers into the white water below. The
jungle's warm breath fogs up eyeglasses and creeps underneath Gore-
Tex jackets, creating portable steam rooms. Once everything is *hecho
una sopa*—soaked like a soup—the temperature drops.

We stopped at a spot called Vista Alegre, which means "Happy View." Everyone parked together under the roof of a three-walled hut, kidding ourselves that the rain might let up. The sky was the color of an anvil. John sat in the corner, head down, rubbing his forehead through the black bandanna. Justo, a man whose charms do not include subtlety, kept shooting glances at me as he babbled in Quechua, evidently explaining how I'd seen a man with bad eyes and neglected to take proper precautions. Overwhelmed by the musk of six unwashed men in close quarters, I wandered off to sit beneath the eaves of the only other structure within our not-entirely-happy view—a one-room wood shack. For a long time I watched the angry rain fall on the hills and listened to the drops clattering on the steel roof. We had no choice but to camp for the night.

John disappeared into his tent at three and didn't reappear until six. This was a bad sign. Justo always served tea at four. John loved afternoon tea. I ate the equivalent of three large buckets of movie popcorn by myself as Justo walked in a circle inside the cook tent, wearing a tight smile, hands clasped behind his back. When John arrived for dinner, he looked ill. He had a ski cap pulled down over the bad eye.

"How's the eye?" I asked.

"It's spasming."

We ate in silence until Justo brought our pudding for dessert.

"John, I'm only going to say this one more time and then I promise to drop it. If you're not better in the morning, I don't care if you have to ride a mule back to Puquiura or find a roadhead somewhere and flag down a taxi to Cusco, I want you to go to the doctor."

John concentrated on his pudding.

"I have a thousand dollars in cash in my backpack to pay these guys," I said, "and I'd imagine that for that kind of money we could hire someone to give you a piggyback ride to Lima. Juvenal probably knows a shortcut, right? I can survive out here for a few days without you, and I can keep Mateo and Julián occupied with engrossing anecdotes about the capricious New York real estate market."

John fought back a smile, which looked like it hurt. "There really isn't anywhere to go," he said. "We're two days from the nearest road. But thank you. I think I'll be okay in the morning."

The next morning, despite having one eye that, with its big red dot, looked like the planet Jupiter, John declared himself fit for action. "Keep these in your pocket, just in case," he said, handing me the eye-drops. We never spoke of the incident again.

TWENTY-EIGHT

When It Rains

Concevidayoc

Our morning celebration of John's recovery was, by necessity, brief. The rain had continued through much of the night, and John and Juvenal's readings of the cloud cover agreed that much more might be in store for us once the temperature rose. The sidewinding trail we followed was a narrow slot canyon carved from reddish mud, its walls sometimes eight feet high, and we traced its contours like pinballs sliding down chutes. The Spaniards had abandoned their mounts nearby before invading Vilcabamba. Bingham had left his pack animals behind shortly before reaching Vista Alegre. Our mules carved spaghetti slalom tracks in the mud. It looked like a mini ski team had passed through before us.

With each looping turn in the path, new signs appeared, signaling that we were about to enter the rain forest. John pointed to a plant with enormous spade-shaped leaves, like a giant violet. "Elephant ears," he said. "The locals pick them to use as umbrellas." A little farther on, John stopped suddenly and aimed his walking stick at a tree branch twenty yards into the forest. "Look, Mark! It's the Cock of the Rock—*tunki* in Quechua—Peru's national bird!" A bird with a bulbous reddish-orange head and black-and-white body appeared to be having an epileptic seizure. "He's doing his male thing, dancing to attract a female," John said. We watched the *tunki* vibrate for a few minutes, but no ladies responded.

"The Peruvian rain forest is the sharp end of the evolutionary stick. See that plant there? It's a vine that wraps itself around a tree and sucks the life out of it until all that's left is a hole where the tree was." John motioned toward another plant with fronds like those my sisters and I used to weave into baskets during interminable Palm Sunday masses. "That one there has spines—if you touch them it'll burn for hours. The lower we go, the more careful you'll have to be about what you touch."

The drop in altitude made John nostalgic for rain forest excursions past. One time he had taken a helicopter trip into the demilitarized zone along the Peru-Ecuador border with a guy who traveled with nothing but a machete—he foraged food along the way and chopped his own shelter out of foliage each night. One day they ran into a group of white-lipped peccaries, the deadly, sharp-tusked wild pigs that roam the rain forest in packs.

"Jaguars and pumas are afraid of them because they *attack*," John said. "When they sense an outsider, they form a group. They make the most awful scraping sound with their tusks as a warning, and you can *smell* them. They give off this unbelievable odor that cuts right through the jungle. This fellow and I had to climb up a tree and hide for an hour and keep completely silent until the peccaries left, or they would have rammed the tree down and gored us. God, that was great."

We arrived at Concevidayoc and made camp on a slope above the river. Juvenal, who referred to this stretch of path as "my trail" because he had been walking the route since he was a boy, said that there had been some Inca ruins in this area but that they had been dismantled to build something, either the old school at the top of the hill or the new school down by the river. He wasn't sure. Any signs of the savage potentate Saavedra—whose bloodthirsty Indian army Bingham had professed to worry about—had vanished as well. Juvenal said that his grandfather remembered Saavedra as an eccentric neighbor who'd moved out around 1930.

The rain started again shortly after we fell asleep, and intensified through the night, with thunder loud enough to wake me more than once. In the morning, the campsite was a bog. The mules splashed up and down the hillside in a single-file line, Julián splashing behind them. Juvenal and Mateo sat on sawed-off logs inside a decrepit shed, warming their hands over a pile of burning sticks. John and I ate breakfast by candlelight. My copy of Bingham's *Inca Land*, which I'd absentmindedly left in an uncovered pocket at Vista Alegre, was soaked through—which seemed appropriate since in the pages describing his journey to Espíritu Pampa, rain followed Bingham like a shadow, drenching his weary party day after day and leaking into his tent at night.

"This is a real Amazon rain," John said, tearing his stale bread in half and picking off bits of mold. "It'll be snowing hard on Choquetacarpo Pass. Those bridges we crossed yesterday? We'd be going over them on our hands and knees today."

According to his account in *Inca Land*, Bingham continued down the trail toward Saavedra's house at Concevidayoc not knowing how he'd be greeted. He sent one of his porters ahead to announce the group's arrival. After waiting a tense thirty minutes, he wrote, "we were startled by the crackling of twigs and the sound of a man running. We instinctively held our rifles a little tighter in readiness." The approaching noisemaker was Saavedra's son, who came to offer his father's warmest invitation. "It was with a sigh of relief that we realized there was to be no shower of poisoned arrows from the impenetrable thickets," Bingham recalled, adding an extra dollop of melodrama.

Saavedra assured his visitors that he could get them to the ruins at Espíritu Pampa, though they'd have to wait for the path to be cleared as the old Inca site was "some distance farther down the valley, to be reached only by a hard trail passable for barefooted savages, but scarcely available for us," Bingham wrote.

For the time being, we weren't going anywhere, either. Mateo, always optimistic, stuck his head in the cook tent to share his opinion that the trail should be okay, because it was mostly rock. This elicited a rare guffaw from John. "He has no idea what he's talking about. That trail we were on yesterday has probably landslided since then because of the rain. If we'd left Huancacalle a day later we'd be waiting back there for a *long* time." He dipped his coca tea bag into his plastic mug. "There are two problems with an expedition in weather like this. Number one, you can't get dry, so you're always cold and at risk of hypothermia. Number two, the soil has no integrity, so it cannot support any weight. Plus, everything gets fungus—your tents, your feet. It'll wear you down, like it did to Bingham. It's better to just wait it out."

Since we were stuck, I thought I'd ask John something that had been puzzling me almost from the moment I'd met him—namely, how a beach-loving engineer from the far side of Oz had ended up wandering alone through the mountains of Peru. He'd brushed off the question on the trail two or three times. Confined to the cook tent, he finally relented. The catalyst, I learned, was a broken heart. It wasn't a girl, though. It was a travel outfitter.

"About 1987, Australia was becoming corrupt, more individual and selfish than it had been compared to the sixties and seventies. In Western Australia, where only a million people lived, we went ten billion dollars into the red. That's ten thousand dollars for every man, woman and child. One day I was watching television and I saw this advert that showed a mass of people all horribly crammed together and one person climbing over them to the top—like that was supposed to be a good thing. And I thought, 'I want out of this.'"

John had seen a brochure for London-based Encounter Overland, one of the first great adventure tour operators. The 1970s and '80s were the glory days of adventure travel, when the Hippie Trail across Asia grew up from a rite of passage for hash-addled hitchhikers into a flourishing tourism business driven by the last wave of pre–*Lonely Planet* wanderers. (In the travel magazine business, this penny-pinching personality was referred to, without affection, as the dirtbagger.) After initially showing skepticism at John's application to work as a driver-cum-guide, Encounter offered him an apprenticeship. "I sold my car, had a great big booze-up, burned my bed. I had thirty or forty thousand dollars and put it all into investments that my tax man recommended. I flew out on Tuesday. Friday was Black Friday in the stock market. I lost half my money. I got the news in London, where I was sleeping on the oil-stained floor of an unheated workshop and earning thirteen pounds a week."

John was assigned an early-1950s vintage Bedford, an open-backed truck with benches and a canvas top, and given charge of his clients for the next three to six months—more or less, since a driver never knew what contingencies might affect the schedule along the way. "One trip might have taken in Kathmandu, Nepal, India, Pakistan, Iran, Turkey, Syria, Jordan, Israel, Egypt, Sudan, Ethiopia, Kenya, Tanzania, Rwanda, Zaire, Central African Republic, Cameroon, Nigeria, sometimes Togo, Niger, Burkina Faso, Mali, Mauritania, Algeria, Morocco. Then back through Europe to London. You never had enough hours to do everything. It was always pressure, pressure, pressure. Ninety percent of the job was hard work. Ah, but the other ten percent . . .

"In Peshawar, Pakistan, all the mujahedin with their AK-47s would come to the hotel and watch the six o'clock news to see how the war was going in Afghanistan. We got permission from the military to go to the black market, where they had Sony TVs, blocks of heroin and ganja. We fired rocket launchers in the arms market of Darra. In the Central African Republic, the thieves were so good, you could have two people watching the truck and in a tree above it there'd be a guy reeling in daypacks out of the back with a fishing pole. The scenery was incredible, of course. But you wouldn't just *see* the gorillas and waterfalls. You'd *live* with the pygmies. Hunt with them. Sleep in their houses. In the middle of the night, dad would roll over onto mom, and do his business—*hooga, hooga, hooga*—and then go back to sleep. God, it was brilliant."

Most people burned out as drivers after a year or two. John thrived. "When I first rolled into Cusco in 1991, I saw three foreigners in three days." By the time he was named Encounter's coordinator for South America in 1998, though, serious adventure travel's moment had

passed, replaced by a bragging-rights mentality. "Travel today is tick-
ing things off: 'Whew, I've done Machu Picchu, now I can get drunk.'

"It used to take three weeks to get people in the right frame of
mind, to un-brainwash them. Now it would take three months just to
get people's heads straightened out. A lot of times, with women especially, these trips would change their lives. They'd go back to London,
quit their jobs and sack their awful boyfriends. It's a real problem
now—people don't know how to enjoy life. They want hedonism,
short-term thrills."

Eventually, John left Encounter. "Hardest decision I ever made," he
said. A couple of years later the company went bankrupt, taking most
of John's savings (and those of his colleagues) with it. Since then, he'd
been making his way around Peru, notebook and cameras in hand,
documenting what was left of the prehispanic culture. "No one followed up on Bingham's work for years," he said. "Maybe we could
have saved more of these Inca sites. I'm trying to nut it all out, put it all
together before it's all gone. There's Espiritu Pampa, Vitcos, Choquequirao and Machu Picchu. Everything else is being torn to pieces.
Look around here. There's *nothing* left here from Inca Concevidayoc.
History is just fading away without being recorded."

We stirred our steaming drinks and stared out at a wet dog that
searched fruitlessly for a spot to dry off, circling past the tent opening
every few minutes to see if we'd changed our minds about letting him
in. Its paws were six inches deep in mud.

"Think we'd better wear our wellies today," John said.

TWENTY-NINE

The Plain of Ghosts

At Espiritu Pampa

E ventually, the downpour slackened enough for us to start walking. Almost instantly, the scenery and climate changed once again, as if we'd pushed open the door to the tropical wildlife room at the Central Park Zoo. "Epiphytes, bromeliads, mosses! This is high rain forest!" John exulted, raising his arms. "Up there are the Andes. Down there is the Amazon." He turned around. "Watch out, Mark, those leaves there will cut your hand like a razor if you touch them."

After two days of waiting in Concevidayoc, Bingham's party departed on Saavedra's newly cut trail. A few hours of walking brought them to "the ruin of a small, rectangular building of rough stone, once probably an Inca watch-tower. From here to Espiritu Pampa our trail followed an ancient stone stairway, about four feet in width and nearly a third of a mile long."

After a few hours of downhill walking we arrived at the same platform and scrambled up on top. Below us, we could see the long stairway that curved down into the thicket below. "Obviously, this is a very important *usnu*," John said, pulling out his GPS. "Manco came up here. His sons, too, after he died. It connected down the valley, up the valley, and straight down into Espiritu Pampa. Imagine how impressive it must've been to look down from here onto hundreds of buildings.

Of course Bingham saw none of that—it would've been a mat of dark green down there." It still was.

Our slow walk down the winding staircase felt like descending into a forgotten world. The sound of moving water had followed us all the way from Vitcos, but the heavy tropical air here was still and quiet. I half expected to hear the roar of a Tyrannosaurus or the shriek of a pterodactyl. It was obvious why Manco had thought he'd be safe hiding here. In the 1980s this dense jungle had also been a stronghold of the Shining Path, the ruthless Maoist paramilitary organization that sought to ignite a revolution by executing thousands of their fellow Peruvians—rich and poor; men, women and children—often for no obvious purpose other than to incite fear. The group's reign of terror came to an abrupt end in 1992 when its charismatic leader, who went by the *nom de guerre* Presidente Gonzalo, was discovered living above a ballet studio in Lima. "There was a long period of time when guys like Mateo and Julián had to work on their farms during the day and hide in the bush at night," John said. "The Shining Path moved after dark and it wasn't safe to be caught sleeping in your house." John had heard that pockets of militants were still based in the area, trafficking cocaine.

John and I signed in at the Espiritu Pampa welcome hut. I scanned the register and calculated that outsiders had been trickling in at a rate of twenty to thirty per month. At the moment, there were exactly two visitors at the lost city Bingham had been searching for when he found Machu Picchu instead. John and me.

John's good humor evaporated when he saw that the mule team had set up our tents in the official campground. At least two dozen vocal turkeys and chickens free-ranged all over our equipment. To me, the accommodations didn't look too bad, and I'd long since given up hope of sleeping anyplace that didn't sound (and smell) like Old MacDonald's farm. There was a running spring to fetch water, an adobe brick shithouse and even a small chapel that didn't look like it saw a lot of business. A territorial rooster hopped atop a rock and screamed its

lungs out at us for about ten seconds, until Mateo, in one smooth motion, picked up a piece of packing rope, fashioned a lariat, lassoed the
annoying bird around its skinny legs and gave it a quick spin through
the air.

John had explicitly asked the muleteers to set up camp inside the
compound reserved for INC workers, which was much closer to the
ruins. Juvenal was prepared with a checklist of reasons why he couldn't
comply with John's orders: "The INC wouldn't allow it. The caretaker
thinks that the mules will eat all the grass. There's no water available
at the other site." He didn't mention one more possibility for his choice:
nostalgia. The Cobos family had once farmed the land we were on.
The caretaker's house directly behind us was Juvenal's childhood
home, now occupied by his cousin and his family.

John fumed. "I camped up there last time and it was *fine*. That does
it. I'm tired of giving the INC everything and getting nothing in return. I'm not talking to anyone from the INC this time." He went inside his tent and noisily unpacked his gear.

"It sounds like he's fighting a llama in there," Justo said to me.

"You think John is angry?"

"No, I think he's crazy. But he'll get over it."

Thirty minutes later, John and I were standing inside the INC
compound, encircled by a dozen young government workers who'd
stopped scrubbing pottery shards to gawk at John's photo album. His
pictures were serious entertainment in a place with no phones, Internet, Xbox or electricity. ("We get a lot of sleep," one fellow told me
when I asked what they did for fun.) The commune, with its thatch-
roofed huts, looked like a remote Polynesian village, and was almost
as isolated. Every worker was male, and between the ages of eighteen
and twenty-five, except for the boss, Javier, who looked about thirty.
One guy was doing bicep curls with a barbell fashioned from a bamboo pole and soda bottles filled with water. Some budding entrepreneur had gathered a bumper crop of achiote leaves, which are sold as
an herbal remedy for prostate problems, and spread them out on the
ground to dry.

We stepped into Javier's office, where he and his lieutenant, Paul, were piecing together an intricately carved wooden drinking vessel, a *kero*, the fragments of which had recently been dug up. John and Javier knew each other from a few years back when they'd crossed paths at an excavation near Machu Picchu. Javier and Paul were thrilled to have a chance to show off their work. "Here, you want to hold it?" Paul said to me, thrusting the fragile four-hundred-year-old artifact into my hands. The woodwork was exquisite, with geometric patterns overlaying one another so tightly they might have been woven. "Just think, an Inca drank out of that," he said.

"Let's take a look at the ruins," Javier said.

Bingham had been escorted to Espiritu Pampa by "two adult savages we had met at Saavedra's, accompanied by a cross-eyed friend, all wearing long tunics." Juvenal had told me that these Indians were Campas, and that as a boy he'd seen them living in the ruins, still dressed like monks; they remained there until the Shining Path scared everyone away in the 1980s. Various subgroups of Campas still lived nearby, somewhere not far beyond the ranges, but the secretive tribe didn't welcome outsiders. "Basically, they're the same people that Bingham met," John said. "God, I'd love to go in there. They could tell a few tales, take you to a few places."

Javier had a slightly less romanticized view. He'd only seen the Campas once, when they came down from the hills, wearing their traditional costumes. That visit was enough for one lifetime. "Mark, if you meet any natives in the forest, run away," he told me. "They live by their own laws."

Unlike the spiffy ruins at Machu Picchu and Choquequirao, the village square at Espiritu Pampa looks like it might have been found last year. Families had hacked out small farms along the entrance path, wherever an acre or two could be reclaimed from the foliage. The welcome sign was a sun-bleached wood plank hand carved in block letters, nailed to the trunk of a looming, hundred-foot-tall *matapalo* tree: BIENVENIDOS A ESPIRITU PAMPA. There was a sense that the jungle was just barely being kept at bay. Small teams of roving teenagers

called *vigilantes*—the name in Spanish simply means "watchmen"—
wielded machetes to make sure it didn't happen. Matapalos trees—the
strangler figs that smother their hosts—had grown over and under and
through buildings, to the point where trees and buildings were insepa-
rable. Many of the stone walls were propped up with two-by-fours.

Bingham's Campa guides led him to "a natural terrace on the banks
of a little tributary of the Pampaconas [River]," a spot they called
Eromboni Pampa. Almost immediately, one Indian showed the explorer the foundation of a huge building, which measured 192 feet in
length. Nearby was a three-spouted Inca fountain. Several hundred
feet away, "hidden behind a curtain of hanging vines and thickets so
dense we could not see more than a few feet in any direction," they
found a group of stone houses whose construction materials and style
"pointed to Inca builders."

The next day, Bingham's cutters found two well-preserved Inca
buildings in good condition and a stone bridge. The buildings were
of "superior construction, well-fitted with stone pegs and numerous
niches, very symmetrically arranged," the explorer observed. There
the discoveries ended abruptly. "Saavedra's son questioned the savages carefully," Bingham wrote. "They said they knew of no other
antiquities."

One minor discovery struck Bingham as "very puzzling." These
were "half a dozen crude Spanish roofing tiles, baked red . . . of widely
different sizes, as though some one had been experimenting. Perhaps
an Inca who had seen the new red tiled roofs of Cuzco had tried to
reproduce them here in the jungle, but without success."

Having seen the high-altitude Inca architecture of Cusco and Vitcos, the insect-choked ruins Bingham found at steamy Espiritu Pampa
were a letdown. The geographical clues he'd found in the Spanish
chronicles indicated that he was standing in the lost city of Vilcabamba.
But Bingham found it difficult to imagine that an emperor who had
settled with his followers in those spectacular mountain aeries could
ever have convinced them to live in a modest jungle exurb. "It does not

seem reasonable," he hypothesized, that such people "would have cared to live in the hot valley of Espiritu Pampa."

After two days the team was exhausted (the Campas had "determined to make the night hideous with cries, tom-toms, and drums," Bingham recalled) and running low on food. Bingham was eager to sort through his discoveries and start preparing for his Mount Coropuna climb. The team retraced its steps to Saavedra's house and began the journey back toward civilization. Bingham would never return to the ghost town in the jungle.

With Vitcos and possibly Vilcabamba in the bag, Bingham turned his attention to his last major objective: climbing the "virgin peak" of Coropuna. (His one other goal, to measure the depth of Lake Parinacochas, was a total bust—he'd brought along a thousand feet of line to plumb a body of water less than five feet deep.) The explorer had met up with his rival, Annie S. Peck, on the ship down from Panama to Peru and claimed to have come away unimpressed. In a letter to Alfreda, he dismissed Peck as "a hard-faced, sharp tongued old maid of the typical New England type." Thanks to her 1909 ascent of Mount Huascaran, though, Peck also happened to be something that Bingham was not: one of the most famous alpinists in the world. Because of Bingham's busy schedule, she also had a head start. A *Boston Post* story published while Bingham was en route to Peru, headlined MISS PECK IS RACING YALE MAN, hinted at his true feelings: "It is an open secret to [Bingham's] friends that he has been chafing under his routine work ever since he heard that Miss Peck had started on the first lap of the race."

Peck was well aware that she had gotten under Bingham's skin. Upon learning that she had a rival for the summit of Coropuna, she had written Bingham a teasing letter inquiring if she might fill him in on any details of the mountain that he proposed to climb. Before sending the note, she inserted a clause noting that unlike *some* people she could name, she had observed Coropuna "from nearer than the railway." Bingham's reply was less than gallant: "Under the circumstances do you not think it would be more sportsmanlike, now that this expedition has been definitely announced and approved by the Yale Corporation, for you to postpone your investigation of Coropuna until we had finished our work?"

When he arrived in Arequipa to begin his assault on Coropuna, Bingham was greeted with the deflating news that Peck had succeeded in climbing the peak while he had been fixated on his glacial bone discovery outside of Cusco. One news account reported that Peck, a strong supporter of women's suffrage, had planted a flag reading VOTES FOR WOMEN at the summit. Yet Peck, who had never shown a reluctance to blow her own horn in the past, was uncharacteristically silent about her triumph. Other than one newspaper story, Bingham couldn't find any further confirmation of her feat. The reason was simple. Coropuna is a horizontal mountain with multiple peaks. Faced with a choice of summits, Peck had selected the wrong one to climb. "No wonder she doesn't talk about it much," Bingham wrote to Alfreda, with no small satisfaction.

Today, most mountaineering outfitters rate the Coropuna climb as moderately difficult and can get a reasonably fit client to the peak and back in a few days. Bingham couldn't have known this, of course, and so deserves credit for possessing the nerve to attempt to reach what he believed was the highest point in the hemisphere outfitted in metal spikes and a bulky cardigan sweater. The climb was miserable. The deep snow near the top melted each day in the afternoon sun, creating a slushy mess in the clouds, and Bingham was hit hard by altitude sickness. On October 15, after some guesswork as to which of Coropuna's peaks was the highest, the team reached the top of what appeared to be its tallest summit. Utilizing two specially made aneroid barometers ("each as large as a big alarm clock," and which gauged altitude based on air pressure) and a hypsometer (a sighting device used to triangulate heights), Bingham made some quick calculations and realized that the peak they stood atop was, in all likelihood, several hundred feet lower than Chile's Mount Aconcagua.

Bingham's son Alfred later wrote an entire book to make the not-entirely-convincing case that his father was more interested in climbing Coropuna than in finding Vilcabamba. But while that seems a stretch, it is true that among all the photographs Bingham was careful to pose for at each of his achievements, the snapshot at the summit of Coropuna is unique. Despite the headache and nausea brought on by *soroche*, the director of the Yale Peruvian Expedition is flashing a tooth-baring grin.

THIRTY

The Old Woman's Secret

At Espiritu Pampa, continued

Espiritu Pampa felt a bit like summer camp for archaeologists: no girls, no grown-ups, lots of guys disparaging one another's anatomical shortcomings and punching one another in the arm. John, Javier, Paul and I walked toward the main site down a tunnel hacked through the jungle. As we rounded a bend, Paul grabbed my sleeve and said, "Hombre, you've got to try this!" A giant liana vine hung down from the canopy into the middle of the path. A tree stump served as a jumping-off point for anyone who wanted to take a Tarzan-style swing, which was, naturally, pretty much everyone. Paul leapt up on the stump, grabbed the vine and hurled himself forward, brushing the ferns on either side of the trail as he swung like a pendulum. When he dismounted, he handed the vine to me. It was like flying.

Being far off the tourism path, Paul and Javier were left alone to excavate, and they were pulling some extraordinary relics out of the ground. As we walked to the site's sun temple, Paul told me about some ceramics that they had found that seemed to tell the history of Manco Inca. "There are pictographs all around the outside," he said. "Sort of like hieroglyphics."

This seemed a little far-fetched. After all, if such a pot were found at Machu Picchu, the discovery would be broadcast around the globe; National Geographic would dispatch a video crew, and Peru's president would appear on TV crowing about this fine example of his country's proud patrimony. (John had taken part in a minor discovery near Machu Picchu a few years back that had generated a flurry of hyperbolic international media coverage.) But archaeologists are just starting to scratch the surface—literally—at Espiritu Pampa. As we stood just below a spot where Bingham once posed for a famous photograph in his fedora, standing rakishly over an Inca doorway, the camp's intern/cook/factotum, a teenager named Roni, leaned over and picked up a piece of ceramic—a pot handle shaped like a puma's head. Beneath our feet were piles of red tiles just like the ones that baffled Bingham. Paul and Javier's team had found intact roofing tiles, hand-painted with symbols. "They are so beautiful," Paul said, holding his hand over his heart.

"Could we see them?" I asked.

"Are you serious? I thought you'd never ask," Javier said.

We walked back to the compound, exchanged greetings and friendly insults with the potsherd scrubbers, and entered a dark, barnlike building. We sat down on benches at a handmade table near a wedge of sunlight that peeked through the open door. Roni served sweet, milky punch in metal cups. Javier ducked under a plastic tarp and started to pull out items. The first piece was a giant roof tile with three serpents painted onto it. He and Paul shouted simultaneously, "*Amaru!*"—Quechua for "snake." "The serpents symbolize the Pachamama," Paul explained. Javier showed off some burned corncobs, possibly leftovers from a four-hundred-year-old dinner. A small pot in the shape of a soup tureen looked like it could have been purchased at Crate and Barrel. Finally, Javier pulled out the Manco Inca pot, which had been glued back together.

"Here, hold it," Javier said, passing the ceramic to John so that he could trace the illustrations that circled its perimeter. "Look, there are the local natives, there's a serpent, there's a Spanish horse. This piece is totally unique. There's nothing like it anywhere else."

The pot was mesmerizing, quite possibly a direct link to Manco himself. At that very moment, Peru and Yale were gearing up for a custody battle over relics that Bingham brought back from Machu Picchu. I'd been to Yale's Peabody Museum and had come away confused; press reports in Lima about the Yale versus Peru controversy had made it seem like Bingham had run off with King Tut's treasure, but nothing at Yale was half as interesting as what John held in his hands.

"Do you know that what you've got here is more impressive than anything Bingham found at Machu Picchu?" I said to the INC men across the table. Javier looked at Paul, then back at me.

"That's ridiculous," he said. Neither he nor Paul could imagine that anything their humble digging had found could compare to the ancient wonders that Bingham was assumed to have unearthed.

In the morning, John, Justo and I made a circuit of the main ruins. Even as a ghost town, Espiritu Pampa keeps growing. Javier had told us that a few years ago archaeologists believed there were four hundred buildings here. Now they knew of at least seven hundred, stretching over an area more than a mile square. "We've been told that there's another settlement hidden in the forest here, a gigantic stone surrounded by buildings," Javier told us. "But no one knows where it is. A Japanese team came here a few years ago especially to find it, and they couldn't do it, either. There are a lot of things still out there."

The abandoned village seemed marginally less spooky in the morning sun. A massive boulder, similar to the one near Vitcos, anchored one corner of the clearing like a sleeping elephant. The rock looked even bigger when Justo stood next to it. He had first come to Espiritu Pampa as the cook on an expedition forty years ago, when the site was virtually unchanged from Bingham's visit. "This looks completely different," he said, swiveling his head to take everything in. "But also the same." Then he wandered off.

Javier asked one of his *vigilantes*, a kid named Juanito, to take us deeper into the forest to get a sense of what Bingham had been able to see. We crossed the plaza and continued into the woods, uphill, and over a river.

This was the most serious jungle that I'd walked through. The ground was a spongy carpet of leaves out of which sprouted trees, vines, and broad-leafed plants that competed for the little sunlight that trickled down from above. The only animals visible were small birds. "The monkeys around here come out mostly at night," Juanito said. We walked close enough to a river for its current to drown out our voices, yet I never saw the raging water. It's no wonder that anthropologists believe that there are still uncontacted tribes living in the Peruvian Amazon.

Juanito told us that there was an *usnu* up ahead, which naturally got John excited. After twenty minutes of thigh-burning work that made me think fondly of the switchbacks at Choquequirao, we stood atop the 750-foot-high slope. There were no ruins, just a nice overview of the site, which stretched on for a couple miles, maybe more—we may never know how big this place was in its heyday. Still, between the fiasco at Huayna Pucará and the lack of drama after this climb, I was definitely starting to doubt that these *usnu* ascents were worth the effort.

Javier had invited us to swing by the weekly Espíritu Pampa soccer match on our way home, but I was exhausted and begged off to go wash up in the spring at the campsite. Like Bingham when he departed Espíritu Pampa, we were headed back to civilization the next day and I wanted to look presentable.

And like Bingham, we were running low on supplies. Justo's conga drums were empty except for dehydrated soy chunks and noodles, which he'd served yesterday. I gave him $10 to buy one of the chickens roaming the campsite, so our valedictory dinner was pasta with soy chunks and stringy poultry that brought to mind the storks Bingham had survived on in Venezuela. As we ate, John pulled out photocopies of pages from *Antisuyo*, a book written by American explorer Gene Savoy after his expeditions to Peru in the 1960s. (Juvenal's father and brothers had been Savoy's guides.) Savoy's work here had helped to start the unraveling of Bingham's reputation, years after the Yale man had died. John was more interested in a story Savoy had told of an old Machiguenga Indian—a subset of the Campas—a woman spurned by her son the chief, who in return for some food had told the explorer:

that if we went to a high, cold place, to a mountain peak (known to us) and to a certain lake that had been guarded by Machiguengas for centuries, we would find great ruins. But she warned us to be careful of the enchantment. Every person that has gone to these two places has coughed blood and died.

John was spellbound by the tale, which wound back all the way to the final hours of Vilcabamba. At 10 A.M. on June 24, 1572, the Spaniards had marched on foot into the last Inca capital. Four hundred houses smoldered in the city center. Stores of food were still smoking. "They found the entire town had been sacked," so thoroughly that "if the Spaniards and [their ally] Indians had done it themselves, it could not have been worse," wrote the Spanish missionary Martin de Murua. Not a soul was to be found. Tupac Amaru had vanished into the Amazon with his pregnant wife. The Spaniards pursued the Inca on rafts and coerced details of his progress from the natives they encountered. After chasing their quarry more than two hundred miles, the Spaniards found Tupac Amaru and his wife huddled over a campfire. They had been fleeing on foot, because she was afraid of the river.

Tupac Amaru was dragged up the steps from Vilcabamba with a golden chain around his neck and led to Cusco for a brief show trial, at which he was sentenced to death. Before a crowd of curious Spaniards and wailing natives in the Plaza de Armas, Tupac Amaru lay his neck on the chopping block. The executioner severed his head with a single blow.

The Spaniards then made a grave tactical error by placing Tupac Amaru's head on a pike in the main square. Rather than take the gruesome display as a warning, natives began to worship the head. Over time, the deaths of Tupac Amaru and his uncle Atahualpa merged into what became known as the Inkarrí myth. This story, passed orally through the generations, foretold the resurrection of a great Inca,

whose severed head would join his buried body to overthrow the conquerors and return Tawantinsuyu to its former glory.[6]

John was convinced that when the Spaniards approached Vilcabamba, the sun king's treasure had been carried off by Indians into the
woods surrounding Espiritu Pampa, to be kept under guard until a
new Inca returned. He pulled out a satellite map of the area and
pointed to a spot near where we were sitting. It was Gene Savoy's secret mountain. Savoy never made it.

"Do you think anyone's ever been up there?" I asked.

"*I've* been up there," John said.

"And?"

"That's *serious* country. There's nothing up there. You have to bring
your own water in. I was carrying eighty-five pounds on my back. I
remember taking off my pack and almost going into shock from the
stress."

"So was the old lady telling the truth?"

"I don't believe there's any major ruins up there—it's too miserable.
That was quite a trip down, though."

"What happened?"

"The day I decided to leave I could see the clouds coming in. *Uh-oh*.
I started plowing through the grass, which was shoulder high. I cut
across a ridge, thinking I'd save a day. The drop-off was almost a thousand feet. I was cutting brush, just barely hanging on sometimes, and
it started to rain. I was carrying a lot of weight, of course. The slope
must have been seventy degrees. And there was a moment when my
foot started to slide. I knew that if I didn't stop it, I was going to die."

"What'd you do?"

---

6 In 1780, a rebel leader who had taken the name Tupac Amaru II led an unsuccessful indigenous revolt. When captured, he was made to watch the executions of his
wife and son in the Plaza de Armas, after which his tongue was cut out and—
following a failed attempt to pull him to pieces between four horses—he was beheaded and his body dismembered. Two centuries later, the Black Panther Afeni
Shakur was so inspired by this revolutionary that she named her son, soon to gain
his own fame as a rapper, Tupac Amaru Shakur.

"I shoved my stick into the ground with as much force as I could and used it to arrest my foot. Then I *very slowly* tied my daypack and backpack to a bush, gathered my strength, and worked my way back up the slope."

"Did your life flash before your eyes?"

"No, no. You have to keep your cool, Mark. Without discipline, you're dead. I can tell you this, though. At the moment my foot started to go, I did think of that old lady and her curse."

A normal person—let's use me as an example—might take such an experience as a sign that it was time to dial back on exploring for lost ruins. John disagreed.

"There are no more Machu Picchus to be found—probably—but there's still a *lot* to be found out there. There was a city full of people here until July 24, 1572. When the Spaniards arrived no one was left—the city was burning! Where did everyone go? The Campas had run into the forest." John looked longingly in the direction of the Indians' no-go zone. "I bet they're *still* guarding things if they haven't forgotten them."

In the morning, the muleteers broke down camp for the last time, amid plenty of giggling and practical jokes. Mateo, who was a very good actor, briefly convinced me that he'd lost a mule. Justo, who couldn't keep a straight face at his mother's funeral, was less successful when he slapped his forehead and claimed that he'd forgotten to boil the water we were drinking—the extremely hot water that he had just poured us out of a steaming kettle. We hiked a few hours out to the roadhead, where Edgar was waiting for us in the Land Cruiser. The town looked like a village of garden sheds. It had been slapped together to meet the newest end of the ever-lengthening road. "None of this was here three years ago," John said.

Mateo and Julián prepped the mules for the walk back to Huancacalle. As a farewell gesture they grabbed Justo, hoisted him over their heads and threatened to lash him to the roof of the truck with the rest of the luggage. I handed out payments, we shook hands—firmly with Mateo, softly with Julián—and the rest of us took seats in the Toyota, except for Juvenal, who climbed in the back among the bags and fell asleep. "Good luck, Papi!" Mateo shouted into our dust, waving as we drove off.

"How about a little music?" Edgar asked.

Among the ideas I'd had time to chew over while walking was a theory about the surfeit of bad eighties music in Peru. Here's my best guess: around 1992, the record companies in New York and London gathered together all the millions of cassettes and CDs that they couldn't sell, even marked down to 99 cents at truck stops, and shipped them off to Peru, where they were air-dropped all across the country. How else to explain the fact that Edgar possessed a copy of the album that Pat Benatar released two albums after the album that had "Love Is a Battlefield" on it? How else to explain the extraordinary "Worst of the Eighties" mix that he played on repeat for the six-hour drive to Quillabamba? "Playing with the Queen of Hearts" was followed by "99 Luftballoons," which segued into "Sister Christian" and "We Don't Have to Take Our Clothes Off." Peru doesn't give out knighthoods, but if they ever start, Kenny Loggins should probably get his tux pressed.

I was contemplating Bingham's complaint that he had to hear someone play "Tonquinoise" on the piano every time he set foot in a new hacienda, when a song came on that I couldn't remember ever having heard before, though it was so awful that I may have simply repressed the memory. It sounded as if Leonid Brezhnev had holed up in the Kremlin with a Casio keyboard and the cast from a junior-college production of *Les Misérables*. John, who had up to this point shown zero interest in any genre of music, sang along with gusto and pounded the back of Edgar's headrest: "Moscow, Moscow, drinking vodka all night long/Keeps you happy, makes you strong/A ha ha ha ha ha!"

"My God, what is this?" I asked John.

"Theme from the 1980 Moscow Olympics. Very big in Australia. You probably don't know it because of the boycott."

I made a mental note to send Jimmy Carter a thank-you card.

THIRTY ONE

Waiting

Near Santa Teresa

We spent a night in Quillabamba, a small city with some features that struck me as overwhelmingly cosmopolitan after two weeks in the backcountry: two-way traffic, restaurants, couples holding hands. Juvenal unfolded himself from the back of the truck, grasped my hand, said, "Good luck, Marco," and walked off into the sunset to catch a bus home to Huancacalle, leaving me to wonder if he'd known my name all along. The only memorable moment of our urban respite occurred when a pharmacist with whom I'd been conversing in Spanish made my year by asking whether I was visiting from Madrid. Because I'd learned to speak Castellano in Spain, I had a habit of pronouncing soft C's with a European lisp that the muleteers found hilarious—a hypothetical order for five beers would come out of my mouth as *"theenk-o ther-vay-thas."*

Not long ago, it had been possible to catch the train to Machu Picchu from our next stop, Santa Teresa. Or rather, from what used to be Santa Teresa. The original town was swept away during the El Niño climate craziness of 1998, by a mud slide caused when a chunk of glacial ice cracked off the side of a nearby mountain. A wave of earth and rocks roared down the valley, wiping out an entire train line, burying a power plant and killing at least twenty-two people. When Edgar pulled over on the highway for a relief stop, we looked down into a riverbed where a gentle current flowed over twisted iron rails and smashed train cars.

There are three ways to reach Machu Picchu, two of which are well known—taking the train from Cusco and hiking the Inca Trail. We were stopping in Santa Teresa to check on the train schedules for the "back door" route to Machu Picchu,[7] a small train shuttle that runs once a day from a hydroelectric plant on the Urubamba River. We'd then spend a day climbing to Llactapata, which has been called the Lost Suburb of the Incas because of its proximity to Machu Picchu. Bingham had found Llactapata during his follow-up Peruvian expedition in 1912. Like a surprising number of his discoveries, it had fallen out of sight for decades—in spite of the fact that it sits just three miles from Machu Picchu and, when cleared of brush, is plainly visible from the more famous site. John had been a member of the team that conducted the first major scientific investigation of Llactapata, in 2003, much of which was based on old coordinates that the explorer Hugh Thomson had found among Bingham's dusty papers at Yale. John therefore had a proprietary interest. "There's some *fantastic* stuff up there," he told me as we did some last-minute shopping in Santa Teresa. "They're just beginning to understand how closely related it was to Machu Picchu."

We drove on through a dry valley to a small cluster of huts at the bottom of a steep slope. John knew some porters we could hire to carry our packs up to a campsite near the top, next to Llactapata. We'd spend a day looking around and then descend to the Hidroeléctrica train station. The afternoon ride to Machu Picchu lasted about forty-

---

7 Incidentally, for those who have the time, this is a much cheaper way to get to MP—you take a bus to the big town of Santa Maria, transfer to a smaller bus at the smaller town of Santa Teresa, flag down a *combi* bus to the train station at Hidroeléctrica and walk along the tracks. As of this writing, a fit person with lots of spare time and a strong back could get to Machu Picchu for about twenty bucks. The conventional trip requires a taxi ride to the train station outside of Cusco (about $15), a one-way ticket on the daily Vistadome ($84), plus bus ticket from Aguas Calientes up the Hiram Bingham Highway ($12). You can walk up to the ruins for free, up the same slope that Bingham scaled in 1911, though almost no one does.

five minutes. I'd be wearing clean underwear and sipping a pisco sour by sundown.

Unfortunately, there was no way of contacting these porters in advance. Spring planting season was approaching, and all the men were off helping burn the nearby hillsides. The entire valley resembled one of those segments on the evening news in which Highway One is shut down near Los Angeles because of wildfires. Every hour or so, John would wander up the road to see if any of his strong-backed buddies had returned home. Each time he came back alone.

We set up lunch in a school yard next to a tiny general store. It was a hot, sunny day, and when I was certain John had gone to check on porters again, I splurged on a bottle of cold water for myself and Inca Kolas for Justo and Edgar. The gearbox on the Land Cruiser was making odd noises, so Edgar went off to examine the underside of the chassis.

"I used to do that with Encounter Overland," John said approvingly when he saw Edgar flat on his back beneath the truck. "Sometimes it's good for the driver to just get under the vehicle and have a good hard look around, study the patterns until the problem pops out at you." Edgar had taken this intuitive method of auto repair to another level by closing his eyes and folding his hands over his chest.

After a long day of near-complete idleness, we officially postponed Operation Storm Llactapata in the late afternoon. Justo and I parked our folding table in the valley's one shady spot, sipped hot tea and tried not to catch each other's eye. Even he was talked out. The only books I had with me were Bingham's, and I'd read them all twice. Not for the first time, I thought about how I'd give a hundred dollars for any one of the four copies of *Great Expectations* buried somewhere in my attic. We all watched some kids play soccer on a dirt field. When the game ended, John headed off again to look for his porter friend Fructoso, whose wife had invited him to come by and wait for her husband. "You should stop by, Mark, they're fantastic people." I lied and said I had some postcards to write.

Two boys, maybe six years old, approached and said their teacher had told them to ask us to collect our mules, which were sticking their noses into the classroom windows. I told them we didn't have any mules. They shrugged their shoulders and walked back to school. When I turned to find out what Justo and Edgar were up to, I saw that perhaps a dozen mules had arrived and were consuming whatever small islands of weedy vegetation remained on the soccer field. The logo of a luxury travel outfitter whose all-inclusive trips I'd checked out online was emblazoned on their gear bags. The tents their mule-teers were setting up next to the general store looked like they'd been bleached, starched and ironed. A distinctly American voice, the first I'd heard in weeks, drifted toward me:

"Offer them fifteen-five. You're authorized to go to seventeen."

I had overheard enough self-important financial conversations in Manhattan to know what to expect as I walked up the small hill that led back from the school yard. And sure enough, there he was: Mr. Super Deluxe Travel Guy. I recognized his boots as the most expensive kind available; the sales assistant at an outdoorsy shop near my home had recommended I buy them only if I were trying to summit Mount Everest. Solo. Without supplemental oxygen. The American was shouting into a cell phone as he walked around trying to find the spot with the strongest reception.

"What? Can you hear me? I'm in the middle of bumfuck Per-ROO! I may not be able to get a good signal until tomorrow." He turned to look for his guide. "Antonio! Do they have cell phone service at Machu Picchu?"

"*Claro!* Of course! Like a crystal!"

Mr. Super Deluxe Travel Guy breathed deeply like he'd taken a hit from his asthma inhaler. "Okay, I'll call you tomorrow as soon as we get off the bus to Machu Picchu."

Sitting cross-legged on a rock off to the side was a slim, pretty woman with a ponytail. Her nose was buried in a book. The book hap-pened to have been written by someone I knew, so I asked if she was enjoying it. When she said that she was, I introduced myself and told her a very embarrassing story about the author. She laughed and invited me to sit down. Her name was Katie.

"Any idea what they're doing up there?" she asked, pointing up at the men lighting the vegetation afire.

"I think they've run out of land to plant on. My friend told me that the easiest way to clear the brush off these mountains is to burn it and hope it doesn't get out of control."

"Seems a shame," she said. "It's so beautiful here, everything is so green. When it's not on fire, that is. Have you been to Machu Picchu yet?"

"I think we're going day after tomorrow. You?"

"We're going tomorrow. I can't wait. Jason and I have been talking about doing this since we were in college." Katie glanced at her husband, who was devouring a PowerBar and shouting a string of numbers into his phone as he continued to pace like a Buckingham Palace guard. "I swear I've had a Post-it that says 'go to Machu Picchu' stuck to my computer screen for about a million years. And finally, we're here. Did you go to Choquequirao? Isn't it incredible? I love it here. Of course he's going crazy because he can't get Yankee scores or real-time commodities prices."

"I haven't been online for a few weeks," I said. "Have I missed anything?"

"I doubt it. We stopped to check e-mail in Santa Teresa. The biggest news story was about some kid who flew into space holding on to a balloon or something. Except maybe his parents made the whole thing up? It was kind of convoluted."

After weeks of conversations that had centered on rocks and mules and bowel movements and the occasional tendency of mules to have rocklike bowel movements, a few minutes of urbane adult chitchat felt like slipping into a hot bath with the Sunday New York Times. Katie and I talked about books in which no one freezes to death or falls into a crevasse. We talked about countries we had both visited, and restaurants we had both eaten at, and movies that she had seen and that I hoped to watch someday when my children left for college and I was again able to stay up past eight-thirty at night.

"Hey," Katie said, "we usually have cocktails before dinner, after we wash up. I'm not sure if I'm authorized to do this, but you know what? I'm paying a fortune for this trip and you definitely look like a man who could use a drink. So stop by if you want. And stay for dinner, too."

I looked over at my companions. Edgar was still snoozing under the Land Cruiser. Justo was trying to persuade a stray dog to eat a tub of rancid margarine. Then I looked across the campsite into Katie's capacious cook tent. A man in chef's whites and a French toque was chopping onions into microscopic pieces. The table probably resembled what Bingham saw at Huadquiña: eight seats, cloth napkins, multiple pieces of cutlery at each place setting. I may never master the machete, but a cocktail party? That's my natural habitat. My mind wandered off in a reverie of ice cubes clinking into glass drinking vessels. Who knows, maybe they even had . . . coasters.

I savored the caramel bite of an imaginary bourbon on the rocks for a few seconds. But I knew that I would never set foot in that tent. I felt bad for lying to John, who was about as honest as Abe Lincoln on sodium pentothal. Having Justo watch me eat another cook's food would have felt like taking part in a live sex act in Amsterdam. But most of all, I realized, I had something I'd rather do.

"I really wish I could," I told Katie. "But I already have an engagement."

John was right about Fructoso and his wife, as he was about almost anything that wasn't an *usnu*—they were fantastic people. Their hut was smaller than some air-conditioning units I've seen in my neighborhood, so between John and me and the Fructosos and their two adult sons, we were quite cozy in spite of a cold rain that had started just after the sun went down. Fructoso apologized profusely for not having been around to carry our packs, and his wife plied us with gigantic mugs of coffee and bowls of *choclo* and a fresh-picked avocado the size of a cantaloupe for each of us. Maybe it was all the organic food they ate, but the whole family seemed to glow with positive energy.

When John inquired how their honeybees were doing, Fructoso stood up and asked excitedly, "You want some honey?" Before we could politely decline, he dispatched one of his sons to fetch some. The son returned with a ten-gallon bucket filled almost to the top with honeycombs. "Eat! Eat! It's fresh! It's fresh!" Fructoso's wife said encouragingly, clapping her tiny hands. John eagerly stuck his hand in and yelled, "Yagh!"

The honey was fresh all right. It still had bees in it.

THIRTY-TWO

A Good Walk Spoiled

At Llactapata

The revised plan was that John and I would walk up to Llactapata alone. Justo and Edgar would drive our packs around to meet us at the Hidroeléctrica train station, where we could catch the train to Aguas Calientes, the tourist town at the base of Machu Picchu. We left at dawn.

About halfway up the mountainside, we encountered a snake in our path, our fourth of the journey by my count. This one was different, because it was alive. John pinned it to the ground with his bamboo pole. "Quick, Mark, take a picture," he said as the snake squirmed angrily to free itself. I leaned in close to get a good shot, then dropped to one knee to zoom in for a few seconds of action video.

"Got it," I said, slipping the camera back into my pocket. "So what was it—another one of those false coral garter snake things?"

"Actually . . . no. Did you notice the diamond shape on its head? That means it was probably poisonous." (When I e-mailed the photos to John later, he confirmed that it was a Bothrops pit viper—which "probably kills more people than any other snake in the Americas.")

An hour later, the slope began to level off. "Bingham saw almost none of what you're going to see," John said, parting some branches near the top of the hill. "He was in too big a hurry." Indeed, Bingham had spent less than a day at Llactapata, both because he was in his usual rush to find the next big thing and because his porters were threatening mutiny. He had poked around, sketched out his customary excellent diagrams of a few buildings, decided that he'd seen "the ruins of an Inca castle," and soldiered on ahead in search of the next item on his checklist. The next day his unhappy crew deserted him.

John and I descended for a few minutes on the far side of the ridge, passing several crumbling structures, until we reached a building that had stonework similar to what we'd seen at Choquequirao. In front of the building was a grassy plaza, and beyond that was a steep drop. Straight across the chasm, laid out like a diorama, was Machu Picchu. The entire complex was sandwiched between the two peaks that mark its north and south ends—it couldn't have been framed any better with red velvet curtains. We sat for a few minutes munching on chocolate bars and trading peeks through John's scope. Yep, that was Machu Picchu all right. We had Llactapata all to ourselves. Across the valley, busloads of tour groups were disembarking outside the main entrance.

John jerked his thumb back, then pointed forward. "There's a direct solstice alignment from the temple here to the sun temple at Machu Picchu," he said.

I started to nod, as I always did when John began talking about solstice alignments. Then I stopped myself. "I have a confession to make," I said, wiping chocolate on my sweaty sleeve. "I know we've been talking about this stuff for two weeks, and I think I get it. More or less. But when you start using words like 'solstice' and 'alignment,' I still don't really know what the hell you're talking about."

John jumped up and led me over to what had once been a long stone hallway of sorts, one that Bingham had mapped and measured in 1912. "For two weeks out of every year, the sun comes straight down this corridor," John said, sweeping his gloved hands backward as if he were a matador ushering in the solar bull. "It's *right* on the June solstice line, the point where the sun rises on the shortest day of the year. And it's a straight shot to Machu Picchu. The Incas probably hung some sort of golden sheet or reflector at the end of it to reflect sunlight back to Machu Picchu. Can you imagine how spectacular that would have been? Machu Picchu would've still been dark, waiting for the sunrise, when the reflection would just *shoot* across the valley!

"And in *that* direction on the summer solstice in December," he said, looking at his GPS and pointing northwest, "you get a near-perfect alignment from Machu Picchu to Espiritu Pampa."

In layman's terms, that meant that some Inca planner had taken the care to ascertain that this corridor would parallel the path of the rising sun—the father of the Sapa Inca himself—on one of the most important days of the year. He or someone like him also planned the locations of at least three important Inca sites—Machu Picchu, Llactapata and a carved rock shrine in the valley below that we were about to visit—to fall on an invisible line that bisected all three. I'd seen pictures of British oddballs dressed up like Druids at Stonehenge waiting for the sun to rise on the solstice, but that hardly compared to what John was talking about. The Incas had plotted these coordinates over thousands of square miles.

Up to now I had been thinking of these places as Bingham had when first starting out, as self-contained lost cities and holy sites, akin to abandoned medieval villages and churches. Trails were just lines on a map connecting the dots. But if John was right, the Incas had seen things very differently. These sites and trails were more like organs and vessels, the circulatory system in a living body. A very big living body.

"Llactapata was *interconnected* with Machu Picchu," John said. "Count the trails!" He walked to the edge of the plaza and pointed across. "One, two, three, four, five, six. At least six Inca trails leading up to Machu Picchu. *Everything was connected!*"

We walked down the mountainside beneath Llactapata and crossed the Aobamba River—an important milestone, because we were now officially inside the Machu Picchu Historical Sanctuary. Technically, this zone is a haven not only for ruins but for the diverse flora and fauna of the region. (This is one of the few safe places for the rare Andean spectacled bear, which looks like a cross between a raccoon and a black bear cub.) There is one important eco-exception—the gigantic hydroelectric plant on the back side of Machu Picchu. John and I walked past dozens of men in matching hard hats and coveralls driving heavy machinery; a funicular ran up the mountainside. KEEP OUT signs were posted everywhere. None of this is visible from the sacred ruins directly above. It was like stumbling upon a Bond villain's secret hideout while hiking in Yosemite.

By twelve-thirty, John and I were at the Hidroeléctrica station, the final gateway to Aguas Calientes. A small, presumably portable bazaar was set up on top of the tracks, where señoras sold meals to electrical plant workers, and bottled water and handicrafts to tourists. The day after his trip to Machu Picchu in 1911, Bingham stopped briefly at this very spot.

The hike John and I had just made up and down from Llactapata—more than a vertical mile in elevation change—would have killed me two weeks earlier. Now it was just another vigorous walk. There was no question that I had taken a huge leap forward in fitness. Despite shoveling five thousand calories a day down my throat, my pants were looser. I'd reached into my back pocket that morning to find something and encountered a hard, grapefruit-like object. It was my butt. So when John mentioned that it was possible to walk the rail line to Aguas Calientes instead of riding the train, it suddenly seemed foolish not to walk through Mandor Pampa, the place where the tipsy innkeeper Melchor Arteaga (whom Bingham noted was "overly fond of 'firewater'") had promised to lead the explorer the following morning up the mountain he called Machu Picchu, Quechua for "Old Peak." This might be my only chance to hike like a serious adventurer, to carry my own pack like a *traveler*, not heave it onto the luggage rack like a *tourist*.

"I can ride a train in New York," I told John.

"All right, then!" he said, thumping his bamboo stick. "We walk to Machu Picchu. Just like Bingham. And twenty dollars in train fare saved!"

Edgar was waiting with the Land Cruiser, leaning against the front grille and talking into his cell phone. He was trying to locate a mechanic who'd drive out from Cusco, and the odds were not in his favor. Justo was doing his worried pigeon walk, hands behind his back. When he saw John and me, he raised his arms and shouted, *"Los aventureros!"* In each hand he held a brown paper bag. "For the final lunch, *un clasico!"* he said. It was an aspirational name for a ham and cheese sandwich. Edgar snapped his phone shut and pulled me aside.

"Hombre, you sure you want to walk?" he asked in a low voice. "You've got a lot of books in this bag. The train will be here soon. You'll be in Aguas Calientes *long* before you'll get there walking." I assured him that I was looking forward to the hike, for historical purposes. After all, what was now the train track had once been the mule trail that led Bingham through these parts, right?

We said our good-byes. When I shook Justo's hand, he smiled broadly enough that I could see the gums above his gold teeth. Tiny *gotas* filled the corners of his eyes. "I hope we see each other again, Señor Mark," he said.

When Bingham had passed through here on his way to the Huadquiña plantation in 1911, he interviewed the proprietor of a small ranch that was called Intihuatana. In *The Incas of Peru*, Clements Markham had translated the word *intihuatana* to mean "place where the sun is tied up or encircled." It refers to a type of carved rock that the Incas are thought to have used in solar observation and worship. From where John and I stood, we could almost see the most famous *intihuatana* ever found, the one up at Machu Picchu.

"There was a major *intihuatana* down here, too," John said. "As good as the one at Machu Picchu, but it's never been studied. There were only the two good ones left—the Spaniards destroyed the rest." This seemed an awfully unlikely spot for important Inca ruins, sandwiched between a power plant and a craft bazaar. John walked over to the hillside, a thicket of banana, coffee and avocado trees that rose at such a steep angle that the train arrived by zigzagging back and forth like a Donkey Kong barrel. "There used to be a trail right here," he said. "What the hell happened?"

John finally spotted a small opening in the brush. "All right, Mark," he said, lifting his bags, "put your big pack on your back. Strap your smaller one on your front. It'll help you keep your balance so you don't fall over." I did as I was told. I looked like a tortoise.

We climbed a hundred feet up the slope, then another hundred, with John occasionally peering into small stands of trees or checking behind a three-sided shack as if he'd dropped something back there. Fifteen minutes into my career as a hard-core backpacker, I knew I'd made a mistake. The muscles between my shoulders felt like they were being slowly torn from the bone. *If this* intihuatana *turns out to be another fucking* usnu, I thought, *I'm going to push him in front of that train.*

"Ah, there it is!" John shouted. "Almost no one knows about this."

I followed him down a short path that led from the train tracks and through an archlike opening in the flora. And I'll be damned if we didn't step out onto one of the most amazing pieces of stonework I'd yet seen in Peru. Carved out of a massive chunk of granite was a sculpture that wouldn't have been out of place at the Museum of Modern Art. Its wide platform top and thirty-foot-high face had been squared off and smoothed. Multiple niches and altars surrounded a set of steps that led up to a geometric base, like a gigantic trophy. It appeared to have once held a gnomon, the vertical part of a sundial.

"The electrical company broke that bit off," John said. "Or so the locals tell me."

After walking around to admire the stone from every possible angle, we sat down, unwrapped our *clasicos*, and gazed up at Machu Picchu, which now seemed close enough to hit with a Frisbee. John didn't even have to use his GPS to show me that we were picnicking atop an invisible axis from Llactapata to the more famous *intihuatana* stone at Machu Picchu, perched atop a stack of terraces like a candle on a birthday cake. Each time there was a break in the crowds up above, I could practically trace its outline with my finger.

Had I not been carrying sixty pounds of belongings, the six-mile walk to Aguas Calientes might have been lovely. We followed the Urubamba River as it looped around Machu Picchu. I tried to match photographs Bingham had taken with what I saw, but it was hard to concentrate when I was stopping every few seconds to shift the weight of my pack. According to the map I had, we were about half a mile, horizontally speaking, from Machu Picchu's Sacred Plaza. In the crazy-quilt world of actual Peruvian geography, we were almost as far beneath it.

We crossed a train trestle above the river and proceeded to the spot where Mandor Pampa should have been. Whatever Bingham had seen there had long since been swept away, replaced by tree ferns.

For three hours, I struggled to keep up with John, who maintained his metronomic pace and paused occasionally to let me catch up. The canyon narrowed until its sides were almost perpendicular to the river, leaving us in shadow. Just when I started to wonder what the logistics were for repatriating a body to the United States, we spotted a depot with a train parked in a siding. On its side was painted HIRAM BINGHAM. Welcome to Aguas Calientes.

THIRTY THREE

Historian Makes History

Mandor Pampa

The morning of July 24, 1911, was a rainy one, and like any serious firewater aficionado, tavernkeeper Melchor Arteaga was in no hurry to seize the day. Bingham dangled a silver dollar reward if Arteaga would guide him to the ruins that he'd boasted about the night before. When Arteaga agreed, Bingham inquired where, exactly, they were going. Arteaga "pointed straight up at the top of the mountain." Bingham's expedition companions from Yale decided to stay behind.

Arteaga, Bingham and his military escort, Sergeant Carrasco, departed Mandor Pampa at 10:07 A.M. About forty minutes later, the trio arrived at a primitive bridge much like those John and I had crossed en route to Espiritu Pampa: "four tree trunks" that had been "bound together with vines" and stretched "only a few inches above the roaring rapids." The Peruvians crossed barefoot, Bingham later recalled, "using their somewhat prehensile toes to keep from slipping," a description that managed to compliment their bravery while not-so-subtly comparing them to monkeys. Bingham crawled across.

The difficult climb up the eastern face of the mountain took about eighty minutes. Much of the journey was made on all fours, Bingham recalled, "sometimes holding on by our fingernails." Bingham was now within the zone known as the *ceja de selva*, the eyebrow of the jungle, where the cloud forest was thick. Tree trunks cut with rough notches served as ladders in otherwise impassable spots. Arteaga warned his guests to watch out for vipers. As it typically does at Machu Picchu, the early cloud cover burned off and the gray day turned hot and humid. Just after noon, the three men arrived at the top of the slope.

The first structure Bingham encountered at Machu Picchu was a Quechua hut. This was the house of the Richarte family, one of Arteaga's subtenants who had settled on the ridge between the peaks of Mount Machu Picchu and Huayna Picchu. Introductions were awkward—the farmers, who had selected the site at least in part because it was an excellent place to elude nosy government officials, were surely rattled by the arrival of a six-feet-four white man with yellow hair and a military escort. Once Arteaga explained the reason for Bingham's appearance, however, the Richartes laid a poncho across a wooden bench and invited the American to sit down. They offered their guest, who hadn't packed a lunch, sweet potatoes and "dripping gourds full of cool delicious water."

Like every first-time visitor to Machu Picchu, Bingham took a few moments to soak in one of the world's most incredible natural settings:

> Tremendous green precipices fell away to the white rapids of the Urubamba below. Immediately in front, on the north side of the valley, was a great granite cliff rising 2000 feet sheer. To the left was the solitary peak of Huayna Picchu, surrounded by seemingly inaccessible precipices. On all sides were rocky cliffs. Beyond them cloud-capped mountains rose thousands of feet above us.

Bingham took note of some well-preserved Inca terraces that the farmers had "cleared off and burned over" for planting, creating an ideal spot for growing tomatoes, peppers, corn and other crops. Decades later researchers would discover that the Inca builders had not only filled these terraces with a thick layer of topsoil, but had also employed granite chips left over from stone cutting to lay down an ingenious multilayered drainage system.

Once rehydrated, the explorer wanted to see the ruins. Arteaga begged off, saying he'd "been there once before" and wanted to hang back and chat with his tenants. The Richartes's young son, never named or quoted in any of Bingham's books but probably the first guide to lead a tour through the ruins of Machu Picchu, was deputized to take the strange guest and his military escort to have a look around.

(In any picture of Machu Picchu taken from its best-known angle, the buildings will fall roughly into two groups, on the left and right, separated by a grassy central plaza.[8] At the rear of the photo will be the rocky green rhino horn of Huayna Picchu. Looking north, the major discoveries of Bingham's July 24 visit took place on the left side, starting in the foreground and advancing toward Huayna Picchu.)

The trio began walking around the side of the mountain, until they reached "a great flight of beautifully constructed stone-face terraces, perhaps a hundred of them, each hundreds of feet long and 10 feet high." Bingham was reminded of the terraces he'd just seen at Ollantaytambo, the same that Manco had once ridden his stolen horse atop. The ones before him were handsome but "nothing to be excited about." Using one of the widest terraces as their path, sidestepping charred tree trunks, the three moved ahead into the "untouched forest beyond."

Inside the green tangle of vegetation, something caught Bingham's attention. The boy had led them into "a maze of beautiful granite houses! The buildings were covered with trees and moss and the growth of centuries, but in the dense shadow, hiding in bamboo thickets and tangled vines, could be seen, here and there, walls of white granite ashlars most carefully cut and exquisitely fitted together."

Bingham had entered the area of Machu Picchu now known as

---

8 An example of this sort of picture can be found on the last page of this book's section of photographs.

the Eastern Urban Sector. He may have been exaggerating slightly about the overgrowth, since the tenant farmers had cleared much of the site to plant their crops. Then again, maybe not. Photographs Bingham took show adult trees growing not just inside and around those now-famous buildings, but *on top* of them as well. "Some walls were actually supporting trees ten and twelve inches in diameter," he noted.

The boy pushed on ahead, ducking nimbly under bamboo and scrambling up terrace walls as Bingham struggled to follow. The explorer seems to have almost collided with his first important find, a cave that the boy pointed out. The cavern's interior chamber was lined with exquisite stonework. At its center were four white stone steps, carved at slightly irregular angles so that they cast enigmatic shadows. Bingham, who over time named the features of Machu Picchu like Adam identifying every beast of the field in the book of Genesis, dubbed this opening the Royal Mausoleum.

Directly above the cave, the Incas had built a high, semicircular wall that formed a tower of sorts; its perfectly curved face contained two small windows. (Bingham named it the Semicircular Temple; it's now commonly known as the Torreon, or Temple of the Sun.) Climbing an adjacent set of stairs, Bingham could see that the curved wall wrapped around until it straightened like the stem on a letter "P," then turned ninety degrees to the left.

The masonry, like that of most Inca masterworks, tilted slightly inward and tapered as it went up. "Owing to the absence of mortar," Bingham wrote, "there are no ugly spaces between the rocks. They might have grown together." The use of white granite had given the walls a luminous beauty that surpassed anything Bingham had ever seen. "Dimly, I began to realize that this wall and its adjoining semicircular temple over the cave were as fine as the finest stonework in the world. . . . It fairly took my breath away."

Bingham followed his guide up a granite staircase to a small clearing that the boy's family had chosen for a vegetable patch. Standing watch over the Richarte family produce were "the ruins of two of the finest structures I have ever seen in Peru." In contrast to the intricate granite brickwork of the Mausoleum wall, these buildings had been constructed from enormous blocks comparable in size to those at Sacsahuaman, some of them "ten feet in length, and higher than a man." Both were three-sided temples. The temple facing south contained a fourteen-foot-long slab of waist-high granite, which sat beneath seven niches set high in the rear wall; Bingham surmised that this spot had been a "sacrificial altar."

Ninety degrees to the right, the other temple seemed in particular to catch Bingham's fancy. "Best windows I have ever seen," he scribbled in his notebook. Three apertures, each measuring four feet by three feet, faced east "over the canyon to the rising sun." The openings looked onto a large central plaza, and beyond to the Urubamba River flowing far below. Straight ahead in the distance, the triptych framed a panorama of skyscraping mountain peaks. Bingham lingered, puzzling over these "three conspicuously large windows, obviously too large to serve any useful purpose." Clements Markham, he knew, had mentioned an important place in *The Incas of Peru*: "the hill with the three openings or windows." Bingham sensed immediately that this structure had "peculiar significance."

Once again, Bingham followed almost to the letter the Royal Geographical Society's *Hints to Travellers* three-step process for "obtaining a record of monument." (Draw a floor plan; shoot pictures; and take copious measurements and descriptive notes.) The explorer sketched the three-windowed building into his small leather-covered notebook. Then he pulled out his camera and tripod and began to document his find, taking care to jot down the details of each shot. While inspecting the temple's interior, he noticed that something had been scrawled on one of the walls: "Lizarraga 1902." Lizarraga, he later learned, was a farmer who rented land farther down the Urubamba Valley.

As the sun began its downward descent, Bingham tried to digest everything he'd taken in. The boy had one more surprise, though. At the site's very highest point—a spot that Bingham would learn the next day was, incredibly, visible from the very mule road that he had been following—stood a large rock carved like a sundial. It had a wide base and a squarish twenty-inch-tall gnomon, shaped like a flat-topped obelisk. Such an Inca carving, Bingham knew from Markham's writings, must be an *intihuatana*. Bingham stationed Sergeant Carrasco and the boy guide next to the carved rock and snapped a photograph, the template for a century's worth of souvenir photos.

With darkness coming on quickly, Bingham returned to the Richarte hut to collect Arteaga and make the descent to Mandor Pampa. The first recorded visit to Machu Picchu lasted less than five hours.

THIRTY-FOUR

Going Up

At Machu Picchu

I f you've ever thought, *The new Times Square is delightful but would be even better if it were more claustrophobic and nearly impossible to leave,* then Aguas Calientes is calling your name. Otherwise, you'd probably find the town—also known as Machu Picchu Pueblo—about as seedy as the old Times Square, another destination where the typical visitor just wanted to rent a bed for a few hours. Like a bloodhound, John sniffed out a couple of ten-dollar rooms. (A person can easily spend two hundred dollars a night on accommodations. Rooms up at the site-adjacent Machu Picchu Sanctuary Lodge, which is like an Embassy Suites with no pool or parking lot but a *great* location, start at eight hundred dollars.) The nice señora who ran the hostel pressed stacks of business cards into our hands each time we entered or exited, begging us to tell our friends about her place.

I was a little nervous about visiting Machu Picchu. See, I'd already been to Machu Picchu once, when I'd brought my son Alex to Cusco. We did the typical day trip, which entails a long (three and a half hours each way), very expensive train ride from the outskirts of Cusco in a frigid car at dawn. After dropping another fifty bucks each on entry fees and bus transport, we arrived at one of the wonders of the world at midday to find it as hot and humid as a terrarium, overrun by plagues of stinging flies and Europeans on holiday. (It was August.) Having shelled out almost four hundred dollars just to get us there from Cusco,

I was in no mood to spend another thirty dollars on a guide, which was a mistake since Machu Picchu has almost no explanatory signs. The buildings were impressive, but not much more so than what we'd already seen that week at Sacsahuaman and Ollantaytambo. I experienced a little of the deflation that other friends had felt when they arrived at the Great Pyramid and saw that the Sphinx could scratch itself against the skyscrapers of Cairo, or made the pilgrimage to Graceland and discovered that Elvis's stately pleasure dome was no larger than a Memphis McMansion.

When I admitted this to John, he looked like he might slap me. "Your problem was that you and Alex only allowed yourselves four hours—four hours to see Machu Picchu!—and you didn't have a *strategy*," he told me over an early breakfast. "You came at the most crowded part of the day, and like everyone on their first visit, you went straight to the most popular spots." Out of his backpack he pulled a thick folder of photocopies, jammed with maps of Machu Picchu and articles about the site in English and Spanish. Even though he'd long since lost count of how many times he'd been here, John believed *every* visit to Machu Picchu was an important undertaking. We were going to squeeze in some last-minute research over our coffee and toast.

"You might want to start with that one," John said. He handed me a special all-Inca issue of a children's science magazine.

There's an old kitchen maxim that squid should either be cooked for two minutes or two hours. A similar rule could be applied to Machu Picchu. With a good guide—there are dozens of them lingering by the front entrance—a visitor who's short on time can see the highlights of Machu Picchu in two hours. A visit of two days, though, allows enough time to take in the site's full majesty. Our plan was to devote one day to retracing Bingham's 1911 footsteps, and a second to seeing some parts of the site that most people never get to.

John and I nabbed the last two seats on a bus heading up to the ruins at seven-thirty. There were more people inside than we'd seen at Choquequirao, Vitcos and Espiritu Pampa combined. The ride up the serpentine Hiram Bingham Highway takes about twenty minutes, and the views almost justify the twelve bucks they squeeze you for. John did a final equipment check before we entered—"camera, video camera, notebooks, pens, batteries, snacks"—and cast an evil glance at the one public bathroom, which charged an entry fee of 35 cents. "I'm fairly certain that's illegal according to the UN Human Rights Commission," he said.

By eight o'clock we were walking along the same path Bingham had taken through the terraces, following a train of photogenic llamas reporting for duty. For whatever reason—our arrival before the big crowds from Cusco, my sense of having earned this visit over the previous weeks of walking, the absence of my sometimes sullen thirteen-year-old son—Machu Picchu was different this time. Even after witnessing the knee-buckling natural settings of Choquequirao and Vitcos, it was impossible not to see almost immediately that Machu Picchu beat them both. The distant peaks ringing the ruins like a necklace were higher; the nearby slopes were greener. And of course the city, laid out before the visitor like a LEGO metropolis atop a billiard table, is impossible to turn away from. For the first time since dropping out of graduate school, I remembered an unpleasant weekend spent struggling to comprehend the philosopher Immanuel Kant's explanation of the difference between calling something beautiful and calling it sublime. Nowadays, we throw around the word "sublime" to describe gooey desserts or overpriced handbags. In Kant's epistemology, it meant something limitless, an aesthetically pleasing entity so huge that it made the perceiver's head hurt. Machu Picchu isn't just beautiful, it's sublime.

As we walked through the stone portal of the Main Gate, John pointed out the sort of detail that I had missed on my first visit. The gate was, essentially, the front door to Machu Picchu and was positioned so that the first thing a guest saw (perhaps as he dusted off his tunic and accepted a cup of *chicha*) was the green thumb of Huayna Picchu's peak, perfectly framed by the portal. It couldn't have been a coincidence.

In a couple of minutes, we were peering inside Bingham's first dis-

covery, the surrealist cave of the Royal Mausoleum. The cavern's natural rock walls had been fortified with elaborate stonework. One
hourglass-shaped section almost seemed to melt into the cave wall, as
if in a Dalí painting. A four-step staircase, slightly off-kilter, had been
carved out of a single piece of granite that grew from the earth near
the cave's entrance. It all obviously had some special significance, but
no one could say what that had been.

"I'd guess those steps were probably for displaying idols of some
sort," John said. "And if you look up"—we took a step backward—
"there's the Torreon."

The circular wall looming above us seemed to have swallowed the
grotto below like the trunk of a *matapalo*. At the center of the Torreon
was a large, flattish rock with a groove cut into its top. The rock doubled as the roof of the Royal Mausoleum below.

"What were the windows for?" I asked John. The tower had three
of them. Two were small and perfectly rhomboid and faced, respec-
tively, east and south. The other, a large portal, was dubbed the Enigmatic Window because of mysterious holes bored through the rocks
at its base. "It is what archaeologists commonly call 'problematical,'"
Bingham wrote, in a rare instance of admitting that he was baffled.

"It's *said* that the small window faces east toward the sun," John said,
somewhat dubiously. The Torreon was also known as the Sun Temple,
both because of this alleged alignment with the sunrise and because of
its uncanny resemblance to the Koricancha in Cusco. "Supposedly, on
the winter solstice in June, the sun rises above a peak over there, to the
east, and then shines through that window and casts a rectangle of light
onto that big rock in the center of the circular building."

"You mean like in *Raiders of the Lost Ark*?"

"Something like that. Now, I have read in a couple of places that the
window doesn't *quite* line up with the solstice, that it's a few degrees
off. That's not really the sort of mistake the Incas would have made."

"Huh. And what about the big window?"

"You might want to talk to Paolo about that." Paolo was the researcher who lived alone in a cabin in Alaska and had yanked Bingham

back into the news when he theorized that a German might have beaten the Yalie to Machu Picchu. "He's been doing a *lot* of work on the subject. He thinks the Torreon might have been Pachacutec's tomb. Paolo even thinks he might have figured out where Pachacutec is buried."

It's almost impossible to spend time at Machu Picchu without asking a question: was there an architectural visionary who can take credit for the city's distinctive, harmonious look? The answer, probably, is yes— Pachacutec, the earth shaker who began the great expansion of the Inca empire. According to one Jesuit missionary's recounting, Pachacutec handed off military responsibilities to one of his sons and turned his attention to building "magnificent temples and palaces and strong castles." In addition to extending the roads of the Capac Ñan, overseeing the transformation of Cusco into a capital worthy of Tawantinsuyu (and the construction of the gold-plated Koricancha at the very center of that empire), Pachacutec apparently supervised the creation or renovation of most of the Incas' greatest hits: Sacsahuaman, Ollantaytambo, and probably even Vitcos.[9] We know that Machu Picchu belonged to Pachacutec because in the 1980s a notation was found in a Cusco archive, dated 1568, that registered a site called "Pichu" as belonging to his clan. Under Inca real estate law, old commanders in chief never died or faded away; because they were immortal, their mummified bodies retained all the benefits they had enjoyed while living, including their real estate holdings. If the Spaniards hadn't arrived, Machu Picchu might *still* belong to Pachacutec.

The stonework at Machu Picchu is just the most conspicuous aspect of its brilliance. The citadel is also, in the words of the hydrologist Kenneth Wright, "a civil engineering marvel." Someone had to have made

---

9   The paleoecologist Alex Chepstow-Lusty has theorized that the Inca empire's growth spurt was made possible in large part by a period of global warming, which melted enough glacial ice to support a huge increase in high-altitude agriculture, which in turn fueled a population boom that provided the labor to make Pachacutec's public works projects possible. Unless current global-warming trends are reversed, most of Peru's glaciers are expected to disappear by 2050.

the climb up to the ridge around 1450 A.D.—historians' best guess—and decided that this remote saddle between two jagged peaks, with dizzying drops on two sides, could be cleared, leveled and made suitable for habitation and agriculture. Whoever planned Machu Picchu also had to construct a royal city that could withstand the sorts of Andean rainstorms and landslides that today are capable of wiping out train lines and entire villages. And let's not forget about earthquakes; Machu Picchu sits atop not one but *two* fault lines.

Yet when Bingham arrived in 1911, after the tropics had reclaimed the site for the better part of four centuries, Machu Picchu wasn't much worse for wear beneath all the bamboo and moss. Even the complex Inca water channels, with a little Roto-Rooter work, functioned like they had in pre-Columbian times. A spring-fed chain of sixteen fountains was designed so that the Inca's hands—or any other part of his sacred being—would be the first to touch the fresh water as it flowed down from a mountain spring. When John and I looked in, a teenage girl was rinsing her long hair in what had probably been Pachacutec's bathtub.

After Bingham followed his boy guide through an old quarry to the Sacred Plaza, the explorer saw the temples that astonished him. The three-sided Principal Temple is the most monolithic structure at Machu Picchu. Constructed of gigantic precision-cut stones, it seems to have been built by an entirely different race of people from those who assembled the Torreon. The blocks are so heavy that one corner of the building, behind the massive stone altar, is slowly sinking into the ground. Just a few steps beyond its open side, terraces staircase steeply down the mountainside for a couple hundred feet before dropping off into an abyss. The power plant was down there somewhere, invisible. In *The Motorcycle Diaries*, Che Guevara wrote about playing a freewheeling game of soccer when he arrived for a life-changing visit to Machu Picchu. It had sounded romantic when I read about it in my early twenties. As I looked over the edge, it seemed suicidal.

"Look at how the Incas built this up to the last possible inch, taking what appears to be unusable ground and making it usable," John said, peering down at the terraces. "A place like Angkor Wat is fantastic," he said, referring to the enormous twelfth-century temple complex in Cambodia. "But they didn't have the problems there that the Incas did here. This place is a statement: *look at how we can tame nature.*"

We turned around and walked over to the Temple of the Three Windows. The view hadn't changed much from the one that had intoxicated Bingham. A low ceiling of clouds hovered around the tops of the mountains straight ahead. John believed the spare stonework had once been dressed up in textiles and precious metals. "It's fantastic now, but imagine this temple covered with gold and silver plate, and colored cloths," John said. "Old Father Calancha would have shit himself."

Noon to three are the busiest hours at Machu Picchu, rush hour for day trippers from Cusco. John led me off to some of the out-of-the-way parts of the complex. "Look at that," he said, as we sat in the shade beneath a spot that Bingham named the Funerary Rock. "There's a trail going off into the bush. It has to lead somewhere, right? Makes you wonder how much there is of this place that we don't know yet."

We munched on quinoa energy bars and watched the parade pass below: American retirees in matching T-shirts; Spanish-speaking men in sport coats and ascots; Japanese tourists proceeding silently, single file, each one carrying a Prada bag; five groovy women dressed like the *Rolling Stone* fact-checking department circa *Frampton Comes Alive!*, walking in a tight group and stopping frequently to stuff herbs into cracks between the stones as they whispered incantations. A college-age couple, with nervous smiles and dilated pupils, tried to look in all directions at once. Four male trekkers arrived from the Inca Trail, speaking German. One of them was wearing a candy-striped cycling cap, red vinyl sleeveless vest unzipped to the navel and blue satin short shorts. Father Calancha would have shit himself.

Over the next couple of hours we made the long walk out to the Sun Gate, the entry point from the Inca Trail, then made another loop around the full site, stopping occasionally at a particularly beautiful building, like the Temple of the Condor. A light rain began to fall, which hastened the daily three o'clock exodus by an hour. Tour groups wearing cheap plastic ponchos gravitated toward the exit like jellyfish attacking a swimmer. John and I returned to the now-empty Sacred Plaza and climbed a few flights of stone steps to the highest point in the main site of Machu Picchu, stopping halfway, while a woman with an unmistakable Long Island accent called her mother on her cell phone.

"Oy gevalt, Mom, I'm calling from nine thousand feet. I can barely breathe. Hold on, I want you to say hi to our guide, Juan." Her pronunciation of WAAAAAAHHHAAAN could have summoned a flock of mallards. We slipped behind Juan, who seemed a little surprised to be connected to Nassau County, and continued to the top. A crowd was milling around the enigmatic carved rock that had been Bingham's final discovery that July day.

Bingham gave this sculptured stone the name Intihuatana,[10] and it almost surely has something to do with the sun. It's also clearly related to the Sacred Plaza right beneath it—the winding staircase up from the Principal Temple ascends to one of those archetypal Inca *ta-da!* moments as the mysterious stone is revealed. Today the rock seemed to be operating as a magnet, pulling toward it the dozen or so mystical tourists who hadn't left with the rain.

"Watch this," John said. "Their guide's going to tell them to hold their hands out to feel the cosmic energy emanating from the rock."

Several sets of hands reached out toward the Intihuatana. After a second or two, the mystics turned toward each other excitedly.

"I feel warmth," said one.

"Me too," said another.

"It's a *rock* that sits in the *sun* all day," John said, loud enough to be heard in Cusco. "Of course it feels warm."

I smiled condescendingly to show John that I was with him one

---

10 Should you mention the name Intihuatana to a Peruvian, you're likely to hear a famous tale—not of Inca architectural glories but rather about how in 2000, a crew shooting a beer commercial allowed a crane to fall onto the sacred stone, cracking off one corner.

hundred percent—what's with these weirdos?—and we started to head for the stairs down toward the bus. But first I pretended I'd dropped something next to the Intihuatana, and, when John wasn't looking, held my hand out to touch it. I couldn't say for sure if it was charged with Pachamama power. I'll say this, though—it was definitely warm.

THIRTY-FIVE

The Big Picture

High Above Machu Picchu

At four forty-five the next morning, John and I were standing in line, in the dark, in a monsoon. Only the first four hundred of the three to four thousand visitors who sign in at Machu Picchu's main entrance each day are allowed to climb to the top of Huayna Picchu, the green peak that anchors its north end. This exclusivity, among a crowd of people who've often waited years to see Machu Picchu and traveled from around the world to get there, makes the idea of queuing for a bus in the predawn darkness seem almost alluring, even when rainwater has leapt the curb and flooded the sidewalk and the feet of all those standing on it. I was exhausted after weeks of fitful sleep at altitude, but excited, too. John had assured me that climbing Huayna Picchu not only provided a gorgeous overview of the site, it also would be the best illustration yet of how Machu Picchu had connected with the rest of the Inca empire. The first bus was scheduled to depart at 5 A.M. The bus drivers began arriving at five-forty.

When the gate to Huayna Picchu was opened a couple of hours later, a number of fit young men were waiting impatiently at the sentry hut, fiddling with their digital watches. Everyone making the climb must sign a waiver relieving the INC of any liability should they fall off; Justo had told me that a Russian with multiple piercings had attracted a lightning bolt recently and taken a nasty fall. Evidently a rumor had swept through the bars of Aguas Calientes the previous night that the record for ascending the peak was twenty minutes. One after another, competitors took off in a sprint. "The real record's probably more like twelve minutes," John said as we signed in. "No need to tell those lads that, though."

From afar, and in photographs, it's difficult to see that Huayna Picchu is covered in stonework, temples and terraces that cling to the slope like baby monkeys. A recent soil analysis revealed that some of its highest terraces were used to grow mate, the nasty caffeinated beverage that people suck through metal straws on the east coast of South America. Sets of granite steps wound like a DNA helix several hundred feet to the summit. Most climbers turned right near the top. John went to the left, where we clambered alone up a final set of stairs angled like a stepladder.

At the top, we waited. And waited. Machu Picchu is cloudy in the morning, and we could only catch glimpses of the city below between the mist. John pointed to the far end of the site, where groups of Inca Trail hikers who'd awakened at four to meet the sunrise at the Sun Gate—virtually every tour company uses this supposedly magical moment as a selling point—were waiting impatiently for their first glimpse of the city.

"The Sun Gate at sunrise is a *complete* waste of time," John said as we looked south. "The sun doesn't actually arrive at Machu Picchu at the sunrise. And when it *does* rise everything's covered in mist. All my clients used to insist on doing it because they'd been brainwashed. And then everyone always used to say, 'That's it? I wish I'd slept in.'"

Directly above us, at the very top of Huayna Picchu, a gaggle of college kids sprawled across a pile of enormous boulders, arguing about who had made it up the fastest and napping away hangovers. Most of the bars in Aguas Calientes, I'd noticed, offered a four-for-one pisco sour special. John prowled the peak, taking GPS measurements as I chatted with a mother and son from Düsseldorf. They thought it was absolutely vital that I know that the Hellmann's mayonnaise in Europe is inferior to the stuff we can buy in the States. "Ours is more bitter," the mother told me, then lowered her head as if she'd unburdened a dark secret.

I should have asked them if there was a twelve-syllable German word meaning "even more sublime." When the fog finally lifted and we could see Machu Picchu stretching out below, the chatter atop Huayna Picchu stopped. From this vantage point it seemed entirely credible that the city had been lost to the outside world for centuries, and that more wonders might be hiding in the cloud forest. Evidently the Incas were fond of the view from Huayna Picchu, too, because several temples and a large *usnu* had been built near the top.

"You'll notice that the temple here looks straight onto Llactapata," John said, pointing west with his right hand. His left was pointed south, so that his arms formed an L shape. "The Intihuatana is due south of here, and Salcantay"—a twenty-thousand-foot peak and one of the Incas' two most sacred *apus*—"is due south of the Intihuatana." I had to take his word for it. Due to low clouds and smog from the seasonal fires, I hadn't caught a single glimpse of Salcantay. On a map, a line connecting the two peaks and the carved rock could be drawn with a ruler. The Incas, leaving nothing to chance, had carved a wedge of rock on the peak of Huayna Picchu that aimed like a compass point due south directly at a wedge-shaped hollow carved into the base of the Intihuatana, which in turn pointed at Salcantay.

The anthropologist Johan Reinhard has observed that the Intihuatana stone may actually be an abstract rendering of Huayna Picchu mountain. If viewed from the correct angle, he says, the shadows cast by the sharp edges of the Intihuatana mirror those that move across the face of Huayna Picchu. Thus the Intihuatana may have been several things at once: a link between two sacred peaks; a sculptural homage to one of those peaks; and a sundial, though not one that marked the hour according to the angle of the shadow it cast. Rather, in the age-old Andean tradition, the time of day could be assessed by reading the shadows on a mountain's face (or a smaller, carved model of the mountain's face)—just as my friend Nati had learned to do in her village as a girl. There were any number of buildings at Machu Picchu that were designed with such multiple uses in mind. And John and I hadn't even discussed how certain buildings were also astronomical observatories by night.

John kept pointing out alignments, but when I tried to imagine all the solstices and trails intersecting with Machu Picchu, the only picture I could conjure in my head was a web of lines intersecting like a gigantic cat's cradle. I felt an overwhelming desire to sit.

By early afternoon, John and I were back down at the main site, resting in the shade of a stone hut with a thatched roof. It was supposed to approximate what buildings had looked like in Pachacutec's day. It reminded me of Juvenal's house. John was crabby. Neither of us had slept well. The live band that performed at the pizza joint across from our hostel had kept going well past midnight, and we'd awakened at 4 A.M. and stood in the rain for an hour. Plus, it was lunchtime and John had only consumed about fourteen hundred calories, starvation rations by his usual standards.

"Well, Mark, I think we've seen almost everything," he said, staring straight ahead. "Except Mount Machu Picchu, of course."

John had been pushing hard for climbing Mount Machu Picchu, arguing that because it was the other bookend of the site—it sits at the south end, opposite Huayna Picchu— the view from its peak was essential for understanding how Machu Picchu connected with other sites. For reasons I still don't completely comprehend, people will line up before dawn to climb Huayna Picchu, but virtually no one who isn't a professional photographer climbs Mount Machu Picchu, even though you're allowed to do so whenever you feel like it. I suppose, for starters, it has something to do with its being more than twice as tall as Huayna Picchu, a steep sixteen hundred feet straight up. There are also no ruins to see along the route, save some granite steps and platforms. Personally, I had little interest in seeing some place that, as far as I could recall, had no special significance for Bingham. But it had turned out to be a beautiful day, and I was sitting in a place that I knew a million people dreamed of visiting but would never have the chance to.

"You know what? Let's climb it," I said.

"Really?"

"Really."

On our way to the peak, we passed through the main site again, reviewing its most famous works as if preparing for a final exam. Shortly after starting our ascent, John lost his footing on some stone steps and stumbled. "Slippery here," he said. "Wish I'd brought my walking stick. Hold on." He stepped off the trail into the thick brush, found a dead stalk of bamboo and wrenched it free. The bamboo was about nine feet long.

"Just give me a minute to cut this down to size." He reached into his bottomless daypack and rooted around for a minute. Then he stood back and scratched his head through his hat. "I must've forgotten my knife at the hotel."

"Wait a sec," I said, unzipping my pack. I dug around for a minute and then handed John my knife.

"That's good preparation, Mark," John said. "Nice sharp blade on it, too." It was, I'm not ashamed to admit, one of the proudest moments of my life. He whittled his stick down to a manageable length and slapped the knife into my palm. We each took a swig of water and moved on.

The trail up had been built with viewing platforms every 150 feet or so, and we paused at each one to take in Machu Picchu from a new angle, the site growing a little smaller at each stop. "These platforms must've been like little stations of the cross," John said. As we neared the summit, we encountered another Inca special effect. Each set of stairs appeared to reach the mountaintop, but then turned at the last minute to reveal another set of fifty or so stairs. Maybe Pachacutec was a practical joker. Or a sadist. It took us ninety minutes to reach the top. Every square inch of clothing I had on was sweated through, including my two pairs of socks, which squished as I walked.

"Looks like we're the only ones up here today!" John shouted. The formula for making John happy could be expressed as $(R + S) \times E$, or Ruins plus Solitude multiplied by Exertion. He was, therefore, ecstatic.

A quarter mile beneath us, traffic on the staircase to the Intihuatana was stop-and-go. We crossed a short, knife-edged ridge to an *usnu*, where someone had planted the rainbow flag of Cusco, which is almost identical to the Gay Pride flag. The view was immense. We could see the Urubamba River coiling around Huayna Picchu, and Llactapata peeking out from the cloud forest across the valley. The ruins of the main site were minuscule. When the high-altitude clouds parted, hints of sacred mountains were visible in the distance. Trails branched out in all directions like the flagellating arms of a deep-sea creature.

We heard singing. Americans singing. Pairs of students from a study-abroad program began to arrive. I worried that they were going to spoil John's afternoon. The opposite happened. These kids were perfect ambassadors for the U.S.A.—multiethnic, well scrubbed, extremely polite, completely uncynical and very curious. They latched on to John almost instantly and peppered him with questions.

"What's the tallest mountain you've ever climbed?"

"Why does the Inca flag look like the Gay Pride flag?"

"Is there really treasure hiding out there or is that just in the movies?"

"Would you like half an orange?"

Mostly, they wanted to hear about the Inca Trail. What was it like? Was walking it hard? Was it the most awesome thing ever?

"It's too bad you don't like the Inca Trail," I said to John.

He turned to me, confused. "I never said I didn't like the Inca Trail. The Inca Trail is *fantastic*."

I thought about this for a moment. John was right. *I* was the one who'd decided that I didn't want to hike the Inca Trail because . . . why, exactly? Oh right, because it wasn't hard-core enough for a serious adventurer like me.

"You can see how the Inca Trail leads out through the Sun Gate," John told his audience. "Up there is Wiñay Wayna—that's a *tambo* where the Inca himself stayed on his way to Machu Picchu. Absolutely brilliant. And beyond that is Phuyupatamarca, some *fantastic* stuff there."

As I watched John excitedly sketch out the highlights of the trail for the study-abroad kids, I realized that I'd learned just enough on this trip to know how much I didn't know. It was true that unlike 99.9 percent of the people who come to Peru, I'd taken the time to see not just Machu Picchu but several other wonders of Inca architecture. I'd carried a real man's backpack long enough to know that I never needed to do it again. As someone with Bingham-like tendencies of my own, who strove to clear his desk at the end of every workday, I'd even developed a fondness for the put-it-up-and-break-it-down rhythms of camping.

At the same time, after walking through the Inca landscape and seeing how their architectural wonders connected to the natural environment—and to one another—I wasn't any closer to understanding Machu Picchu. Anyone who has ever studied string theory in physics may have some idea of how I felt. You walk into class one day confident that you live in a three-dimensional world. An hour later you walk out with only the faintest grasp of the concept that there are actually nine or ten dimensions and, quite possibly, parallel universes on top of our own.

The cheerful gathering atop Mount Machu Picchu broke up. John and I caught a late afternoon bus back down the Hiram Bingham Highway. We hopped off at the point nearest to the new Machu Picchu museum, housed in a handsome building that almost no one visits because it's a half mile from Aguas Calientes, at the end of a shadowy dirt road. I was curious to see how the official history would credit Bingham's achievement.

It doesn't. Not directly, anyway. Amid the typical museum displays (what the Incas ate; their metallurgical techniques) were two dedicated to undermining any claims that what Bingham had accomplished on July 24, 1911, was in any way special. The one nearest the entrance, labeled MACHU PICCHU: KNOWN TO SOME, explained how plenty of local people had known about the ruins before you-know-who showed up with his camera. This was indisputable, of course—

there were people *living* at Machu Picchu when he arrived. I did find it a little odd, however, that the brief explanation on the wall referred to the Yale explorer by the single name Bingham, as if he were Pelé or Cher. Or Mussolini.

In the next room hung six portraits of men who had influenced the history of Machu Picchu over the last hundred years. One of the men featured was Albert Giesecke, the University of Cusco administrator who suggested Bingham stop and see Melchor Arteaga at Mandor Pampa. Beneath the framed picture was a quote from Giesecke about how he and Bingham had often discussed the likelihood of finding ruins down the Urubamba Valley.

Something seemed to be missing. I looked around the room, and then made two circuits of the museum. Strangely, of the hundreds of photos on display, not a single one was of Bingham. The first man to photograph Machu Picchu had been airbrushed out of its official visual history.

When I returned to Giesecke's smiling face, I noticed a display beneath that delved into some "highly irregular" dealings that Bingham had gotten involved in when *he* became fixated on solving the mystery of what Machu Picchu had been. Apparently, it wasn't what Bingham did in 1911 that pissed people off; it was what he did when he returned the next year.

I was starting to think I might need another visit, too.

THIRTY-SIX

A Star Is Born

New York and Washington, D.C.

Bingham's arrival in New York City aboard the steamship *Metapan* on December 21, 1911, could not have been better timed. Newspaper reporters were awaiting word of a victor in the Scott-versus-Amundsen race to the pole and had spent months whetting the public's appetite for adventure stories. Bingham had cleverly churned the waters with the interviews he'd given prior to departing, promising lost cities. He had also telegraphed news of the Coropuna triumph at the first possible moment. His peers in the Royal Geographical Society received a sneak preview of his discoveries, with photographs, which Clements Markham published in the society's December *Geographical Journal*, along with the encouraging comment, "I trust that [this] is the forerunner of a fuller topographical description of the Vilcabamba region."

Though Bingham could, and did, boast about the expedition's many achievements—the Cusco bones, the proof of Vitcos, the Coropuna climb—the news angle that received the most play in newspapers from Oshkosh to Topeka was his encounter at the lost city of Machu Picchu. *The New York Sun's* headline was typical: EXPLORERS FIND CITY THAT WAS: WHITE-WALLED TOWN OF THE INCAS DISCOVERED IN PERU SNUGGLED UNDER CORNFIELDS. YALE PROFESSOR ASTOUNDED AT BEAUTY OF ARCHITECTURE. Had the explorer returned with any samples of this incredible stonework? "Nothing would have suited us better than to have brought specimens of the architecture home with us," Bingham assured the mob. "This could not be done, however, as the Peruvian Government expressly forbids it."

Bingham's discovery immediately raised a number of questions: Who among the Incas built this palace in the sky? What was the significance of the unusual buildings? Why did the Incas choose such a dramatic location? And how had Machu Picchu been lost for centuries? Bingham seems to have been pondering the answers to some of these questions on the way home. The London *Observer* offered one possible answer. Bingham had found "what are believed to be the ruins of the Peruvian town referred to in the writings Sir Clements Markham as 'the hill of the three-windowed temples.'"

In Markham's book *The Incas of Peru*, which surveyed more than fifty years of study and had deeply influenced Bingham's plans for the 1911 expedition, the former RGS president had recounted the story of Tampu Tocco—the Incas' creation myth. "The legend relates that out of a hill with three openings for windows there came three tribes," Bingham wrote in an article for *Harper's*, his first attempt to explain Machu Picchu's significance to the American public. "These tribes eventually settled at Cusco and founded the Inca empire." At Machu Picchu, of course, Bingham had been transfixed by the building he named the Temple of the Three Windows. Since the structure was so extraordinary, and since no archaeologist had yet found the ruins of Tampu Tocco, then perhaps, just maybe, Machu Picchu and Tampu Tocco were one and the same. "It seems to me that there is a possibility that . . . Machu Picchu is the original Tampu Tocco, although this is contrary to the accepted location," he wrote. The site was generally believed to have existed a few miles from Cusco and nowhere near Machu Picchu. "I may be wholly mistaken in this," Bingham stressed near the end of his *Harper's* story, "and I shall await with interest the discovery of any other place that fits as well the description of Tampu Tocco, whence came the Incas."

Among the persons most intrigued by Bingham's reports on Machu Picchu was Gilbert Grosvenor, the head of the National Geographic

Society in Washington, D.C. Grosvenor, a little man with a tidy mustache and big plans, had been handpicked at the boy-wonder age of twenty-three by the society's founder, the telephone inventor Alexander Graham Bell. His assignment was to transform *National Geographic* from a dry, scholarly periodical into a general-interest magazine that would deliver information about science and the natural world to a wide audience. In the first decade of the twentieth century, Grosvenor succeeded brilliantly, growing the circulation from one thousand to more than eighty thousand. He possessed the rare editor's genius at divining popular tastes—in 1910, after much trial and error, he gave *National Geographic* the eye-catching yellow border that is still instantly recognizable a hundred years later.

Grosvenor had made his magazine a success largely by pursuing two strategies. First, after making a study of famous travel narratives (such as Richard Henry Dana's *Two Years Before the Mast*), he began to emphasize stories about heroes and their triumphs; the society helped to sponsor Robert Peary's successful ride to the North Pole. Grosvenor's second editorial innovation was to devote more pages to photography. A 1905 photo essay about the hidden mystical city of Lhasa, Tibet, had helped kickstart the magazine's growth spurt. Grosvenor was now considering throwing a third innovation into the editorial mix. The relatively new science of archaeology was becoming popular and *National Geographic*'s editor saw potential in adding to the magazine tales of ancient cultures rediscovered.

Grosvenor had politely declined earlier inquiries from Bingham asking the society to sponsor his South American peregrinations in 1906 and 1908. After reading about Machu Picchu, however, Grosvenor immediately sensed that Bingham's story was perfect for his magazine. Within days of Bingham's return, Grosvenor had solicited a long story from the explorer about his adventures in Peru, with plenty of photographs. The project would require a return expedition, which the National Geographic Society would help fund. Bingham had hardly returned from Peru before he was planning another, bigger trip back.

This time, no Mitchell family money would be required. Back in New Haven, Bingham the junior faculty member found that the 1911 expedition had improved his status on campus as well. A column in *The Wall Street Journal* predicted that the bones found near Cusco would provide a "new chapter" in the paleontological work begun by Bingham's fellow Yale scholar Othniel Marsh. In January, Bingham presented his findings before a meeting of the members of the Yale Corporation, a group that included President Taft. Bingham must have been convincing, because Yale agreed to split the costs of a new expedition with the National Geographic Society. By May 1912, Bingham was once again steaming southward to Peru.

THIRTY-SEVEN

Digging for the Truth

In and Around Machu Picchu

One of the major factors in the rise of archaeology had been the birth of the public museum. Starting in the eighteenth century, antiquities that had been stashed away in private collections across Europe were converted into public property, accessible to the general populace. The British Museum in London and the Louvre in Paris were just two repositories of culture founded on the accumulated trophies of wealthy hoarders. As Daniel Boorstin notes in his book *The Discoverers*, the very word "tourist," which had come to represent the decline of serious adventure travel in the eyes of John Leivers, was popularized after 1800 to describe the "mobile community of transient spectators" who made a grand tour of these new collections. The Smithsonian Institution was founded in Washington, D.C., in 1846, soon to be followed by natural history museums in most major cities and on several college campuses. The acres of display space in these new institutions needed to be filled.

At Yale, where the pioneering paleontologist Othniel Marsh had encouraged a wealthy uncle to fund the Peabody Museum, there was great hope that the hastily arranged "Peruvian Expedition of 1912, Under the Auspices of Yale University and the National Geographic Society" would provide such artifacts. If Machu Picchu had really eluded the Spaniards and vanished into the jungle since the sixteenth century, there was no telling what archaeological treasures might be hiding beneath its granite temples. "We all hope that you will be able to excavate and bring back a shipload of antiquities for your museum at Yale," Grosvenor wrote to his new contributor.

Grosvenor's cheerleading, unthinkable today, would have seemed unremarkable at the time. Peru's artifacts had been shipped out of the country with few restrictions since Francisco Pizarro's ransom deal with Atahualpa. By the early twentieth century, American museums were among the world's most eager customers for pre-Columbian treasures. One New York newspaper reporter, receiving a tour of a new exhibition at the American Museum of Natural History's Peruvian Hall in 1906, observed merrily that the "choice personal ornaments of gold and silver, rich garments, pottery, etc.," on display "were wrested mainly from ancient burial sites."

As the 1912 expedition came together, however, attitudes in Peru toward its national heritage were changing almost week to week. Bingham's very public search for Manco Inca's lost capital had mobilized Peruvian intellectuals, who were fighting to preserve their country's indigenous treasures. Within days of his 1911 visit to Machu Picchu, Bingham had received word from the prefect of the Cusco region that he was forbidden to undertake any excavations, a warning that Bingham brushed off because he wasn't planning to do any digging. (An indication of how fast the atmosphere was changing in Peru: the order came from J. J. Nuñez, the same official who had invited Bingham to Choquequirao two years earlier to observe the treasure hunting that Nuñez had undertaken with explosives.) A second, stronger governmental decree was issued from Lima as Bingham returned from Espiritu Pampa. The exportation of artifacts from Peru without official consent was now "absolutely prohibited."

As he hurried to assemble the 1912 expedition, Bingham reached out once again to President Taft, asking if the White House might help convince President Leguia to grant an exception to Yale, allowing Bingham to excavate and bring the Peabody Museum whatever artifacts he found. Taft was happy to oblige, and a deal was quickly negotiated. Bingham would receive a concession to dig, and he would split any unearthed antiquities fifty-fifty with Peru. From his half, Bingham also agreed to turn over one third of any "treasures, monuments and whatever other riches that might be found" to the owner of the land on which Machu Picchu sat.

Bingham's desire to prove that the bones he found near Cusco were those of a prehistoric man was so well known that it had become fodder for jokes. "Prof. Bingham might be better engaged if he started out to find the prehistoric woman instead of the prehistoric man," wrote one popular gazette. "We do not believe that the prehistoric woman belonged to a woman's club, although she may have wielded one in the interests of the family." To Bingham, confirming the age of the Cusco Man (as some were calling the glacial bones) was serious enough that he arranged to bring George Eaton, the Peabody's curator of osteology, on the expedition. Preliminary estimates had ranged from ten thousand to fifty thousand years. Determining when, exactly, humans had migrated to the Western Hemisphere was one of the most hotly debated topics in the sciences at the time. The Smithsonian Institution's Aleš Hrdlička, the most prominent anthropologist in the United States, had recently journeyed to Argentina to view some skeletal remains that scientists hoped would establish South America as the cradle of humanity. Hrdlička returned unconvinced that *homo sapiens* had inhabited the Americas for more than a few thousand years.

When Bingham's team arrived in the Andes, a close examination of the bones was made almost immediately. Eaton reviewed some animal remains found in the deposit, which Bingham had excitedly hypothesized were those of a long-extinct bison hunted by the Cusco Man. After a reconnaissance mission to a local butcher shop, Eaton decided that they were actually the bones of a modern domestic cow. The finding negated Bingham's theory that humans might have inhabited South America going back to the Ice Age. He wired his editors at *Harper's*, pleading with them to kill a suddenly obsolete article he'd written about the bones' likely historical importance. It was the first sign that 1912 wasn't going to be a replay of 1911.

Bad news continued to pile up. The native laborers Bingham con-

scripted were unenthusiastic about clearing the ruins at Machu Picchu, which had vanished again under tropical foliage in less than a
year. One of Bingham's key assistants lost his footing while climbing
Huayna Picchu and nearly plummeted two thousand feet to his death;
he was falling toward the Urubamba River when he grabbed a
mesquite bush, almost tearing his right arm off. A week of "back
breaking" digging at the Principal Temple yielded nothing, Bingham
wrote. "Not even a bone or potsherd." The dearth of discoveries, plus
ample evidence of looting, made it clear that Yale's was not the first
expedition to search for whatever had been buried at the abandoned
city. A 50-cent reward that Bingham offered to "any workman who
would report the whereabouts of a cave containing a skull, and who
would leave the cave exactly as he had found it" spurred the quick
discovery of dozens of graves. Most were located by Alvarez and Richarte, two of the Machu Picchu farmers who had welcomed Bingham
to their mountaintop the previous year. When Alvarez disappeared for
a few days, though, osteologist Eaton was told by another laborer that
"Alvarez's trouble is in his testes, and that the other Indians say the
trouble has been inflicted by the spirits of the dead Incas whose graves
Alvarez was robbing." Then Richarte vanished, too. "Perhaps they really are afraid of the spirits," Eaton wrote in his journal.

Bingham left the excavation of Machu Picchu under Eaton's supervision and went off in pursuit of new discoveries in the nearby cloud
forest. When he paid a return visit to the nearby hacienda Huadquiña,
the son-in-law of the proprietress, an "enthusiastic amateur archaeologist" named Tomás Alvistur, delighted Bingham with a report that
"some of the Indians on the plantation knew of three localities where
there were Inca ruins, so they said, that had not been visited by white
men." These "feudal tenants," as Bingham called the Huadquiña laborers, had zero interest in leading Bingham to these sites. As their over-
lord, Alvistur gave them no choice.

The first site the team encountered after climbing five thousand
feet was Llactapata. Bingham hastily measured and photographed
what he called the "relatively unimportant" ruins, pausing just long

enough to wonder "what connection the people who built and occupied this mountain stronghold had to the other occupants of the
valley"—the residents of Machu Picchu. Bingham pressed on through
a second unpleasant day, at the end of which the explorer was shown
another site, known as Palcay. There, in the middle of the night, the
Huadquiña workers deserted. The discoverer of Machu Picchu needed
a young boy who lived in a hut near the ruins to guide him back to the
nearest town.

Bingham's sophomore slump continued. Vitcos, the most promising site he had found aside from Machu Picchu, had been picked clean
long before he arrived in 1911. "The existence of scattered boulders
and torn down walls would seem to show a violent attempt at treasure
hunting in the past," Bingham wrote in his journal. The entire region
along the Vilcabamba River had been swept by deadly plagues of
smallpox and typhus, and the native workers Bingham was able to
round up were "insolent." A week's work turned up not a single artifact of note, only "a handful of rough potsherds."

Back at Machu Picchu, Bingham was taking no chances. The crew
carefully shielded its museum-quality finds from the prying eyes of its
government overseer. The Yale team strip-mined the site, following
the director's instructions to note carefully where every bone chip and
pot fragment had come from. Among the best finds were several small
bronzes, a few pots, two carved stone boxes, some silver shawl pins
and a copper bracelet. The vast bulk of what workers packed into
ninety-three boxes at the end of the dig were broken ceramics and
human remains.

Upon returning to Lima, however, Bingham learned that he might
not be leaving Peru with any artifacts at all. Yale's concession had
been arranged with President Leguia as a sort of gentleman's agreement. Bingham had presumed that Leguia—a political strongman
whose unpopular dictatorial tendencies would, years later, lead to his
incarceration—could arrange for the Congress to approve the fifty-
fifty split when the legislature opened for business in July. It was a serious misreading of Peru's political climate. Antipathy toward Leguia

was so strong that a national uprising forced him out of office. When Bingham met with the new populist head of state, Guillermo Billing-hurst, the president informed the explorer that he considered Yale's concession to be "a disgrace." Anticipating the legal trouble that would arise a century later, Lima's newspapers portrayed Bingham as a Yankee imperialist looking to steal the country's treasures and dispatch them to Yale. "I am blue, blue, blue," Bingham wrote to Alfreda. "This has been the hardest, most discouraging and least productive of my expeditions."

Just as the expedition was devolving into a complete disaster, Bill-inghurst offered a surprising solution. Yale would be required to stop excavating as of December 1, earlier than expected. At that time, Bing-ham would be allowed to export, pending a thorough inspection, not just the half of the objects that he had agreed to, but *everything* that Yale had found.

There was one catch with the new agreement. Peru reserved the right to "exact" from Yale "the return of the unique and duplicate ob-jects that it has extracted." In other words, the Peabody Museum was welcome to display the fruits of Bingham's labors at Machu Picchu. But Peru could demand them back whenever it wanted.

Hiram Bingham III, photographed during his 1911 search for Vilcabamba, the legendary Lost City of the Incas. He found Machu Picchu instead. *(Courtesy of the National Geographic Society)*

John Leivers, the author's guide. He'd survived more than one brush with death while indulging his passion for exploring Peru's forgotten ruins. *(Courtesy of Paolo Greer)*

Francisco Pizarro, the Spanish conqueror of Peru. His shrewdness was exceeded only by his ruthlessness. *(Library of Congress)*

After Pizarro captured the Inca emperor Atahualpa in 1532, the prisoner offered one of the richest ransoms in history—a large room filled once with gold and twice again with silver. The entire Inca kingdom was mobilized to collect precious metals. *(Author's collection)*

Pizarro executed Atahualpa, installing Manco Inca Yupanqui as puppet king of the Incas. Their friendly relations were short-lived—this early sixteenth-century illustration shows Manco attempting to burn a Spanish church. *(The Royal Library, Denmark)*

Many of Cusco's ancient architectural wonders still stand, including the gargantuan walls of the Sacsahuaman complex. *(Courtesy of John Leivers)*

An example of the precise Inca stonework inside Cusco's Koricancha sun temple. *(Courtesy of Pierre Boucher/Wikimedia Commons)*

The collision of Spanish and Andean cultures can be seen in this famous eighteenth-century Last Supper painting. Its centerpiece is the traditional mountain delicacy *cuy*, or guinea pig. *(Antonio Zapata Guzmán/Wikimedia Commons)*

The mule whisperers: Julian *(with his ever-present bag of coca leaves)*, Mateo and Juvenal, a living legend of Peruvian exploration. *(Courtesy of the author)*

Justo prepares dinner at Valentin's farm in the clouds. *(Courtesy of the author)*

One section of the very vertical trail to Choquequirao, a six-mile distance that requires two grueling days of walking to cross. *(Courtesy of the author)*

Choquequirao, often called Machu Picchu's sister site, was the original candidate for Lost City of the Incas. *(Courtesy of the author)*

Only one quarter of Choquequirao's ruins have been excavated; these terraces adorned with llamas were discovered in 2005. *(Courtesy of the author)*

Justo on the deserted stone path that runs from Choquequirao to Vitcos. John Leivers called it "one of the finest stretches of Inca trail in all of Peru." *(Courtesy of the author)*

One of the clues that aided Bingham in his search for the Lost City of
the Incas was a sacred carved boulder, known as the White Rock. He
snapped this photo in 1911. *(From* Inca Land)

The White Rock's backside,
as seen today. *(Courtesy of John
Leivers)*

An optical illusion built into the central doorway at the palace of Vitcos *(as photographed by
Bingham in 1911 and as seen today, occupied by John Leivers)* seems to narrow as one enters
from either direction. *(Archival photo from* Inca Land; *other courtesy of the author)*

The hand-carved welcome sign at Espiritu Pampa, nailed to a *matapalo* strangler-fig tree. *(Courtesy of the author)*

Espiritu Pampa was once capital of the Inca empire-in-exile; today machete-wielding teenagers are employed to prevent the jungle from once again swallowing the ruins. *(Courtesy of the author)*

Government archaeologists at Espiritu Pampa display newly excavated Inca artifacts. *(Courtesy of the author)*

The overgrown ruins of Machu Picchu were inhabited by farmers when Bingham first saw them. *(© H.L. Tucker/National Geographic Society/Corbis)*

Though Bingham made several important discoveries on his wildly successful 1911 expedition, press reports in the United States zeroed in on the mist-shrouded mountaintop citadel the explorer had found. *(The New York Times, December 22, 1911)*

National Geographic's ambitious young editor Gilbert Grosvenor saw potential in the story of Machu Picchu; his magazine made stars of both Bingham and his discovery. *(Library of Congress)*

The least convenient but cheapest way to reach Machu Picchu is to arrive via the "backdoor" route atop train tracks. The sign to John's left reads DANGER: DO NOT WALK ON TOP OF RAILS. *(Courtesy of the author)*

The railway to Machu Picchu follows the same route Bingham followed through the Urubamba Valley in 1911. *(From* Inca Land*)*

Hidden on a hillside below Machu Picchu is a giant carved *intihuatana*, which aligns perfectly with the angle of the sunrise for a few days each year. *(Courtesy of the author)*

The Torreon at Machu Picchu, a sun temple where a mysterious beam of light shines through a window on the June solstice.
(Courtesy of the author)

The Torreon sits atop the Royal Mausoleum, a cave lined with surrealistic masonry; Bingham theorized that this was the birthplace of the Inca civilization.
(Courtesy of the author)

The two as photographed by Bingham.
(From Inca Land)

The abstract Intihuatana stone sits at the highest point within the main ruins of Machu Picchu. Its shape mirrors the holy peak of Huayna Picchu, which lies due north of the stone; other important peaks stand directly to the south, east and west. *(Courtesy of the author)*

Bingham surmised that the east-facing Temple of the Three Windows was the key to solving the mystery of Machu Picchu's origins. *(Courtesy of the author)*

Bingham carefully cultivated his swashbuckler image and frequently had himself photographed in dashing poses, such as this one at Espiritu Pampa. *(Yale Peruvian Expedition Papers, Manuscripts and Archives, Yale University)*

Bingham's best-known book, *Lost City of the Incas*, inspired the 1954 B-movie *Secret of the Incas*, a major influence on *Raiders of the Lost Ark*. *(Courtesy of the author)*

Newly unearthed film production memos indicate that the connection between Bingham and Indiana Jones is closer than previously known. *(© Sunset Boulevard/Corbis)*

Decades after his death, Bingham made headlines again in 2008 when Peru's former first lady Eliane Karp-Toledo *(shown with her husband, President Alejandro Toledo)* prodded Peru to sue Yale University for the return of artifacts Bingham had taken from Machu Picchu. *(© Paolo Aguilar/EFE/Corbis)*

The same year, Alaskan researcher Paolo Greer published an article that raised new doubts about Bingham's status as the discoverer of Machu Picchu. *(Courtesy of Paolo Greer)*

A section of the hand-drawn map that led Greer on a twenty-year odyssey. *(Courtesy of Paolo Greer)*

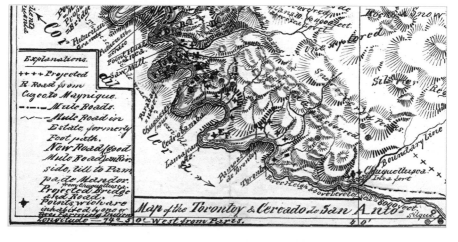

Bingham located the Inca Trail during his final attempt to prove his Lost City theory. The agricultural settlement of Patallacta, near the trail's start, fed multitudes at Machu Picchu. *(Courtesy of the author)*

The author takes a break with his Inca Trail guide, Efrain Valles. One of these men has walked the trail three hundred times. *(Courtesy of John Leivers)*

John Leivers approaches the Sun Gate, the pilgrim's entrance to Machu Picchu. *(Courtesy of the author)*

On the morning of the June solstice, a beam of sunlight shoots down this corridor in the ruins of Llactapata. A gold reflector at its end may have blasted the light back across the valley to Machu Picchu. *(Courtesy of John Leivers)*

The same day, the sun can be seen from Machu Picchu rising directly over the top of Cerro San Gabriel. *(Courtesy of the author)*

Mystically inclined visitors congregate at Machu Picchu for the solstice. *(Courtesy of the author)*

Machu Picchu today. The Torreon, scrubbed to its original brilliant white, can be seen in the bottom right corner. The Intihuatana stone is halfway up on the left. The Sacred Plaza, including the Principal Temple and the Temple of the Three Windows, is at the base of the small terraced hill on which the Intihuatana stone sits. *(Courtesy of the author)*

THIRTY-EIGHT

Yale v. Peru

Near Washington, D.C.

To understand how Bingham's actions in 1912 dragged his beloved Yale into court a hundred years later, I had to travel about four thousand miles to the café of a Barnes and Noble in suburban Washington, D.C., where I met with Eliane Karp-Toledo. In a country populated by circumspect brunettes, the former first lady of Peru was almost as famous for her fiery red hair and flamboyant native-inspired accessorizing as she was for her far-left politics and inability to keep her strong opinions to herself. Her strawberry tresses (the closest shade in the Crayola palette would fall, appropriately, somewhere between Outrageous Orange and Radical Red) were held up by a pair of mirrored sunglasses, and she was wearing Stanford sweats (she had recently taught there) and an olive-drab military-style shirt that from twenty paces appeared to be emblazoned with that dewy-eyed portrait of Che Guevara. Lady Bird Johnson this was not.

I have no idea if any president in Peruvian history other than Alejandro Toledo has been married or not, because no one has ever expressed an opinion to me about any first lady other than Karp-Toledo. The day we met she had been gone from Peru for four years and people there still talked about her *all the time*. She was usually compared to one of three women: Eva Peron, probably because she had political ambitions and was suspected to be the real power behind her husband; Imelda Marcos, because she sometimes seemed ridiculous and was suspected of living luxuriously on taxpayer money (charges were filed but never proven); and Marie Antoinette, for reasons that didn't really make sense except that she was unpopular. She did, though, offer me a very cake-like muffin when I sat down.

I wanted to meet Karp-Toledo because she was widely perceived—largely through her own efforts—to be Hiram Bingham's worst living enemy. In 2002, the Yale scholars Richard Burger and Lucy Salazar had approached Karp-Toledo about Peru's cooperation in an exhibition they were assembling around Bingham's Machu Picchu artifacts. Karp-Toledo agreed to a meeting with her own agenda in mind. She had asked some Peruvian researchers to look into the Bingham situation and came away convinced that the 1912 edict that Bingham had agreed to in order to get his relics out of the country required Yale to return the artifacts. "We provided talking points that represented the position of the president," Karp-Toledo told me. "Everything started with two points: One, we wanted to take an inventory of the pieces at Yale. Two, everything had to come back to Peru. We said, 'Nothing happens if you don't start with those two points.'" Yale declined, and the Machu Picchu show toured without Peru's assistance. Karp-Toledo kept pushing the subject. In the meantime, the National Geographic Society reviewed their records and sided with Peru—in their opinion, Yale should send everything back. "In 2005, my husband, in front of the board of directors of the National Geographic Society, picked up the phone and said to the president of Yale, 'We need to discuss this.' The president of Yale never returned the call, from the president of a sovereign nation. That's very disdainful."

Karp-Toledo was certain that Yale had waited for the clock to run out on her husband's administration. In September 2007, a year after the Toledos had left Peru for Stanford, Yale and Peru announced that a "memo of understanding" had been reached under which the Bingham items would be returned. Initially, it sounded like a good deal for both sides. Yale would give back more than three hundred "museum-quality" pieces. For the time being, the university would hold on to a less exciting-sounding "research collection." Yale would reassemble the Burger-Salazar show, which would make a new tour of museums to help pay for a new Machu Picchu Museum and Research Center in Cusco. (Peru would pick up the rest of the tab.) With a little elbow grease, both parties could look forward to a 2011 ribbon cutting. The memo stated that "it is intended that the international opening of the new Museum will coincide with the centennial celebration of Bingham's rediscovery of Machu Picchu."

"Do you know what they did?" Karp-Toledo asked me, her dainty hands throttling her gigantic herbal tea. "They sent a cartoonist to do the negotiating with Yale!" (Actually, the negotiator was Peru's minister of housing, who'd written children's books that were made into animated movies.) "I found this 'memo of understanding' on the Web, and I couldn't believe it!" The fine-print details did seem to favor Yale. While the university acknowledged Peru's title to all the artifacts, they reserved the right to keep the "fragments, bones and specimens" for use in "ongoing research," which turned out to mean for an additional ninety-nine years.

Karp-Toledo was out of power but she wasn't powerless. In February 2008 she wrote an Op-Ed column for *The New York Times,* in which she said the agreement reflected Yale's "colonial way of thinking." The subsequent uproar made the deal politically untenable. By the end of 2008, Peru was suing for the artifacts in U.S. district court, on the grounds that Bingham's concession clearly stated that the relics would be returned when requested. Yale rejected Peru's claims as "stale and meritless." And so, fifty years after Bingham's death, Yale and Peru were fighting in court over his inheritance.

I'd heard a radio interview in which Karp-Toledo had referred to Bingham as a *huaquero,* a grave robber. Did she still feel that way?

"Of course. What's the difference between Bingham and a *huaquero* at this point? Nothing. Bingham was very clever at marketing himself. He managed to make himself look like the discoverer. That's a legend that needs to be completely thrown out."

At that moment a short man, wearing a dark blue suit with no tie, approached us, introduced himself and sat down with some colleagues at an adjacent table. It was Alejandro Toledo, the ex-president of Peru. I felt like I was meeting with the Peruvian government in exile, which had set up headquarters between Cookbooks and Self-Improvement.

"In 2007–2008 the INC was finally allowed to go to the basement of the Peabody and do a proper inventory," she said. "Yale said there were five thousand pieces; the INC counted more than forty thousand." Karp-Toledo's allies in Peru had since made quite a bit of hay with this alarming-sounding discrepancy; news accounts in Peru some-times hinted that Bingham had secreted away a hoard equal to Ata-hualpa's ransom. The truth, as Karp-Toledo acknowledged, was just a difference in accounting. What Yale counted as a single lot of human remains, Peru might count as dozens of fragments.

Karp-Toledo roiled the waters further in 2009 when she was invited to speak on campus by the Yale Political Union. From the podium she brandished a 1916 letter from Bingham to Gilbert Grosvenor that read: "The objects found do not belong to us, but to the Peruvian govern-ment, which allowed us to take them from the country under the condition that they be returned." He wasn't, in fact, referring to the specific items he excavated in 1912, but Karp's insinuation was clear— Bingham knew that what he'd taken from Peru was a loan, not a gift.

Aside from a small group of scholars, administrators, and lawyers at Yale, almost everyone with an interest in Machu Picchu agreed that the artifacts Bingham took should be returned. There has long been, however, some (politically incorrect) doubt about Peru's ability to take proper care of its antiquities. The National Museum in Lima was notoriously robbed of hundreds of irreplaceable objects in the late 1970s. The Museo Inka in Cusco had twenty-two gold pieces stolen in 1993. One well-known explorer I spoke with recalled handing mum-mies and artifacts over to the INC, only to return later and learn that they'd been lost or stolen. In 2008, a pair of vendors operating a souve-nir shop off the main plaza in Cusco was found with 690 Inca and pre-Inca artifacts; they'd been hawking them on the Internet. Even Karp-Toledo agrees that thanks to the thriving *huaquero* industry, it's an open secret in Peru that artifacts can be bought easily. I'd seen collections in private homes that rivaled what the Peabody owned.

Which is not to say that Yale's stewardship had been flawless. Bingham sent boxes of remains from his 1914–15 Expedition back to Peru without any documentation, making them almost useless to researchers. When Burger and Salazar first saw the Bingham collection in the 1980s, much of it was deteriorating after decades of neglect. Karp-Toledo had no doubts. "It's absolutely certain that Peru can take care of these artifacts."

The latest chatter I'd heard in Lima was that Karp-Toledo was pushing the conflict over the Bingham pieces to keep her husband's name in the news as he contemplated another run for the presidency. I asked as diplomatically as possible if perhaps Bingham was being used as the whipping boy for other interests.

"He has been demonized by some specialists—fairly," Karp-Toledo said, but declined to name any names.

In that case, could she think of anything nice to say about Bingham?

"I think the politician in him ate the adventurer in him. That's too bad. If I were to give Bingham credit for one thing, it was that he brought knowledge of Machu Picchu to the world."

We stood to leave. I noticed that her military T-shirt had writing on it. "What does it say?" I asked.

Karp-Toledo pinched the hem and pulled it down so I could get a good look. It wasn't El Che. It was a picture of an ancient Peruvian warrior framed by the words INCA POWER. "Do you know who that is?" she asked, smiling.

"Pachacutec?"

She shook her head no. "It's him," she said, and pointed at her husband, who was still huddled with his associates. Inca. Power. The next day I would read that he was running again for president.

Karp-Toledo insisted that I take a muffin for the road.

THIRTY-NINE

Action Hero

Within the Pages of *National Geographic*

Bingham sailed again into New York Harbor almost a year to the day after his triumphant return in 1911. This time, in lieu of swashbuckling tales of lost cities and conquered mountain peaks, he came bearing excuses, grudges and thirteen-year-old Juan Leguia, the son of the former president, whose toxically unpopular father was shipping him off to military school in Virginia. According to the version of events that Bingham chose to tell reporters, Yale's concession had been all but forced upon him by the elder Leguia. The sudden opposition to his expedition removing artifacts had been stoked by "men who were in the business of exporting and buying archaeological things." The officials who handed down the decree allowing him to depart with his boxes had been "as insulting to us as they possibly could be." The whole affair had left Bingham bitter. "I can now say freely that we don't propose to go to Peru in the near future," he said.

Down in Washington, D.C., Gilbert Grosvenor evidently saw things a little differently. After viewing Bingham's photographs from Machu Picchu, the editor decided immediately that *National Geographic* would devote an entire issue to the story, the first time in the magazine's history that it would do so. Grosvenor also arranged the seating chart for the society's annual dinner, held in January 1913, so that Bingham dined at the head table. There he was joined by the evening's main attractions: toastmaster and North Pole hero Robert E. Peary, who told the assembled attendees that Bingham's discoveries had "astounded the scientists of the world," and the Norwegian explorer Roald Amundsen, recipient of the year's Explorers Gold Medal for winning the race to the South Pole. (The world was still a few weeks from hearing the news that the frozen body of Amundsen's rival Captain Scott had been discovered.[11]) Dressed formally in white tie and tails, Bingham delivered a brief speech that focused on the triumphs of 1911, not the disappointments of 1912. "Buried in the jungle, we found a city called Machu Picchu," he told the evening's six hundred distinguished guests. "That is an awful name, but it is well worth remembering."

"I do not think even you realize the sensation that the article will make," Grosvenor wrote to Bingham shortly before the Machu Picchu issue appeared that spring. (Readers' expectations may not have been especially high. The lead story from the previous edition had been "Oysters: The World's Most Valuable Water Crop," by Hugh M. Smith, who'd previously penned "Making the Fur Seal Abundant" and "Brittany, the Land of the Sardine.") Anyone picking up the April 1913 *National Geographic* edition would have seen immediately that it was something special. The entire magazine consisted of one long article, catchily titled "In the Wonderland of Peru." A brief introductory editor's note set the tone: "What an extraordinary people the builders of Machu Picchu must have been to have constructed, without steel implements, and using only stone hammers and wedges, the wonderful city of refuge on the mountain top." The story and its accompanying photographs—including a panoramic view of the entire site, printed as a foldout—conveyed a romantic tale of exploration and discovery that would endure for almost a century: an intrepid young American professor, searching for the capital of a vanished kingdom, discovers an immense city in the clouds, lost to the jungle for untold centuries.

---

11 Bingham isn't the only Inca expert whose reputation has suffered over the intervening years. Historians have laid much of the blame for Scott's death at the feet of Sir Clements Markham, who pushed Scott and his team to use sledges pulled by men instead of dogsleds, as Amundsen did.

As always, Bingham's storytelling tended toward the dry side, his narrative weighed down by lists of maladies suffered by expedition members and tedious details about building a temporary bridge. (Incredibly, his first draft of the article seems to have skipped over the details of the 1911 discovery; Bingham added them only after Grosvenor gently pointed out that "our readers will want to know how you found it.") The photographs, however—250 in all—were astonishing. Bingham managed to capture the vastness of the Andes and the precision of Inca masonry; his black-and-white images of the new mule road through the Urubamba Valley have the spellbinding etched-mirror allure of Ansel Adams's work. The before-and-after pictures of the ruins as they were transformed from an overgrown ghost town to the mystical city known today make clear, in a way that Bingham's stiff prose never managed to, how it was possible for such a set of buildings to simply disappear into the jungle.

If the reaction of the press had been enthusiastic in December 1911, Bingham's visual aids now pushed writers to hyperbolic new heights. In a long story titled "The Greatest Architectural Discovery of the Age," *The New York Times Magazine* was particularly effusive:

> Just now, when we thought there was practically no portion of the Earth's surface still unknown, when the discovery of a single lake or mountain, or the charting of a remote strip of coast line was enough to give a man fame as an explorer, one member of the daredevil explorers' craft has "struck it rich," struck it so dazzlingly rich, indeed, that all his confrères may be pardoned if they gnash their teeth in chagrin and turn green with envy.

Perhaps the most extraordinary thing about that extraordinary sentence is that it happened to be true.

FORTY

The Sacred Center

Between New York and the Appalachians

One morning I was sitting with John Leivers in a Cusco café, nibbling on coca cookies and watching a parade sponsored by the Peru-Cuba Alliance. Less than twenty-four hours later, I'd been sucked through the CUZ > LIM > JFK pneumatic tube and found myself in midtown Manhattan, standing bewildered amid the scurry of commuters in Grand Central Terminal. My cell phone, after weeks of homesick scanning for a signal, recognized where it was and vibrated to life in my pocket. I called Aurita and went straight to voice mail. Without really thinking, I bought a coffee and a bagel and hopped on the 9:37 local train home. When my car emerged from underground, I noticed that the trees had lost their leaves while I was away.

Aside from a lingering tendency to walk down stairs splayfooted, I lapsed into my old routine within a day or two. I drove the boys to school, took long shopping trips to the supermarket and stopped glazing my hands with sanitizer every ten minutes. To my former colleagues I bragged a little about the trip—"of course you've got to be careful traveling with mules at high altitude"—but the satisfaction was ephemeral. For a few weeks my wandering mind seemed to tune in intermittently to a staticky Andean radio station; at stoplights, random thoughts of devil goats and *intihuatanas* popped into my head. Whenever I started to wonder if my memory was playing tricks on me, I pulled out two souvenirs I'd brought home as reminders that Peru was simply a different world. One was a ten-sol note, Peru's equivalent of a five-dollar bill. On the flip side, where the august Lincoln Memorial would be printed on a sawbuck, was a picture of a Peruvian war ace flying his plane. Upside down. The other memento was a postcard of Cusco's most famous painting, which hangs in a cathedral on the central plaza. In it, Jesus and the twelve disciples are seated at the Last Supper. At the center of the table, paws up, is a roasted guinea pig. Of course, having been raised Catholic, I immediately felt guilty for seeing humor in a painting that others saw as holy. Even if it was pretty funny.

My ambivalence toward supernatural matters wasn't particularly helpful when I sat down to untangle everything John had told me about why Machu Picchu had been built where it was—all the alignments and solstices and the worship of the sun and the mountains. When editing adventure travel magazines, I had always rolled my eyes at press releases that crossed my desk promising "healing excursions" or "sacred getaways" to Machu Picchu; a never-ending parade of New Age kooks always seemed to be marching through the site, waving crystals and absorbing the positive vibrations. Through most of my trip with John, a quote from Shirley MacLaine, patron saint of pop occultism, had been stuck in my head like a bad fast-food jingle:

> I went to Machu Picchu in Peru with a man who said he had had a love affair with an extraterrestrial. He said he was still being guided by her and could call on that guidance anytime. He proceeded to do just that.

Still, I had to admit that when I stood atop Mount Machu Picchu and saw how the site aligned with the natural features surrounding it, I'd felt a twinge of . . . something. Awe? Transcendence? I felt ridiculous even trying to think in such terms.

Unfortunately, I didn't know any extraterrestrials who'd have sex with me, but there was one obvious way to find some of the answers I was seeking. I called Johan Reinhard.

Reinhard is the author of *Machu Picchu: Exploring an Ancient Sacred Center*, the book that had sent John searching for alignments all over Peru (and which had kept me waiting for over an hour at a Cusco bookstore). He also happens to be an explorer who has summitted more than a hundred seventeen-thousand-foot peaks. He's probably best known for finding the Ice Maiden, the mummy of an adolescent girl who had been left hundreds of years ago atop Peru's 20,700-foot Mount Ampato as a human sacrifice to the all-powerful mountain gods. Reinhard had been searching for Inca ruins amid the *apus* south of Cusco when he realized that the heat from a volcano erupting nearby might have revealed new artifacts beneath Ampato's ancient snowcap. When he and his climbing partner, Miguel Zárate, scaled the mountain, they found the frozen body of a young woman, laid out on a burial platform and surrounded by unbroken ceramics and gold and silver figurines of humans and animals. She wore a feather headdress. Reinhard intuited immediately what they had found. "We were looking straight into the face of an Inca," he later recalled.

In addition to Reinhard's mountaineering and academic credentials—he has a PhD in anthropology—he specializes in the emerging field of sacred geography. This is but one of many disciplines grouped together under the umbrella term "archaeoastronomy," or the study of how ancient peoples incorporated the sun, moon and stars into their daily lives. (Amateur practitioners devote a lot of time to trying to prove that the Mayas predicted the world would end in 2012.) Reinhard has spent much of his life in South America and Asia studying how mountain peoples integrate the landscape in which they live into their spiritual beliefs. He drew on this experience to formulate his sacred center theory.

"The Western idea is that you look at something like a mountain and you see a physical object," Reinhard told me when I reached him at his home in West Virginia. (I'd assumed that anyone named Johan

Reinhard would speak like Henry Kissinger; as it turned out, Reinhard had grown up outside Chicago, like me.) "Among traditional peoples—in the Andes, in China, in the Himalayas—we've found that certain features of the landscape—mountains, rivers, lakes, caves—are seen as physical, but they're also imbued with sacred power in one way or another. For example, a mountain might be the place where their ancestors originated, or the place where the dead go. A mountain might be perceived as the deity that controls fertility in all its different aspects, everything from the welfare of animals to the fertility of humans and, of course, the fertility of crops." Which makes sense on a purely phenomenological level—in the Andes, Reinhard said, elements such as rain, snow, thunder and lightning all seem to originate in the mountains. The effect is multiplied by Peru's insane weather. "I was in the Sacred Valley in 1983 when a hailstorm knocked out ninety percent of the corn crop in fifteen minutes," he said. "So if your perception is that the mountains control weather, you're going to try to make those mountains happy."

If there were a Geiger counter for geographic sacredness, the topographically rich site of Machu Picchu would bury the needle. Mountain worship was one of the cornerstones of Inca religion. Among the pantheon of *apus* scattered throughout the Andes, the Incas revered two peaks above all others. One was Ausangate, which stands above Cusco and the glaciers of which are the source of the sacred Urubamba River. "The Urubamba does a very unusual thing at Machu Picchu," Reinhard said. "It loops *around* the promontory that the site is built on." The other key *apu* is Salcantay, which not only overlooks Machu Picchu but is directly linked to it by a long ridge, like the tip of a root on an old oak tree. Salcantay's glaciers are the source of the sacred Aobamba River—which unites with the Urubamba near where it folds itself around Machu Picchu. "Wherever you have water coming out of a mountain slope, people perceive it as coming out of the mountain's own body," Reinhard said. Machu Picchu was also "situated in the transition zone between the highlands and the Amazon jungle," which heightened its importance.

All of these natural convergences would have made Machu Picchu's site "especially powerful," says Reinhard, but the Incas also, of course, worshipped the sun. The Sapa Inca—"not only a secular ruler but also the head of the state religion," according to Reinhard—relied on his status as the son of the sun to support his claim to power. For this reason, the cardinal directions (north, south, east, west) were crucial to Inca beliefs, according to the Spanish chronicles. "The *particularly* unusual thing about Machu Picchu," Reinhard explained, "is that in all the cardinal directions, you had sacred mountains." I'd seen this when I'd climbed Huayna Picchu with John. Because Huayna Picchu was due north of the city, an Inca priest standing atop its peak would have faced south toward the major *apu* of Salcantay. Similar important peaks stood directly to the east and west of the city.

The night sky above Machu Picchu held even more clues. The Southern Cross, one of the most important constellations in the Incas' religion, appears directly above Salcantay on the December solstice— the longest day of the year and the start of the rainy season. The Milky Way was a celestial river mirrored by its earthbound counterpart, the winding Urubamba. Or as Reinhard put it to me, "Machu Picchu is sort of like the Inca cosmos written on the landscape."

Looked at through the telescopic lens of archaeoastronomy, the question isn't why Pachacutec chose to build Machu Picchu where it is, but rather how he could have placed it anywhere else.

The structures and carvings at Machu Picchu, too, were designed to complement all this sacred geography. The Intihuatana stone, carved out of solid granite attached to the Salcantay massif, connects Huayna Picchu to the main peak of Salcantay. Bingham's Temple of the Three Windows looks due east toward the rising sun. The building that intrigued me most was the Torreon. The upper curved part seems to have been modeled on the Koricancha sun temple, the most sacred building in the city of Cusco. The cave below, with its psyche-delic stonework and carved stone stepladder, faces the sunrise on the winter solstice, the shortest day of the year. One small east-facing window is positioned perfectly to observe the Pleiades cluster of stars, whose appearance heralded the turning of a new agricultural year. This was the same window that I'd been told cast a beam of light onto the carved rock within. (Reinhard had also heard of this phenomenon, but hadn't witnessed it.) It occurred to me that making a return trip to Machu Picchu to see that solstice alignment—visible for only a few days in June—might be my one chance to see the sacred center theory in action.

Our discussion of the infinite mysteries of space reminded me of another universal law: when people speak to a writer for the first time, they must ask him where he gets his ideas. Naturally, I asked Reinhard if he recalled how he'd come up with the sacred center theory.

"I was trekking in on the Inca Trail on a brilliant day," he said, "and I pulled out my compass and it all started coming together."

"The Inca Trail?" It seemed a little soft for a man who'd carried a ninety-pound mummy down from the peak of a twenty-thousand-foot mountain on his back.

"Oh, *absolutely*," Reinhard said, and proceeded to rattle off the names of the structures that John had described to the study-abroad kids atop Mount Machu Picchu. All of them, Reinhard said, were adjacent to the main trail and had been constructed near water sources. "Each site is so unique," Reinhard said. "These are *not* standard Inca sites. They were built for a purpose. Where else in the Inca empire do you find a path leading to these sorts of sites?"

"What does this mean in regard to understanding what Machu Picchu was?"

"It means you can't just take Machu Picchu in isolation—you have to see it in context of the sites leading up to it."

"So the Inca Trail isn't just a pretty shortcut that Pachacutec took on his way to his summer home?"

"Mark, you can't finish the Inca Trail and *not* know that this was the end point of a pilgrimage."

FORTY-ONE

What's the Big Idea?

New Haven

Having achieved his dream of becoming a famous explorer, Hiram Bingham III remained as driven as ever. A log that he maintained in early 1913—let's pause for a moment to wonder just how many people were using time-management strategies in 1913—shows that he spent precisely six hours each week on "class exercises" for his teaching work; twenty-four and a half hours on writing "books and articles"; eight hours on "walks and squash and tennis"; and five hours on "reading for fun." A second log subdivided his reading by category.

Bingham felt a growing urgency to determine once and for all what Machu Picchu had been. And he knew that he needed to figure it out relatively quickly. With both poles claimed and Machu Picchu's discovery drawing the spotlight to the ancient wonders of South America, explorers were concentrating their efforts as never before on the once-neglected continent. William Farabee, whose map of his Harvard expeditions had helped guide Bingham to Machu Picchu, embarked on a three-year trip in and around Peru, during which he assembled a formidable collection of pre-Columbian artifacts for his new employers at the University of Pennsylvania. Bingham's onetime companion through Venezuela and Colombia, Dr. Hamilton Rice, was exploring the jungles of the Amazon (and, according to press reports, performing emergency surgery on his own knee by lantern light). Even one of

Bingham's heroes, former president Theodore Roosevelt, embittered after his failure to retake the White House as a third-party candidate in 1912, departed the following year on a perilous adventure to navigate a mysterious Brazilian waterway known as the River of Doubt.

For Bingham, the most jolting news coming out of South America emerged from the mouth of J. Campbell Besley, a dashing English mining magnate, equally famous as a world-class polo player and a soldier of fortune who'd fought with Lord Kitchener's scouts in the savage Boer War. Stung by a broken engagement to one of Los Angeles's leading debutantes, Besley departed for Lima at the head of what one newspaper called "a red blooded party in search of a lost expedition into the Peruvian wilderness." (The missing persons were a pair of explorers from Chicago, who vanished while searching for Inca cities.) When Besley returned to New York City in February of 1914 (accompanied by a tiny, mischievous monkey named Changa), he claimed to have found something even grander: three lost Inca cities near Cusco. These Besley modestly judged "equal in conception and execution to anything that is to be seen at present in the world of civilization." He had also brought back, according to one newspaper, "a valuable collection of cinematographic pictures of the lost capital of the Incas, Machu Picchu." Bingham pooh-poohed Besley's claims about the new ruins— and nothing approaching the immensity of Besley's descriptions has ever been found—but he surely knew that more serious fame-seeking adventurers were to follow.

"Somebody is going to solve the mystery connected with these ancient peoples," Gilbert Grosvenor wrote to Bingham in early 1914. "Let us get there first."

Bingham's competitive fires didn't need much stoking. He was already planning his largest and most expensive expedition yet, one that would take two years to complete—one year of preparatory work by underlings and another of fieldwork under his supervision. In February, his chief Peruvian nemesis, President Guillermo Billinghurst, had been deposed, exiled and replaced by a military junta. Bingham dispatched an advance party to establish a new headquarters at Ollantaytambo, which was given the faux-Quechua name Yankihausi, or House of the Yankees. From this base they could continue mapping the region around Machu Picchu. Bingham planned to follow in 1915.

The official handbook that Bingham assembled for the Peruvian Expedition of 1914–15, under the Auspices of the National Geographic Society and Yale University, was his masterpiece of micromanagement. Almost every conceivable subject and contingency was covered, from "Care of Rifles" to "Treatment of Snakebite" to "Instructions for the Care and Selection of Mules." ("Avoid mules with extra long heads, also those with hollow or dish faces.") Considering the level of detail that Bingham was willing to go into regarding minutiae, his plans for 1915 seemed uncharacteristically scattered. Whereas in past years Bingham had been diligent in drawing up bullet-pointed lists of objectives, he described the goals of the new expedition in vague, grandiose terms. As Bingham was departing, the *Hartford Courant* explained that his expedition's mission was to "complete the work of uncovering the mysteries of Inca civilization."

A handwritten to-do list that Bingham scribbled inside his own copy of the 1914–15 handbook indicates that the one unifying thread of his plans was his desire to prove once and for all his theories of why Machu Picchu had been built. Under the heading "Must Be Done," Bingham's top priority was to examine Pacaritambo, a site near Cusco that was generally agreed to be the location of Tampu Tocco, the three-windowed hill believed to be the fountainhead of the Inca dynasty.

In the February 1915 issue of *National Geographic*, published just before Bingham departed for Peru, the explorer made clear that he was no longer *suggesting* that Machu Picchu might be Tampu Tocco, the birthplace of the Inca civilization; he was all but convinced of it. Bingham's growing certainty relied on a somewhat shaky foundation, a history of the Incas published in 1642 by a priest named Fernando de Montesinos.[12]

---

12 Montesinos compiled an extraordinary amount of original research on the Incas, which he then turned around and used to try to prove that they had descended from the great-grandson of the Biblical ark-builder Noah.

Bingham's argument boiled down to this: The first Incas, because of their small army (Montesinos estimated their number at five hundred), would have needed to live in a place with excellent natural defenses. Machu Picchu was, of course, almost inaccessible. Montesinos reported that one of the early Inca rulers banned the use of writing. Bingham thought that enigmatic stones with rounded edges (sort of like poker chips) that had been excavated at Machu Picchu in 1912 might have been used for record keeping in the place of letters.[13] Tampu Tocco was believed to have contained a wall with three windows—just like the Temple of the Three Windows at Machu Picchu—and to have been situated near a cave. "It is well to remember that there is no cave, large or small, at Pacaritambo," Bingham wrote. "At Machu Picchu there are several large caves, one of them lined with very beautiful masonry." In other words, the Royal Mausoleum beneath the Torreon was the holiest spot in Tampu Tocco—the very place from which the founding Incas had emerged.

It was a pretty far-out argument, even for a man described by one New York newspaper as "the foremost authority in this country on South America." But Bingham wasn't finished. The ruins of Machu Picchu were *so* impressive—might they not also constitute the elusive Vilcabamba, Manco's jungle refuge, the true Lost City of the Incas? Going back into the Spanish friar Antonio de la Calancha's *Coronica Moralizada*, the seventeenth-century book whose clues had led him to Vitcos, Bingham reviewed Calancha's description of Vilcabamba and the "University of Idolatry" contained within its city limits. A century before Calancha put quill to parchment, two Spanish monks who

---

13 One of the most fascinating topics of study in Inca anthropology is that of the *khipu*. These were knotted cords used to register information down to "even one pair of sandals," according to one sixteenth-century observer. The knots were decipherable only to a special class of *khipu* keepers, which is why none of the six hundred *khipu* known to have survived the conquistadors' purge of Inca records has been fully decrypted. Harvard professor Gary Urton has theorized that the knots used a system analogous to a computer's binary code—which leaves open the possibility that the *khipu* were used to record historical information as well as accounting data.

wished to see this unholy place had traveled three days on foot from Puquiura, near Vitcos, to get there. According to the *Coronica*, Vilcabamba was a hidden city, situated so that the priests could be kept quartered just outside its limits for three weeks without ever catching a glimpse of the blasphemous rituals being conducted within. While the monks bided their time, the new Inca, the rebel Manco's son Titu Cusi, sent out wave upon wave of beautiful women "to tempt and try the monks and to endeavor to make them break their vows of celibacy," Bingham wrote. According to Calancha, among the ranks of these temptresses were some women from Peru's coastal tribes, renowned for their beauty.

When Pizarro and his gang of thugs arrived, Bingham explained in his 1915 *National Geographic* story, "the most precious objects" to be hidden away were not "the gold and silver images that the Spaniards craved, but the Sacred Virgins of the Sun." (The sexy name was Calancha's coinage.) These were the beautiful young women who "from their earliest childhood had been educated to the service of the temple and to ministering to the wants of the Inca." Finding the hidden road by which Manco and these Virgins had fled to Vilcabamba from Cusco was #2 on Bingham's hastily scrawled to-do list.

Machu Picchu had certainly been laid out so that a pair of monks waiting at the base of its mountain would have had no idea what was happening in the clouds above. Could it be reached from Puquiura (and Vitcos) in "three days' journey over rough country," as the friars had described it? Bingham planned to find out (item #3). As for the Virgins, an analysis back at Yale of the human remains from Machu Picchu had led to an interesting discovery. "The large majority of the skeletons are female and *some are coast types*," Bingham wrote, emphasizing what he saw as a key piece of evidence.

One question had hounded Bingham from the moment he'd first run his fingers along the flawless stonework behind the Torreon: "What could this place be?" An answer was finally emerging from the mists—Machu Picchu was *both* Tampu Tocco and Vilcabamba, the Lost City of the Incas. It was as if some intrepid Bible scholar had lo-

cated an interesting hill outside of Jerusalem and concluded that it
was not only the Garden of Eden but also Mount Calvary, site of Jesus
Christ's crucifixion. Such a sweeping theory would take an enormous
effort to prove. The staff for the 1915 expedition was twice the size of
1911's, and the budget had mushroomed five times, to more than
$50,000. Hundreds of square miles of new territory would need to be
mapped. Untold miles of trails would have to be blazed through knotted cloud forest in areas Bingham had labeled "unexplored" on his
maps. New excavations were to be undertaken, and every ruin that
had been mapped needed to be reviewed. Few archaeologists accomplish that much in their careers. Bingham hoped to get it done in six
months.

Gilbert Grosvenor, in a note marked "personal" from February
1915, seemed to recognize that he may have encouraged Bingham to
spread himself too thin.

> On the strength of our friendship, I am going to take the
> liberty of giving you a friendly tip. . . . You are overworking
> yourself to an extent that is unwise; you are overdrawing
> your reserve in your enthusiasm for your researches. You've
> got a problem on your hands that will require years of study
> before the solution is gained. . . . Every year your reputation
> and the fame of your achievements will increase like a
> snowball, but remember that physical strength is limited. I
> fear you are getting reckless, working too much nights and
> worrying for too quick results. . . . I've seen a great many
> men in my work here in the past fifteen years, of whom
> some of the brightest passed to the great beyond and *obliv-*
> *ion* because they forgot that a man's strength is limited and
> if overtaxed will break as easily and as quickly as a thread.

Hiram Bingham wasn't interested in slowing down, though. He
had presented to the world his Grand Unified Theory of Machu Picchu. Now all he had to do was prove it.

FORTY-TWO

Second Chances

Between New York and Lima

John and I exchanged a few e-mails in the weeks after I got home, then he disappeared on one of his long excursions into the mountains. A couple of quiet winter months passed, during which the only communication I received from him was a short note saying he was spending a few weeks in Lima. This seemed a bit out of character as John wasn't particularly fond of big cities. Then one morning my e-mail inbox pinged and there was a message from him, with the subject "TRIPLE CABG!"

"Hi Mark," the note began. "How are you? It's now been a month since I had a major health trauma, i.e., serious problems with my left coronary artery."

Just after we'd parted, John had been walking up a flight of a few hundred stone steps in Cusco when he felt a dull pain behind his sternum. A few similar episodes followed while he was engaging in his usual strenuous recreational activities. It was during a four-hour cycling trip through the mountains of Suriname (riding a one-gear bike, naturally) that the pain spiked enough for John to realize he'd better get to a doctor. A cardiologist in Lima gave him a stress test. "The angiogram showed I had three serious blockages of my left coronary artery," John wrote in his e-mail. "Two of the blockages were greater than 85 percent." He went in for an eight-hour triple bypass operation a week later.

"Those first couple days after the procedure were awful," John told me on the phone the day after his e-mail. "I woke up with a tube down my throat, completely unable to move, coughing blood. There was a nun reading the Bible over my bed."

If John felt any just-happy-to-be-alive euphoria, it was fleeting. "What they don't tell you about heart surgery is that you get depressed," he said. "I was in bad shape for a month afterward, physically and mentally." He still sounded a little blue. John was proud of his ability to defeat any physical challenge through effort and concentration; the heart trouble had obviously left him rattled. He'd been told his days of carrying eighty-pound packs uphill were likely over.

"My surgeon says it's genetic—not enough HDL cholesterol, the good stuff," he told me. "All the sport and walking in the Andes that I've done might've been what saved me. My heart was stressed so hard when I was younger that whenever my problem started, my circulatory system began building new pathways to pump the blood through. As it is I'll be taking five pills a day for the rest of my life."

John paused. "You know, my father died at fifty-seven, same age as me. He was always so busy, vice president of his firm, president of the Royal Perth Golf Club. I was twenty-four when it happened. I felt like I hardly knew him.

"It's funny, for the last five years, as I got closer to fifty-seven, that's always been in the back of my head. You wonder if your heart is telling you, 'I'm not working properly.' I'm always aware of gut feelings. They usually mean something."

I'd never heard John sound so melancholy. "Did you have anyone to look after you in the hospital?" I asked.

"Well, it's a little hard with no family around. You really need someone there twenty-four hours a day for the first two or three weeks. I have one Peruvian friend who's been a bit helpful. And Paolo's been here in Lima, of course. He's visited a few times."

Paolo was Paolo Greer, an old friend of John's from the expat community in Cusco. He'd been the person who suggested I contact John about my original Bingham trip. Paolo was the retired Alaskan gold prospector and dogged amateur researcher who'd made a splash in 2008 when he published an article in the *South American Explorer Magazine* titled "Machu Picchu Before Bingham." The story described Paolo's discovery of a hand-drawn nineteenth-century map in the Library of Congress. The map wasn't labeled, but appeared to be of the area near Machu Picchu. "It took me another twenty years to find out who had drawn the map and why," Paolo explained in his article.

The evidence that Paolo dug up over those two decades supported an accusation that people had been making for years—that the site Bingham identified as the Lost City of the Incas might not have been nearly as misplaced as he'd made it out to be. I had exchanged dozens of e-mails with Paolo and found him to be, by far, the best-informed expert on the subjects of Hiram Bingham and Machu Picchu. Having seen his research twisted in the press, he was also suspicious. Whenever I inquired about visiting him in person to discuss Bingham's role at Machu Picchu, he seemed to vanish into his isolated cabin near Fairbanks, which had neither phone nor electricity. I'd come to understand that if I was ever going to meet Paolo, it would probably be easier to track him down during one of his long visits to Peru.

"Is Paolo still in Lima?" I asked John.

"No, he's gone back to Cusco. But I think he'll be back through Lima for a few days in June before he returns to Alaska. Says he's very keen to have a chat with you."

The feeling was mutual, which gave me an idea. I'd made a small discovery of my own, one that seemed head-slappingly obvious once it sunk in. Somehow in all my reading I had failed to recognize that an ancient highway leading to Machu Picchu that Bingham uncovered in 1915, one that he was convinced proved his Vilcabamba theory, now went by a more familiar name. For it was on his last expedition to Peru that Bingham found the Inca Trail.

"When do you think you'll be ready for hiking again?" I asked John.

"The doctors tell most people to avoid strenuous exercise after a procedure like this."

"Uh-huh. And you?"

"Well, I *have* been doing some special exercises to close this hole in my chest. It's supposed to take six to ten weeks to heal up, but I think I've been able to do it in five. I felt it seal—it was like plastic setting."

"You think you'd be up for doing the Inca Trail by June? I've been thinking that I'd really like to see what happens on the solstice."

"I haven't done the trail in, it must be twelve years."

"Think it's changed much?"

"Oh yeah. And unlike most things in the world, for the better. It used to be a mess, porters carrying a hundred pounds of gear, people shitting everywhere, bugs from the cattle that roamed the farms next to the trail. All that's gone now; they've got regulations. No more than five hundred people per day are allowed on the Trail, including guides and porters. Speaking of which, we'll have to get you a Peruvian guide, licensed for Machu Picchu—I can't take you by myself."

"Anybody you'd suggest?"

"There's one fellow I know from Amazonas Explorer named Efrain—he's very, very good. Speaks Quechua and English, knows his history. I'll see if we can get him." I heard the click of a ballpoint pen. "We'll need porters . . . and a cook. Might be a little tricky."

"Is there a problem?"

"It's my new diet. I don't know how I'll ever explain low-fat cooking to one of these guys."

I asked John if he'd like anything special from the States.

"Actually, yes. A good heart rate monitor."

FORTY-THREE

The Last Crusade

Far Down the Urubamba Valley

When we'd been sitting out the rainstorm en route to Espiritu Pampa, John had explained to me what might be called Leivers's Law of Expedition Entropy: "The bigger the expedition, the greater the chance of something going catastrophically wrong." Bingham's 1915 expedition offered an excellent case study. Things began well enough at Patallacta,[14] a site of "half-moon terraces" that had been located on the 1912 trip. Bingham's team had collected two hundred skulls in the area. Many showed signs of trepanation, the medical practice of punching holes in the cranium, often to relieve pressure on the brain. In an extraordinary photograph published the following year in *National Geographic*, one expedition member appears to be wading through a pond filled with white bowling balls.

Bingham's first project for 1915 was to investigate a trail that seemed to lead out of the south end of Machu Picchu. One of the expedition's native assistants had found an old Inca road that might extend to the citadel from the opposite direction. The region in between was completely unexplored. From Patallacta, Bingham and a

---

14 Astute readers may notice a similarity to the name Llactapata. Both mean "high place." As we've seen in the case of "Vilcabamba," residents of the Andes have never placed a high priority on differentiating places by name. There's a theory that Patallacta was also the original name of Machu Picchu.

small team passed through "a picturesque primeval forest" and encountered the ancient stone highway.

The path climbed to an extraordinary height. At the crest of the
ridge they found ahead of them "a lovely abandoned valley," in which
not a single creature stirred. As the group descended into this untouched paradise, Bingham spotted a circular ruin where, he wrote to
Alfreda, "We pitched our tent . . . and enjoyed the lovely view, which
the Incas had before us."

The trail plunged precipitously the next day, briefly vanishing "in
a maze of boulders and the remains of a fairly recent landslide." Here
the highway forked. The left branch ascended a set of steps to a rock
outcrop like the prow of a ship. Atop this perch the Incas had constructed a labyrinth of stone buildings, including a bullet-shaped structure with nine windows. After a wet night and two hours of walking
the following morning, Bingham recalled, "I at last came out on a
ridge from which a great part of the grand canyon of the Urubamba
was visible—and in the distance the familiar outlines of Machu Picchu
Mountain—but oh so far below us!" Bingham then encountered a
third striking set of unknown ruins. The impressive stonework—
including five stone fountains—was crowned by an Inca overlook that
took in Salcantay and most of the other important peaks near Machu
Picchu. He sensed that he was getting close to his goal.

"We walked along the ridge by the old trail for a couple of hours
until at last the ruins of Machu Picchu itself came into view," Bingham
wrote. Then, "within rifle shot of the city," the trail vanished, buried
by "rotting vegetable matter." Bingham detoured down to the Intihuatana ranch (now the location of the Hidroeléctrica train station) and
climbed to "dear old Machu Picchu" from the west. The explorer
"nearly wept to see how it had gone back to jungle and brush" in just
three years. "Even the Sacred Plaza was so dense we had to cut our
way into it with a machete," he wrote to Alfreda. Only one group of
buildings was clear—"and that occupied by six pigs!"

To prove that his city in the clouds was indeed Manco Inca's Vilcabamba, Bingham next needed to trace the route to Machu Picchu

that Manco would have taken from Vitcos when the Spaniards surprised him there in 1537. As an Indian guide led them through the boggy no-man's-land between Puquiura and Machu Picchu, the trail passed a large, dark green lake. Bingham inquired what its name was. "The answer gave me a thrill," he remembered. The guide had said "Yanacocha"; Bingham convinced himself that he'd meant to say "Ungacacha." ("They look so different on paper that it is somewhat difficult to realize how closely the Indian pronunciation of one approaches the other," he later rationalized.) Ungacacha was the name of a lake that Father Calancha had reported his two friars passing on their way from near Vitcos to Vilcabamba, where they were assaulted by battalions of lovelies from the Peruvian coast. Bingham reasoned that it was the monks who had heard the name incorrectly, rather than he. When the trail ended at the familiar hacienda of Huadquiña, just a half day's walk from Machu Picchu, Bingham was certain that he'd compiled enough evidence—the Inca highways from Cusco and Vitcos, the skeletal remains of the chosen women, the architectural splendor of Machu Picchu—to prove beyond the shadow of a doubt that the city he'd found in 1911 was indeed Vilcabamba, the Lost City of the Incas.

Bingham's logical next move was to visit the cave near Pacaritambo, where he could refute once and for all the notion that Machu Picchu was not also Tampu Tocco. His victory march was halted by an unlikely culprit—an organizational screwup. Considering the size of the 1914–15 expedition and the unpleasant exit that Bingham had made in 1912, it seems obvious that someone should have secured permits to excavate before digging up two hundred skulls. Unfortunately, this was one detail that Bingham had delegated. When Bingham arrived back at Yankihausi on June 15, 1915, he was informed that he faced charges of excavating and exporting artifacts illegally. One of his accusers, the archaeologist and newspaper editor Luis Valcárcel, had published reports in his Cusco paper El Sol that the Bingham expedition was smuggling gold from Machu Picchu out of the country through Bolivia. Bingham rushed off to Cusco to attempt to clear his name and salvage his expedition. As if fulfilling Gilbert Grosvenor's bleak prophecy, Bingham collapsed into a hotel bed, fevered and exhausted, unable to move for a week.

In Cusco, Bingham discovered that the Peruvian rumor mill had been working at full capacity. "Among other things," Bingham wrote wearily to Grosvenor, "we were charged with having brought a steam shovel from Panama." The expedition was more or less exonerated of the more serious charges, but Bingham was ordered not to undertake any new digging. And because the investigation was still open, government inspectors would be appointed to monitor any future work. Chief among Bingham's new babysitters was his accuser, Luis Valcárcel. Bingham briefly worried that he might not be allowed to leave the country.

The irony of Bingham's prosecution is that he really *was* smuggling artifacts out of the country, hundreds of them—just not those that Valcárcel had accused him of. The previous year, the historian Christopher Heaney has written, Bingham had negotiated the purchase of 366 Inca artifacts from Tomás Alvistur, the son-in-law of Huadquiña's owners. After a bit of haggling, the antiquities were smuggled out of Peru and arrived in New Haven, where they outshone the pieces that Bingham had excavated at Machu Picchu. At the same time he was under suspicion of smuggling gold in 1915, Bingham purchased another collection in Lima and shipped the artifacts out under a false name.[15]

In the end, it was hard not to view the 1914–15 expedition as a near-complete failure. The year's only bright spot was the old Inca highway that Bingham had blazed anew, along with the three sets of strange ruins that he had found en route to Machu Picchu. As far as Bingham was concerned, he had proven his theory. After exiting the legal circus

---

15 Bingham's purchases were folded into the Machu Picchu collection at Yale's Peabody Museum. Several of the finer artifacts still on display when I visited were identified as having been "acquired by Bingham in Cusco." The explorer's nemesis, Luis Valcárcel, went on to become one of Peru's leading archaeologists and a world-renowned expert on Machu Picchu. He and Bingham later struck up a mutual admiration. At the Machu Picchu museum, Valcárcel's picture hangs above a glass case containing details of Bingham's 1912 troubles.

in Cusco, he had returned to Ollantaytambo and retraced his steps along the now-completed Inca Trail. "I had the satisfaction of going into 'Vilcabamba the Old' over the very road used by the Virgins of the Sun when they fled here from Cusco and the conquistadors," he later wrote. His work in Peru was finished.

FORTY-FOUR

My Dinner with Paolo

Lima

When I arrived in Lima in June, my first thought was how lucky John had been to have had his heart surgery during the sunny half of the city's annual climate cycle. The same geological cacophony that wakes El Niño draws the *garúa*, a thick cloak of clouds over the capital city that blots out the sun for weeks at a time, creating near-perfect laboratory conditions for an epidemic of seasonal affective disorder. Visitors to what Herman Melville called "tearless Lima, the strangest, saddest city thou cans't see" search the skies for a cathartic storm that never comes. The clamminess is maddeningly consistent. When I'd checked the Lima weather report before leaving New York, the forecast was identical for each of the next seven days: high of 65, low of 63, cloudy and humid.

Counterbalancing the gloom was a ray of good news. Finally, after a year, I was going to meet Paolo Greer. In a roundabout way, Paolo's investigations had launched my Peruvian odyssey by dragging Bingham back into the news fifty years after his death. Paolo had been extremely helpful in my own research. There was something vaguely unsettling about him, though. Maybe it was the mildly combative tone of his e-mails—more than once he challenged me to "call his bluff" with a list of tough questions that I think he was expecting me to spring on him, *60 Minutes*-style. He believed that he'd made powerful, shadowy enemies in the Peruvian bureaucracy. I couldn't figure out if his choice to live alone in the woods had more in common with Thoreau's desire to commune with nature or the Unabomber's need to wall himself off from society. And then there was Paolo's photo, which I found on a Web site devoted to Inca history. In it he faced the camera defiantly, as if he were about to challenge the photographer to a knife fight.

So when I arrived outside the high metal gate of the South American Explorers Club around five o'clock on a gray Sunday afternoon and saw that no lights were on inside, a small part of me hoped that Paolo had skipped town. I walked around the side of the building, searching for an after-hours bell. Then I heard someone call, in English, "Hey, Mark, is that you?"

The front gate of the clubhouse creaked open and out stepped someone who was not at all what I'd been expecting. In his frayed windbreaker and rumpled plaid shirt, Paolo looked more like an absentminded classics professor who'd misplaced his Seneca than a sociopathic street fighter. He pressed a DVD into my hand and started talking as if he'd been waiting for someone, anyone, to listen to his story.

"That DVD's got two hundred and sixty books and articles about Machu Picchu on it, stuff that's hard to come by in Peru. Both in English and Spanish." He turned his head and leaned an ear in my direction. "If you want me to hear what you're saying, you'll have to speak up—I'm half-deaf. I read lips." He removed his ball cap for a second, ran his fingers through his short salt-and-pepper hair and looked me straight in the eyes. "So, you want to go sit down somewhere and talk about Bingham?"

As we walked through the crowded sidewalks of Lima's fancy Miraflores neighborhood, searching for a café, Paolo explained how a retired Alaska pipeline laborer and gold prospecting hobbyist had become the most controversial scholar in Machu Picchu studies. He'd spent twenty-seven years working on the pipeline. ("When I went in for my physical before starting, the doctor asked me, 'You know you've got TB, tuberculosis?' Now when I go to the doctor in Peru they ask me, 'You know you've got holes in your liver?'") Like John, he had never married or had children, which left plenty of time to root around in libraries and archives. He actually lived in *three* cabins outside of Fairbanks, one of them devoted to "nothing but papers and maps and books." He lived only a short drive from a University of Alaska campus and spent a lot of time taking adult education courses. Whenever he built up a "grubstake," Paolo said, he'd head off to the Peruvian Andes to have a long look around.

"Never filed a claim, though," he told me as we finally found a place to sit down, an arty-looking coffeehouse filled with college students. "It's all about the prospect. After twenty years of looking for lost gold mines, researching Machu Picchu was a piece of cake."

In 1978, while doing some research at the Library of Congress, Paolo came across an intriguing prospecting map drawn by hand in the 1870s. He recognized that the sketch, which was untitled but labeled in English, was of the area around Machu Picchu. The spot where Aguas Calientes now sits was identified as "Saw Mill."

"Of course the name had changed by the time Bingham got there," Paolo said.

Over the next twenty years, Paolo pieced together clues in libraries on two continents. The map had been drawn by an associate of Augusto Berns, a German mining prospector who'd purchased a ten-mile stretch of land across the Urubamba River from Machu Picchu in 1867. The diagram Paolo had found was actually the inset to a larger map that Berns himself had prepared, on which he'd labeled the area of Machu Picchu—land he didn't own—as "Inaccessible."

"In other words, he was saying 'Don't even try to cross the river,'" Paolo said. Keep out. The spot marked "Saw Mill" appears on later maps as "Maquina," the rusted piece of machinery that Bingham had seen near Melchor Arteaga's hut at Mandor Pampa. Paolo believed that the machine in question was a sawmill that Berns had planned to use to make railroad ties.

"What you have to remember is that Berns was an *estafador*, a scammer," Paolo said. After failing to scare up investors for his dubious claims of silver and gold, Berns changed his strategy. He established a company to loot the *huacas*, or holy places, of the Incas, where he could unearth their priceless relics. "Helped by my professional knowledge and casual circumstances," Berns wrote in a prospectus sent to would-be investors in 1887 (about a year before Hiram Bingham III made his first attempt to escape Hawaii), he had been able "to discover the existence of significant rustic buildings and underground structures that had been closed with stones, some of them carefully carved, which will undoubtedly contain objects of great value, and form part of those treasures of the Incas."

To Paolo, the inference was obvious. "Berns was a crook. He lived across the river from Machu Picchu pretty much constantly for four years, from 1867 on. He knew where every family lived on the opposite side of the river—all twenty-four huts are on that map. He searched for ruins, specifically to loot them, using locals as guides."

For years, Paolo shared his theory with anyone who would listen. Professional academics mostly condescended to him. Then he published his Bingham story in 2008.

"And suddenly you were famous as the guy who proved that Bingham hadn't discovered Machu Picchu," I said.

Paolo got agitated and spilled his coffee. "I don't give a shit about fame!" he said, mopping up the mess with napkins. "All these newspapers said that I said that Berns discovered Machu Picchu. I don't like that word."

"What word?"

"Discovered. No gringo discovered Machu Picchu. Machu Picchu was never forgotten."

Paolo talked for a while about various persons in Peru who were trying to steal credit for his research, but a jazz combo started tuning up and Paolo couldn't hear a word I was saying. We walked back through the damp night to the South American Explorers clubhouse. The building was a converted home. We sat down in easy chairs, beneath an enormous map of Peru, in what had been the living room.

Like Bingham himself, Paolo had moved on from asking lots of little questions about Machu Picchu to trying to answer the Big One— what had Machu Picchu actually been? And like Bingham, he thought he might have found the solution to this riddle in the writings of a Spanish chronicler with an unusual personal history. Juan de Betanzos was considered the Spaniards' finest interpreter of Quechua and married an extremely well-connected widow named Doña Angelina Yupanqui. She had been the child bride of the emperor Atahualpa and was with the Inca before and after he was captured at Cajamarca. After his execution, she later became the mistress of the man who ordered his death, Francisco Pizarro, with whom she had two sons. So when Betanzos wrote his comprehensive history *Narrative of the Incas,* published in 1557, he had pillow-talk access to inside information. Most of Betanzos's work was unknown to Bingham; a copy of the last forty-six of the *Narrative*'s sixty-four chapters turned up in a private collection on the Mediterranean island of Palma de Mallorca, in 1987.

What's fascinating about the new Betanzos information, in conjunction with the discovery that Machu Picchu was likely part of Pachacutec's estate, is that Betanzos's work may shed some light on why Pachacutec might have ordered Machu Picchu's construction. Paolo had just spent several weeks out at Machu Picchu as the guest of the chief INC archaeologist. He was so excited about what he'd seen that he could barely stay in his seat.

"You go into Machu Picchu and you sit down in front of the Torreon and it *clicks,*" Paolo said. The Torreon, Paolo believes, was designed to represent the Koricancha sun temple in Cusco, the holiest building in the most important city in the empire. According to Betanzos, after Pachacutec's death, the emperor "was taken to a town . . . where he had ordered some houses built in which his body was to be entombed." In addition, he "ordered that a golden image made to resemble him be placed on top of his tomb . . . to be worshiped in place of him by the people who went there."

The very idea was straight out of Indiana Jones—a gold statue of the greatest of all Incas, standing inside a temple devoted to the sun, which possibly aligned with the sunrise on the most important day of the Inca calendar. A recent excavation inside the Torreon had revealed another possible clue: a tomb with beautiful stonework was located just outside the circular wall. Paolo had pictures of himself down in the hole.

"You know what it is?" he asked. "It's Pachacutec's tomb!"

I was reminded of the two small windows in the Torreon, one of which was believed by some to face the solstice. The third window in the tower is the larger, oddly shaped opening that faces north, which Bingham named the Enigmatic Window. Paolo thought that *this* opening was the important one, and that it was used to give offerings to the golden statue of Pachacutec. "On both sides of the Enigmatic Window are secret stones that pull out of the wall. The chief archaeologist just showed me this. The Incas had something inside, something that tightened up and turned. I've got pictures!"

"So what happened to the gold statue?" I asked.

"It was brought up to Cajamarca for Atahualpa's ransom."

The circular part of the Torreon had been built to wrap around a large rock with what appears to be a chunk chiseled out of its center. This rock has befuddled archaeologists for a hundred years. Bingham was the first to note that it looked burned. "At some time or another a really extraordinary amount of heat must have been applied," he wrote. The prevailing theory, according to Paolo, was that the rock had been struck by lightning.

"It wasn't done by lightning," Paolo told me, shaking his head. "I was just up inside there. Granite doesn't conduct lightning that well, and it's cracked as hell on the inside. Atahualpa's people came in to get that golden statue. They filled the entire place up with firewood and they torched it." The intense heat would have had a similar effect to a lightning bolt, cracking the rock quickly. "Apparently they were in a hurry," Paolo said.

Paolo's not the only one who thinks this, incidentally. Luis Lumbreras, one of the most respected archaeologists in Peru, has argued that the Torreon and the cave underneath were probably Pachacutec's royal crypt.

"It's all *right there* if you examine it," Paolo said. "Play Sherlock Holmes. It all fits together really well."

Now we were getting somewhere: Maybe the Inca Trail had been a pilgrimage, leading to gold statue of Pachacutec—which was illuminated by the rising sun on the holiest day of the year! I asked Paolo what he thought of the sunlight-through-the-window theory.

"That little window doesn't mean shit," he said. A friend of his had taken a digital compass reading that indicated the position of the window didn't quite align with the angle of the solstice; it was off by a few degrees.

"Oh." Admittedly, this took a little wind out of my sails. Paolo must have noticed my disappointment.

"Well, who cares if it does or it doesn't? Let's go eat."

We moved on to dinner at an Italian restaurant, where Paolo explained a way to prove his theory. Berns wrote that the Indians near Machu Picchu possessed a "large stone statue of an Inca," which later vanished. Paolo thought the statue was buried in some terraces on the back side of Machu Picchu, beneath a rounded wall that he insisted was "the best wall in Machu Picchu."

But, assuming the statue was found, how could we possibly know it was the Earth Shaker? Paolo had that covered, too. "Find the mummy."

According to one Spanish chronicler, the mummies of at least three Incas, including Pachacutec, were transported to the San Andrés Hospital in Lima in 1560. The last person to report having seen them was Bingham's old pal Father Calancha, in 1638. A few attempts have been made to search for the mummies, none successful.

"Did I tell you how I found Pachacutec? That's a weird story." Paolo looked at me across his gnocchi to see if I was prepared. I wasn't, but since I had flown in on the red-eye and had downed a glass of wine, at this point I was pretty much defenseless. "One day a friend of mine confided in me; she said, 'You know, Paolo, I'm a dowser.'"

"You mean like someone who searches for water with a stick?"

"You can dowse for anything. I gave her a new map I had of Machu Picchu, a *good* map, and told her I was looking for a stone statue of Pachacutec. When she dowsed it, she picked the *same spot* I did."

The look on my face must not have conveyed complete credulousness, because Paolo immediately added, "I'm a skeptic. I like details." When his friend next came up to Lima, Paolo arranged for them to visit the old hospital grounds. "She starts sensing things, and she zeroes in on the patio. Then she pulls out this special dowsing thing. I gave her a piece of chalk and said, 'Mark the ground.' She starts making marks, x x x x x x x. Then she says, 'This must be wrong—it's a shape about a meter long. How can he be a meter tall?' I said, 'Incas were mummified in a sitting position.'" They found three possible mummies, one of whom Paolo surmised had been cremated. Paolo took a photo of the three sites and then the two of them marked up the patio with fifteen more body shapes with chalk x's to hide their discovery. "It looked like the crime scene for a mass murder." He was concerned that time might be running out—the charity that administered the hospital grounds had begun leasing out lots for commercial purposes.

I wasn't exactly sure what to say. On the one hand, I'd always found Paolo to be unimpeachably well informed about Machu Picchu. On the other, well, as far as I know, Emily Post never addressed the subject of how to keep the conversational ball rolling when your dinner guest starts talking about dowsing for mummies. So I asked Paolo if he'd like dessert. Over crème brûlée, I tried to get a fix on what he thought of the trouble Bingham had stirred up between Yale and Peru. "Frankly, Bingham didn't find shit. He bought the Alvistur stuff." This was the collection of 366 artifacts from the son-in-law of Huadquiña's owner.

"Machu Picchu was completely sacked before Bingham was born. Far and away the best stuff that Bingham got out of Machu Picchu he didn't find—he bought. The funny thing was, Bingham snuck that stuff out and they wanted to keep it a dirty secret. But that stuff legally they can keep. It's the other stuff that has to come back."

Earlier in the evening, Paolo had described his skill at reading satellite images for signs of undiscovered ruins. "Do you think there's anything else left to find near Machu Picchu?" I asked.

"Plateriayoc, the lost city of Machu Picchu," he said without hesitation. The name sounded familiar. Bingham's polo-playing rival Captain J. Campbell Besley had reported finding a phenomenal city by that name. Plateriayoc means "place of the silver" and is sort of shorthand for the El Dorado of the Andes. In other words, Plateriayoc is a myth.

"There are *other* Plateriayocs," Paolo explained. "No one knows about this one. Berns was there. I was close three weeks ago. I had a hell of a time getting there. There's a wall over a thousand meters long—Berns called it 'steps' but it's not that. It's covered over now, big-time; the ruins are buried in the jungle."

Every explorer I'd spoken with in Peru had one secret site that he was hoping to find someday. Paolo was the only one who willingly shared what he was looking for. Why?

"I have to assume that grave robbers are already there. Bingham was no hero, but what he did which was good was that he stopped for a short time the *huaqueando*—the grave robbing—till the INC took over. Now I'm bugging the shit out of the INC trying to get them to protect Plateriayoc."

"And you think you'll get there?"

"I can *show* you where Plateriayoc is."

Later on, he did just that, showing me how the thousand-meter wall aligned almost perfectly with two famous Inca landmarks. And for just a moment, I felt the itch that Bingham—and Paolo, and John—knew well: the urge to drop everything, set off and find something lost and waiting behind the ranges.

FORTY FIVE

Major Revisions

All Over the Map

Hiram Bingham's career as a professor-cum-explorer burned brilliantly but extinguished its fuel in less than a decade. The fall 1916 semester was his last teaching at Yale. He struggled to finish a third big article for Gilbert Grosvenor, who was understandably eager to publish another adventure tale from his magazine's star correspondent; *National Geographic*'s circulation had more than doubled again in the wake of Bingham's 1913 Machu Picchu story. The editor was appalled by the quality of Bingham's initial efforts. "You can do such fine writing when you want to but I am at a loss to understand the present heterogeneous collection of scraps," he wrote after reading a first draft. *National Geographic*'s half a million subscribers "would murder me if I gave them anything as irrational as this story."

Bingham was probably preoccupied with his new passion: politics. Encouraged by one U.S. president, his conservative mentor Theodore Roosevelt, and motivated by his antipathy toward the sitting White House occupant, his former Princeton boss Woodrow Wilson, Bingham lobbied successfully for a role as an alternate delegate to the 1916 Republican National Convention in Chicago. As war raged in Europe, he channeled his organizational skills into the "preparedness" movement, urging the United States military to be ready to join the battle against Germany. At age forty-one, he volunteered to join the Yale Corps of the

Connecticut National Guard, which he hoped would pursue the Mexican revolutionary Pancho Villa, who'd attacked an American cavalry unit in New Mexico. Instead, Major Hiram Bingham put his new pilot's license to use starting in April 1917, when he was deputized to organize flight schools to train America's first generation of military airmen. By Armistice Day in 1918, eight thousand men were under his command in France.

After the war, Bingham endured a forced health sabbatical like the one that had led him to South America in 1906. He was struck by the great Spanish flu epidemic, then was diagnosed with tuberculosis, and then underwent an operation for gallstones. "Some of these symptoms must have been psychosomatic, aggravated, if not caused, by anxiety and self-doubt at a turning point in his life," his son Alfred later guessed. During a recuperative visit to his mother-in-law Annie Mitchell's estate in Miami in the first part of 1922, the retired explorer finished his first book about his discoveries in Peru, *Inca Land*.

Bingham claimed to his publishers, Houghton Mifflin, that he'd written "a new kind of travel book—a combination of adventure, exploration and historical research." In truth, he'd baked an unremarkable casserole from the leftovers of his stories for *National Geographic*, *Harper's*, and various other periodicals. Reviews were tepid, as were sales. A planned sequel was scrapped.

Less than two weeks after *Inca Land* appeared in bookstores, Bingham began the third act of his remarkable career. He had long cultivated the powerful Republican Party chairman of his conservative home state of Connecticut. His wooing paid off in November of 1922, when Bingham was elected lieutenant governor. Two years later, he was tapped to run for governor. Bingham's Yale credentials and fame as a man of action made him unbeatable in 1924, a very good year for Republicans' Calvin Coolidge–led ticket. Before Bingham could occupy the governor's mansion in Hartford, however, Connecticut's senior U.S. senator committed suicide. Party bosses chose the governor-elect to run in a special election for the Senate seat. Bingham won again. He was sworn in as governor on January 7, 1925, and over the next twenty-four hours gave what was described as "the longest inaugural address in the history of the state"; appeared in a parade with full military escort; and hosted a governor's ball at which he made his entrance flanked by two columns of men standing at attention, as a band played "Hail to the Chief." So as not to be forgotten, he had commissioned the biggest portrait of a Connecticut governor ever to hang in the state's official gallery. On the second morning of the Bingham administration, the governor resigned, and as one reporter recalled, "was off to Washington, his jaw set in broad self-satisfaction."

Bingham's eight years in the capital, during which the press dubbed him "the Flying Senator," would have provided the raw material for an excellent *March of Time* newsreel. Here comes the handsome, silver-haired senator, landing on the steps of the Capitol in a blimp. There he goes, from almost the same spot, folding his six-feet-four frame into an autogiro—a sort of hybrid airplane/helicopter equipped with both rotors and a propeller—taking a recess from senatorial duty, golf clubs looped over one shoulder. Moments after sitting down for lunch at the exclusive Metropolitan Club, the senator from Connecticut hears the hum of the airship *Graf Zeppelin*; he hails a taxi to the nearest naval air base, changes into a flying suit, hops behind the controls of a plane and races to greet the first commercial transatlantic flight before the craft lands in New Jersey. When the chairman of the National Aeronautics Administration weds in Washington, D.C., best man Hiram Bingham is matched by an equally famous matron of honor—Amelia Earhart.

Such activities made Bingham wildly popular with reporters. Senior Senate colleagues who'd had their Spanish pronunciation corrected or received long lectures on aviation were less enamored of the Flying Senator. So when Bingham was caught secretly placing a lobbyist for the Connecticut Manufacturer's Association on his Senate payroll, his fellow senators "fell upon him with a malevolent enthusiasm which can only be explained as a compensation for their own unhappy inferiority," *The American Mercury* reported. Goaded by his colleagues to admit wrongdoing, Bingham refused, saying, "I have nothing to apologize for." The other senators voted overwhelmingly to censure him, the first time the body had used such harsh punishment in twenty-seven years, since the two members of South Carolina's delegation had physically attacked each other in 1902. His reputation blackened, Bingham was voted out during the FDR landslide of 1933.

Machu Picchu's fame grew a bit more slowly than that of the man credited as its discoverer. For almost twenty years after Bingham's last visit, the site was left untended yet again, until the Peruvian government ordered one final clearing in the 1930s. In 1939, the American songwriter Cole Porter, smitten by a story about the ruins that he'd seen in *National Geographic*, made the journey up to the location on horseback. "When they reached the top, a 'hotel' with three rooms and no bathroom was the only facility," wrote one Porter biographer. Guests washed themselves with bowls of water and heeded nature's call in the forest. Dinner was a chicken killed and cooked by their guide, "which when they ate it was still partly unplucked."

Foreign interest in Machu Picchu—especially American interest—began to grow somewhat faster after 1948, when Hiram Bingham published a revised account of his adventures, *Lost City of the Incas*. To reshape what would become the most famous version of the story, Bingham wisely edited out the least interesting bits of *Inca Land*. Gone were the long-winded soliloquies on the deficiencies of canned goods and two entire chapters about climbing Coropuna. In their place was a narrative with three parts: an explanation of who the Incas had been, a description of Bingham's search for their lost city, and a summation of the discovery of Machu Picchu and Bingham's attempts to explain its significance.

The elemental facts covered in *Lost City of the Incas* differ little from Bingham's previous works. What's different is the tone. As the new title indicated, the book was much more a classic adventure tale than his earlier works. The reason was probably twofold. Bingham had passed seventy when he sat down to write the book, and knew that, despite his other achievements, he'd be remembered posthumously as the man who found Machu Picchu. As always, he wanted to have the last word.

Bingham also, not unreasonably, would have wanted to sell some books. His previous full-length efforts to describe his work in Peru, *Inca Land* and the 1930's more scholarly *Machu Picchu: A Citadel of the Incas*, were flops.

Anyone who has read James Hilton's 1933 classic *Lost Horizon* (or, more likely, seen Frank Capra's film adaptation) can't help but notice that in *Lost City of the Incas*, Machu Picchu seems a little more like the fictional Shangri-La than it did in Bingham's earlier attempts. Bingham may have seen something of himself in *Lost Horizon*'s diplomat Hugh Conway, whose plane crashes in the mountains of Tibet. (Conway's first sight of Shangri-La: "It might have been a vision fluttering out of that solitary rhythm in which lack of oxygen had encompassed all his faculties. It was, indeed, a strange and half-incredible sight.") In *Lost City*'s version of events, Bingham downplayed all the detective work he'd done; he ratcheted up the tension of a story whose ending was already known by making it seem as if he hadn't expected to find anything on the abandoned mountaintop. From there he segued into language that the explorer-historian Hugh Thomson has aptly described as "hallucinogenic, spiraling":

> Suddenly, I found myself confronted with the walls of ruined houses. . . . It seemed like an unbelievable dream. . . . What could this place be? Why had no one given us any idea about it? . . . Surprise followed surprise in bewildering succession. . . . The sight held me spellbound.

A more telling editorial change from 1922 to 1948 is Bingham's failure to share credit. The truth is that even Bingham admitted—for a while anyway—that he hadn't been the first person to see Machu Picchu. Three families were living at the site when he arrived; it would have been ridiculous for him to argue otherwise. On his very first visit to Machu Picchu, he'd seen writing scrawled on the wall of the Temple of the Three Windows, the words "Lizarraga 1902." I'd seen the words he penciled in his 1911 notebook the day after his famous encounter:

"Agustin Lizarraga is discoverer of Machu Picchu." (In his 1913 *National Geographic* account, Bingham complained—somewhat comically in light of the controversy that would follow—that it took two days to scrub the graffiti out of the temple.) Lizarraga lived at the Intihuatana ranch on the Urubamba River, where the explorer had paid him a visit. Later, in his 1922 book *Inca Land*, Bingham described seeing Lizarraga's name and surmised that "some one must have visited Machu Picchu long before that; because in 1875 . . . the French explorer Charles Wiener heard in Ollantaytambo of there being ruins at 'Huaina-Picchu or Matcho-Picchu.'" The same year *Inca Land* was published, in a letter to a schoolmaster in Honolulu, Bingham candidly admitted:

> I suppose that in the same sense of the word as it is used in the expression "Columbus discovered America" it is fair to say that I discovered Machu Picchu. The Norsemen and the French fishermen undoubtedly visited North America long before Columbus crossed the Atlantic. On the other hand it was Columbus who made America known to the civilized world. In the same sense of the word I "discovered" Machu Picchu—in that before my visit and report on it it was not known to the geographical and historical societies in Peru, nor to the Peruvian government.

Not that it really matters. No one has any idea how many people—whether they spoke Spanish, French, English or any other non-Quechua tongue—beat Bingham to the top of Machu Picchu. Almost from the moment he announced his discovery, a handful of other claimants—most notably an English missionary and a pair of German explorers—emerged to say they'd been there first. They were almost certainly wrong.

What had been a general impression that Bingham hadn't strained especially hard to disprove became cemented into presumed fact when Bingham published *Lost City of the Incas* in 1948. In this final version,

Lizarraga was written out of the story. The long description of Charles Wiener's "detailed map" was cut and replaced by the claim that Bingham didn't even know of its existence until after his return to New Haven. The tip from Albert Giesecke, the University of Cusco administrator who urged Bingham to pay a visit to Melchor Arteaga, wasn't mentioned. Instead, Bingham inserted a condescending note that when he arrived in 1911, "the professors in the University of Cusco knew nothing of any ruins down the valley."

The unanswerable question is *why?* Bingham was already rich and famous. Was it simple mendacity? An editing oversight? Perhaps as good an explanation as any can be found in a stanza near the end of Kipling's "Explorer," the same poem that sent Bingham marching off to search for the lost city "behind the ranges" forty years earlier:

> *Well I know who'll take the credit—all the clever chaps that*
> >   *followed*
> *Came, a dozen men together—never knew my desert-fears*
> *Tracked me by the camps I'd quitted, used the water-holes I'd*
> >   *hollowed.*
> *They'll go back and do the talking. They'll be called the*
> >   *Pioneers!*

Though Bingham's Grand Unified Theory didn't go uncontested during his lifetime, *Time* magazine was correct in stating, five years after Bingham's death in 1956, that he had compiled "the best known—and most romantic—history of Machu Picchu." And so it remained until 1964, when another handsome young explorer, Gene Savoy, arrived in Peru determined to prove Bingham wrong. Savoy was convinced that the Lost City of the Incas had actually existed at Espiritu Pampa, not Machu Picchu. Like Bingham half a century before him, Savoy had reviewed all the clues in the old Spanish chronicles as to the whereabouts of Vilcabamba, and like Bingham he had no special training as an archaeologist. He did have some advantages over his predecessor, though. He had the aid of the Cobos family, which owned a farm next to the ruins. He had plenty of time and money; in the kitchen of the Sixpac Manco hostel, Juvenal Cobos told me that Savoy had hired forty *macheteros* to cut through the jungle at Espiritu Pampa. And he had a colossal ego that dwarfed even Bingham's. After retiring from exploring, Savoy founded his own religion.

On his very first day at Espiritu Pampa, led by Juvenal's older brothers Benjamin and Flavio, Savoy was able to see everything that Bingham had seen during his visit, including the strange ceramic tiles that had baffled the Yale man. Over the coming days, the *macheteros* hacked through vines and *matapalos* trees to find one new structure after another: houses, temples, storage facilities and fountains. The discovery of a giant stone like the White Rock near Vitcos, he wrote, "suggests we are inside an important ancient Inca community; for such stones were used for oracles."

When Savoy found clay tiles, he made a connection that Bingham had not. They were evidence that Manco Inca's guests at Vitcos, the Spanish refugees who later stabbed him in the back (literally), had taught the Incas an improved form of roofing technology, which they had employed in building their new capital. Savoy believed that he'd found Vilcabamba, but his thesis wasn't confirmed until the historian John Hemming linked the evidence of the tiles to documentary sources that had come to light since Bingham's exploring prime. The architect-adventurer Vince Lee made several trips to Espiritu Pampa in the 1980s—often with the help of Juvenal Cobos—and returned with evidence that not only had this been the site of Manco's Vilcabamba, but that it had been a thriving metropolis with thousands of residents. Bingham had been there and missed it all.

The final load-bearing beam of Bingham's Vilcabamba theory collapsed when John Verano, a physical anthropologist at Tulane University, reexamined the bones that had been exhumed in 1912. Contrary to Yale's original findings, the ratio of men to women was roughly even, and many of the female skeletons showed evidence of childbirth. Thus the mythical Virgins of the Sun vanished once again, this time probably for good.

As for Bingham's Tampu Tocco theory, it relied on the assumption that Machu Picchu had been constructed by the Incas' predecessors, perhaps a thousand years before Pizarro's arrival. Further excavations and comparisons to other masterpieces of Inca architecture indicate that a more probable date for its construction was around 1450. Such a date would place its founding squarely in Pachacutec's reign. Most experts now agree that the likeliest location of Tampu Tocco is Pacaritambo, the spot near Cusco that Bingham had been keen on visiting in 1915 before his expedition imploded. The evidence here is thinner than it is for Vilcabamba. John Leivers told me he'd visited Pacaritambo but didn't see any proof that it had been Tampu Tocco. Locals who lived in the vicinity told him that they knew of no cave nearby.

The artifacts that Bingham had sent back from Machu Picchu in 1912 sat gathering dust in the Peabody Museum until 1981, when the Andean specialists Richard Burger and Lucy Salazar arrived at Yale. The pair thoroughly reexamined the Bingham collection and, largely based on that research, decided that Machu Picchu, "far from being the Inca birthplace, was merely one of a number of personal royal estates built by an Inca king in the remote countryside," Salazar later wrote. Burger has described the site more succinctly: "It was Pachacutec's Camp David." As for all the temples and such, that stuff just came with the job. "The Inca was considered descended from the sun, so there would have to be a religious component," Burger told *Time* magazine. "But the Incas probably spent just as much time hunting or drinking corn beer on the plaza." From Bingham's lofty romantic vision of Vilcabamba, Machu Picchu had now sunk to the level of a sportsman's lodge, the lost tap room of the Incas.

Even before the controversies sent Bingham's reputation as a hero into steep decline, his role as America's greatest swashbuckling explorer had been superseded by an even more indelible adventurer: Indiana Jones. There have been any number of attempts to prove that Bingham's life was the source material for the movie hero: both are university professors who dabble in archaeology, both search the blank spots of the map, looking for important relics, both wear fedoras. The opening scene of *Raiders of the Lost Ark*, in which Indy outruns a gigantic rolling boulder, takes place in a part of Peru that looks like it could be within walking distance of Machu Picchu.

The most direct connection between Indy and Bingham is a 1954 B-movie titled *Secret of the Incas*. The movie features two good-looking stars: Charlton Heston, who plays Harry Steele, a hard-boiled treasure hunter based out of Cusco; and Machu Picchu, playing itself. Deborah Nadoolman Landis, who designed the costumes for *Raiders*, has said that she and her team watched *Secret of the Incas* multiple times and based Indy's look on Harry Steele's; both treasure hunters have a weakness for earth tones, leather jackets and, of course, fedoras. The most obvious connection between the two films, however, is *Raiders'* famous map-room scene, in which Indy holds the staff of Ra and catches a beam of sunlight to reveal the location of the Ark of the Covenant on a scale model of the lost city of Tanis. In *Secret*, Steele consults a tabletop reproduction of Machu Picchu—for which, much like Indiana Jones, he happens to possess the key missing piece—then employs an ancient Inca reflector to direct a shaft of light to the spot where the coveted golden sunburst is hidden.

The link from Indy to Harry Steele is obvious—the beam-of-light trick in *Raiders* is pretty clearly a winking homage to the earlier film, the sort of thing Quentin Tarantino fans applaud in their favorite auteur. This hasn't prevented cinema conspiracy buffs from pointing out that *Secret* and *Raiders* were both produced by Paramount and that *Secret* has never been released on DVD. (Producer George Lucas and director Steven Spielberg have always maintained that Indy was inspired by innumerable old adventure movies, a claim that is largely backed up by the transcript of the meetings in which they, along with screenwriter Lawrence Kasdan, hashed out the film's plot.)

The leap from Harry Steele to Hiram Bingham is a little harder to make. What puzzled me the first time I watched *Secret of the Incas* was that it was loaded with slightly off-key references from actual Inca history, remnants from a not-quite-erased earlier story peeking through like a palimpsest. The American archaeologists' Quechua helper is named Pachacutec; the foreigners are excavating at Machu Picchu in hopes of finding the tomb of Manco Inca; everyone in the movie is searching for the sun disk, the holiest relic from the Koricancha, which supposedly has been buried at Machu Picchu. Bingham's *Lost City of the Incas* would have been far and away the most accessible source of this information. (From *LCI*, chapter nine: "The great golden image of the Sun which had been one of the chief ornaments of the temple in Cusco was probably kept here at Machu Picchu after Manco escaped from Cusco.") The screenwriter Sydney Boehm, however, told the *San Francisco Chronicle* that he got the idea for *Secret* after meeting the Peruvian-born chanteuse Yma Sumac, who also appeared in the film, at a party.

The full story is a bit more complicated than that. Buried in Beverly Hills amid the hundreds of thousands of files in the archives of the Academy of Motion Picture Arts and Sciences are the production notes of *Secret of the Incas*. In late 1951, Boehm (who had just written the screenplay for the noir classic *The Big Heat*) and a partner submitted three loose ideas to the head of production at Paramount. One of them was titled "Lost City of the Incas." The film was planned as an adventure yarn set in Peru. Bingham's widely publicized book of the same name had been published less than three years earlier. In another memo written a few months later, Boehm's lead character had been fleshed out. Stanley Moore was a Yale-trained archaeologist, "a tall, slender man with an abstracted face" who was carrying out excavations at Machu Picchu.

By 1953, for whatever reason—a potential lawsuit from Bingham doesn't seem entirely out of the realm of possibility—Boehm's story emerged from the Hollywood sausage grinder with a new title and a new lead character, the rough-edged Harry Steele. Stanley Moore was stripped of his Yale credentials and relegated to a supporting role as the sap that doesn't get the girl.[16]

So in a roundabout way, Indiana Jones almost certainly *had* been inspired by Bingham's discovery of Machu Picchu. Unlike Bingham, however, Indy knew his archaeoastronomy.

---

16 In another fun coincidence, a scene from the generally reviled 2008 sequel *Indiana Jones and the Kingdom of the Crystal Skull* was filmed in Yale's Sterling Memorial Library, just down the hall from the Rare Books and Manuscripts Room, where a certain author examined Bingham's notebooks and expedition papers. Jones makes an impressive entrance, skidding across the library floor on a motorcycle piloted by his son Mutt; on his way out he instructs a mousy student, "You want to be a good archaeologist, you've got to get out of the library." The team behind *Crystal Skull* might have benefited from a few more hours in the library, since the story is riddled with embarrassing errors, not the least of which is Indy's greeting at a Peruvian airport by a Mexican mariachi band.

FORTY-SIX

Roxana Begs to Differ

Cusco

S hould you find yourself in Cusco en route to Machu Picchu, I highly recommend that you stop for a drink at the Cross Keys Pub. Not only is it the best place to get a beer in town, but just inside the second-floor entrance, to the right, are some old scrapbooks that are well worth a look. In one of them is pasted a photograph of a handsome man in his early forties, athletically built, with a gigantic stogie clenched between his teeth. The beverage awaiting him on the bar appears not to be his first of the evening.

"Thought you might enjoy seeing that one, Mark," the man in the photograph said to me as we flipped through the album.

This was the second interesting set of plastic-covered photos that John Leivers had shown me since meeting me at the airport. Earlier, he'd pulled out a four-by-six laminated card that was illustrated on both sides. On the front was a color snapshot of his cracked-open chest, heart beating within; on the other was a black-and-white line drawing that looked like an electrician's diagram for rewiring a rather lumpy circuit breaker; little arrows explained just how the triple-bypass worked. In the flesh, John was a little bit thinner than when I'd last seen him. He looked more like Hiram Bingham than ever.

"I think that photo was taken not long after I walked the Inca Trail for the first time. Did I tell you about that? That must have been the first time I did it in bare feet, too."

"Correct me if I'm wrong, but isn't the Inca Trail covered in rocks?"

"Oh, it's not too bad if you've trained your feet for it. Feels good to have your soles in contact with the earth. All the porters kept complimenting me for being connected to the Pachamama, the Mother Earth." For the record, John had walked it twice in bare feet and four times in flip-flops. He was planning to wear boots this time.

We strolled down the cobblestones of Triunfo Street, through the Plaza de Armas, where the annual Inti Raymi festivities were in full swing. This celebration, which dates back to the Incas, originally honored the bond between the sun and his son the Inca. It also marked the new year. Every street surrounding the main square was filled with garishly dressed marching bands, girls in traditional costumes and boys wearing ukuku masks, which look like ski masks with clown faces knitted onto them. It was as if the Colorblind Junior Majorette Society of Greater Cusco had scheduled a social mixer with the Future Bank Robbers of Southern Peru.

Our plan was to start the Inca Trail on June 18, arrive at Machu Picchu on the twenty-first, and ride up to the ruins early on the twenty-second to see the sunrise over the sacred peak and, with any luck, the light beam shooting into the Torreon. (The solstice lasts from the twenty-first to the twenty-fourth.) I'd read everything I could find on the subject but hadn't encountered anything conclusive. John had checked his personal archives and confirmed that while various anecdotal reports testified to something interesting happening at the Torreon on those mornings, digital compass readings indicated the window didn't align with the same solstice angle—roughly sixty-five degrees—that shot straight through the center of Machu Picchu to the riverside Intihuatana shrine and the corridor at Llactapata. And the Incas, I'd been told repeatedly, simply didn't make engineering mistakes.

There was one potential hitch in our plan. A group of farmers outside of Cusco, angered by the price of cooking gas, was calling for a paro, or general strike, on the day we were scheduled to leave town. In New York, the word "strike" conjures up a picture of people with picket signs parading in front of an office building, slightly inconveniencing any smokers who stepped outside to light up. If things get serious, the strikers might bring along a giant inflatable rat to express their displeasure with nonunion laborers. Evidently the word has a somewhat stronger meaning in Peru. All roads inside and outside of Cusco were blockaded by farmers, who rolled rocks into every throughway wider than a mule path and then sat sentry over those barricades, fortifying their political convictions by drinking heavily all day. Schools were closed during general strikes. All trains, including those to Machu Picchu, were canceled. Attempts to sneak through a checkpoint were generally frowned upon. "You really don't want to drive through one of these blockades," John told me over a vegetarian lunch. "Every time there's a strike, you see pictures in the next day's newspaper of cars and buses burning."

One of the most famous strikes in Cusco had taken place in 1999, in reaction to a government plan to build a cable car to Machu Picchu. Theoretically, the number of persons admitted to the site each day is limited to twenty-five hundred, though I've never heard of anyone being turned away. The planned funicular would have allowed as many as five thousand daily visitors. Several years ago, UNESCO recommended that to limit damage, no more than seventeen hundred sightseers should be allowed at Machu Picchu each day. The number of annual visitors had doubled in the last decade, from about four hundred thousand to more than eight hundred thousand, though entry tickets had more than quadrupled in price during that time.

The 1999 strikes were successful, in part because local protesters were able to frame the proposed construction as a violation of their cultural and religious heritage. The strikes did not, however, halt the stream of crazy ideas to maximize traffic to the site. One recent proposal suggested installing an elevator that would convey passengers up sixteen hundred feet to Machu Picchu's central plaza. Another recommended placing a dome over the citadel, around which would be constructed a catwalk from which tour groups could look down onto the Intihuatana and the Sacred Plaza as if watching the trained seals jump through hoops at an aquarium.

Such plans are based on the assumption that in the future the government of Peru will still own Machu Picchu. At least one person in Cusco was working hard to challenge that assumption. As it turned out, Yale was not the only party suing Peru over Machu Picchu.

Roxana Abril was a curator at Cusco's Museo Inka. We met at the fountain in the Plaza de Armas, cut through the revelers and took seats at a second-floor café. It was an arctic day by Cusco standards, about sixty degrees, and after Roxana unwrapped herself from a thick red wool coat, I asked her to explain why, exactly, she was the rightful owner of Machu Picchu.

"Okay, let's start at the beginning," she said, and gave me a sad half-smile, as if to say she'd told this story before and didn't always get the response she hoped for.

According to Roxana, her great-grandfather started buying up properties on the left side of the Urubamba River, where Machu Picchu sits, in the years before Bingham arrived. He eventually accumulated a parcel that included all of Machu Picchu and much of the Inca Trail. Bingham struck a deal to give the landowner one third of any treasures that he found on his property. Since Machu Picchu had long since been picked over by grave robbers—and Bingham snuck out his teammates' few valuable finds—Roxana's great-grandfather wound up with nothing from the dig. After Bingham left, interest in Machu Picchu subsided and the site became overgrown again, an attraction only to huaqueros who almost surely went home empty-handed.

"In 1928, my grandfather, Emilio Abril, said that it was too hard for private people to take care of archaeological properties," Roxana told me. "The owners of the land cannot prevent the huaqueros. So he offered to sell Machu Picchu to the government of Peru. In 1935, they gave an answer—'Okay, we'll buy it.'"

"Wait, they took seven years to respond?" I asked. "Why?"

"Mark, here in Peru things take a very long time."

Should Roxana ever write her autobiography, that would make an excellent title. Her grandfather gave the chunk of land on which Machu Picchu sat to the state, and over the coming decades, her family continued to farm its property around the ruins, which were still relatively obscure. Roxana remembered walking parts of the Inca Trail as a girl and visiting its various sites. In the 1940s, her grandfather sold off much of his remaining land. (The family that purchased the Abril land is now also claiming title to Machu Picchu. It gets a little complicated.) According to Roxana, all her family ever received from the government in return for what became one of the most valuable pieces of land in South America were some worthless bonds. One of Roxana's most vivid memories from her girlhood is of her father and brothers going to Lima to ask for the money they felt they were owed. "They never got an answer!" Roxana dug her phone out of her purse and dialed a number. "You should talk to my lawyer," she said, cupping the mouthpiece. "I have a *very* good lawyer. He says that half of the pieces at Yale belong to my family because we had not sold the property when Bingham came. *Alo?*" We sat staring at each other across the table for a minute while she listened to someone on the other end.

"His secretary says he's out of the country on business."

"When did you start your legal proceedings?" I asked.

"I sent my first letter in 2003."

"And what did they say?"

"I'm still waiting to hear back."

"What sorts of damages are you asking for?"

"I want to ask for one hundred million dollars. The price of three years of entry fees at Machu Picchu."

"What would you do if the government said, "Okay, Roxana, you win. We're going to give Machu Picchu back to you."

"Well, I would stop letting in so many tourists. And I'd get rid of that highway for the bus." This was the Hiram Bingham Highway, the zigzagging road up the eastern face of the ridge. Roxana folded her arms across her chest. "If people want to visit, let them go by foot like the Incas used to."

FORTY-SEVEN

On Bingham's Trail

Ollantaytambo and Beyond

The *paro* was due to begin at midnight Wednesday. John called my hotel at around three o'clock that afternoon. We were going to make a run for it. "Everything's packed. We'll pick you up at six," he said. Edgar would drive us out to Ollantaytambo in the Land Cruiser. From there we could either haul our stuff the ten miles to the Inca Trail or hope that the strikers were being a little less vigilant outside of Cusco and would let a taxi through. Whether our guide, Efrain, who had our entry tickets, would be able to make it was a question that would have to wait for an answer. He was out of pocket, guiding another trip somewhere.

The seriousness of our situation was made clear when Edgar showed up a mere forty-five minutes late. Evidently, strikes were the only events in Peru that began in accordance with Greenwich Mean Time. As we drove out of town in the dark, Edgar passed the time the way he usually did, by quizzing John about his world travels.

"So, John," he said, looking into the rearview mirror, "what's the craziest thing you've ever eaten?"

"Oh, you know. Ants. Monkey."

Edgar nodded his head in agreement. "Monkey is *riquisimo!*"—delicious. "Come on, John, everyone knows your famous appetite. You mean to tell me that's the craziest thing you've ever eaten—monkey?"

"I once ate a cockroach, but that was on a bet back in Australia. I also once, after quite a lot of beer, ate a kilo of butter." He leaned forward between the front seats. "Won ten dollars on that bet."

"Which you then spent on twenty loaves of bread, I hope," I said.

"Actually, I seem to remember something about a three-foot sausage after that. Sort of a salami."

"Did your heart surgeon happen to ask if you'd ever consumed an entire lifetime's worth of trans fats in one evening?"

"Like I said, we drank a *lot* of beer that night."

Ollantaytambo is perhaps the last inhabited town in Peru that has maintained its street grid laid out as it was under the Incas. This makes it a historically interesting place to pay a visit but, considering that the Incas didn't use wheeled vehicles, not a great place to drive. During a typical day, swarms of taxis and motorized rickshaws crowd the narrow streets, spewing diesel fumes and honking their horns as they swerve around the souvenir vendors who spill from the sidewalks. Nighttime is, if anything, worse, as trains collect and disgorge tourists coming and going from Machu Picchu. After waiting in traffic for an hour and moving only about twenty feet, John and I hopped out of the Land Cruiser and walked uphill to the town past rows of stopped buses and vans, all filled with unhappy faces, nervously awaiting the witching hour.

The next morning, Ollantaytambo was a ghost town. Every vendor but one had taken the day off. The only vehicle I saw in operation was a BMX bike upon which a kid was doing tricks in front of the one open café. It felt like a snow day. In the afternoon, I poked my head into the building that had once been Bingham's Yankihausi (nothing remained) and spent a long time staring up at the empty ruins where Manco Inca had made his final stand on horseback against the Spaniards, before escaping to Vitcos and Vilcabamba.

The following morning I woke before dawn, uncertain how—or if—we were going to meet our porters at KM 82, starting point of the Inca Trail. The last we'd heard from Efrain, Cusco was in lockdown and he was thinking about sneaking out of town on a motorbike.

As I walked out of my room, I almost bumped into an Andean-looking fellow in a red ski hat who was heading up the stairs.

"*Buenos días,*" I said, trying to diagram the next Spanish sentence in my foggy head. "Do you know if it continues strong, the strike?"

"You look like Clark Kent," the fellow replied, in English. Efrain had made it.

We went down to the hotel dining room for a much-needed coca tea. Efrain had left Cusco at 2 A.M. in a tiny Tico taxi, a vehicle that Peruvians call a coffin on wheels, but they exaggerate; it actually looks more like a washing machine on wheels. Efrain had traveled between midnight and dawn, when the strikers were sleeping off the day's libations. Each time his taxi approached a roadblock, he'd asked the driver to kill the lights. He then rolled away the boulders, waved the Tico through, and put the rocks back where he'd found them.

"Isn't that a little dangerous?" I asked.

"Nah. The last time I did it the strikers were a lot angrier," Efrain said. "I had to bring bottles of pisco, and cartons of cigarettes." Whenever he stopped, he'd hand out packs of smokes, stuff a few ten-sol bills into shirt pockets and do shots of brandy with the strikers. Eventually, someone would shout, "This guy is all right!" and wave his taxi through. "By the time I met my clients in the morning, though, I could barely stand."

Efrain walked into the hotel's kitchen and sweet-talked the motherly cook in Quechua, until she laughed and poured him a large mug of what looked like weak beef broth. He said it was *maca,* an old Andean energy drink made from a root that grows at high altitudes. After one mugful, he sat up straighter and started speaking more clearly. (I later learned that *maca* has a reputation for being stimulating in other ways. In the United States it's marketed as "organic Viagra.") Thus fortified, he walked into town to get a sense of how serious the local strikers were about enforcing the *paro* on the second day. To my great relief, the fervor had cooled a bit and we were able to hire a car to take us to KM 82 to start the hike. There we met our team of six porters, who would be carrying everything we needed on their backs—

tents, cooking gear, even a portable toilet. (Regulations now limit each porter's burden to fifty-five pounds, but I wondered if wages were pro-rated to reflect the nature of one's burden.) We introduced ourselves, and they hoisted their loads, each the size of a small bookcase, and walked rapidly away.

"We used to pull ourselves across here on a sort of cable," John said when we approached the bridge spanning the Urubamba. Accord-ing to Peter Frost's excellent guidebook *Exploring Cusco*, for years the only access to the trail was via a metal basket with a pulley system, operated for a fee that was often renegotiated as the hiker was halfway across the Urubamba River. The footloose days when a traveler could arrive in Cusco and decide at the last minute to hike the Inca Trail have long since passed. I'd had to book our spots three months in advance.

Efrain was thirty-three and handsome, with a smile that looked like it could bite through a corncob. He knew the Inca Trail about as well as I knew the path from my kitchen sink to the refrigerator. He'd walked it three hundred times, more or less. (He'd lost count.) He'd *run* the Trail twice, as part of the Inca Trail Marathon, which is about a mile longer than a regular marathon. (He finished in just over four hours, which would be a very respectable finish for 26.2 miles at sea level.) Efrain had a Dickensian life story: He'd been born in the Ama-zon jungle and grew up speaking Quechua for the first few years of his life. When the Shining Path began terrorizing Peru's countryside in the late 1980s, his mom was unable to feed all her kids, and so left him in an orphanage in Cusco—he was nine—and went off to Lima with his siblings. The orphanage was run by a woman from California, whom Efrain called his "second mother." This explained why even though he'd never been to the States, he spoke English like a guy from Orange County. Efrain had worked his way through school selling crafts, and later took a job as a porter to save money to earn a degree as a guide. ("On my first trip the load was so heavy that I cried," he told me. "The other porters laughed.") He was working at a luxury hotel when a guest asked if he knew the Inca Trail. Efrain lied and said yes.

"At KM 82, I told the client that I'd be right back, went around the corner and started asking everyone, 'Hey, do you know how to get to the Inca Trail?'" Now he was one of the most sought-after guides on the trail; he'd recently led a minor member of the British royal family on a trek, along with her bodyguards.

John, Efrain and I walked for two or three hours along a well-marked trail, passing the occasional dry-goods mini *mercado* selling nuts and bottled water, or *chicha* stand, where teams of porters rehydrated. The midwinter landscape was arid and the air dry. Efrain had two little girls back home in Cusco, and his guiding style was more fatherly than John's. He checked frequently to make sure I was carrying water and wearing sunscreen. He also asked some general probing questions to get an idea of what sort of client I was—a know-it-all *norteamericano*? A bucket-list tourist? A woo-woo spiritual seeker?—and filled in some more details of his life story. He'd made peace with his mother after the whole orphanage thing, and had started a foundation of his own to help send homeless kids to school.

"You're not a Catholic, Mark, are you?" he asked.

"Well, yeah, technically, yes, I am."

"Great! So you understand that everything happens for a reason."

Near the end of the afternoon, we approached what appeared to be a slight ridge. "Okay," Efrain said, then walked a few steps ahead, turned toward John and me and held his hands up. "You and John link arms." I raised an eyebrow. I'm pretty sure John groaned. "Trust me," Efrain said. "Now close your eyes and walk forward twenty paces. I said *trust* me." We did as told. "Okay, about ten more paces. Don't open your eyes or you'll ruin the surprise. Now five more, slowly." A gust of cool wind came up from somewhere and nearly blew my hat off. I heard the sound of rushing water.

"Okay, open your eyes. This is my way of saying, 'Welcome to the Inca Trail.'"

Below us were the ruins of Patallacta, where Bingham's men had excavated many of the skeletal remains found by the 1915 expedition. The site was immense. It looked as if someone had filled the Roman

Colosseum with wet sand and dumped it onto the side of a mountain, and then built a small village on top of the new plateau. A river flowed in front of the ghost town like a moat.

When I signed up for this trip, John had told me that I had two choices—a four-day trip or a five-day one. He strongly recommended the longer (and far less popular) option. It didn't make sense to fly thousands of miles to hike the Inca Trail, only to rush through it, but the vast majority of people preferred to hurry. Now here we were, at what Efrain called "the most important site between Ollantaytambo and Machu Picchu," and there wasn't a single other hiker in sight.

The day's last sunlight was scratching the tops of the mountains, and John and I had just enough time to run down to the river in our bathing suits for a quick wash. I stood on a rock along the bank and splashed the frigid water on myself in the deepening blue light. John waded out into the current and sat down on a boulder. He removed his jacket and then to my great surprise his hat—the big reveal was that he was a little bald on top—and then doused himself with the glacial water. "Look at this, Mark!" he shouted, pointing to his chest. There was a red scar running down the center, about the size of a pocket comb, where the surgeon had cracked open his sternum. "I think I'm getting some feeling back in the left side of my chest!"

Patallacta is now believed to have been a satellite of Machu Picchu, a settlement where several hundred laborers resided and much of the food consumed at Machu Picchu was grown. We sat down to what may have been the first low-fat meal served there since the death of Atahualpa. Actually, it was more a low-fat *style* meal, since John noticed an empty can of condensed milk next to the suspiciously rich potato soup. "Looks like I better take an extra statin," he said, pulling a vial of heart pills from his jacket.

After dinner, John went straight to bed. I put on my headlamp and followed Efrain into the blackness of the immense valley, across the river and into the ruins. The most impressive building at Patallacta was a sun temple with rounded walls, which looked like a rustic replica of the Torreon at Machu Picchu. There was even a small cave underneath.

"Come here, Mark," Efrain said, pointing his flashlight into the crevice. The rock was charred and the ground strewn with the remnants of a fire. "Mountain people are *very* traditional. They come here to make offerings when the INC is away." In the embers I saw candy wrappers, seashells and an empty wine bottle.

"This is the cheapest stuff," Efrain said, picking up the bottle. The label said VINO FORTIFICADO—the Peruvian equivalent of Wild Irish Rose. "Supposedly they're paying it to the Mother Earth, but they drink the wine themselves." He poked the ashes with a stick. "A llama fetus is a very good offering. Sometimes you can find little metal shapes that represent things, like a new house or people getting married." I'd seen these for sale in the market in Cusco. They looked like tiny Monopoly pieces.

We entered the Torreon, which, if less beautiful than the one in Machu Picchu, was more obviously utilitarian. Efrain pointed out two small windows much like those in the more famous sun temple tower. "June twenty-first is approaching, right, the solstice? The stars move counterclockwise. Right up there is the Corona Borealis. You see it?" The size of the night sky was—sorry, but there's really no other word for it—astronomical. "The Incas had specialists who kept track of the stars. On the winter solstice you can see the Corona from this window, which points northeast." He traced his fingers around the window to the left. I looked at the constellation through the thick stone frame. "By the summer solstice on December twenty-second, the Corona has moved to that window on the right."

"Wow, I don't think I've read about that anywhere," I said, half hoping Efrain might direct me to a printed source. He kept a running bibliography on every topic that we touched on, from Inca weaving to Bingham's skill as a photographer, and I'd already written down the names of half a dozen books that he thought I should read.

"A lot of people don't believe things they can't read in a book," he said. "So many of the things I've learned in the mountains—like how to navigate by the stars—can't be found in books." The clear night air was freezing, and the stars' brilliance deepened as the minutes passed.

"What you might know as the constellation Scorpio, mountain people call the Condor. When you see those really thin clouds—I forget the name in English."

"Cirrus?"

"Those kinds of clouds mean that there's going to be frost. If you hear all the frogs singing, you can be sure it's going to rain. If the birds put their nests near the water, it's going to be a dry season. These are the sorts of things that fathers teach their sons."

We wandered through the alleyways of Patallacta, then crossed back over the river to the cook tent, which glowed in the dark like a jack-o'-lantern. The six porters were huddled inside, laughing about something.

I'd been wondering something ever since Juvenal and Justo had complained about Mateo's snoring. "Do these guys ever get sick of sleeping all together?"

"No way," Efrain said. "If you made an offer to a team of porters or muleteers—'Here, we'll give you a tent for two people'—they'd always say, 'No, thank you, we'd rather sleep together.' They stay warm, review what happened during the day, and make fun of everybody." Someone shouted something in Quechua, followed by a loud laugh. Efrain stifled a smile.

"Like the clients, for example," I said.

"Good night, Mark," he said. "I hope you sleep well."

FORTY-EIGHT

Pilgrims' Progress

On the Inca Trail

"Not far from Patallacta," Bingham wrote in his last article for *National Geographic*, "we located the remains of an old Inca Road leading out of the valley in the direction of Machu Picchu." As we picked up that same trail in the morning, a positive sign appeared overhead—two condors soaring above the mountain into which Patallacta had been built. I had read—and Efrain confirmed—that condors, which were becoming rare sights in the Andes, were traditionally believed to be *apus* that had transformed into animals. This was my third trip to Machu Picchu, and I had yet to catch even a glimpse of the great *apu* Salcantay. It was as if a twenty-thousand-foot peak was avoiding me. Maybe one of the condor pair was the elusive mountain, on a reconnaissance mission to check me out.

On a purely practical level, the Inca Trail doesn't make much sense. Anyone in a hurry to travel from Cusco or Ollantaytambo to Machu Picchu—even someone borne on the shoulders of his subjects in a golden litter—could have more easily followed the original route Bingham took, next to the Urubamba River. The Inca Trail hooks around at a right angle, like a giant check mark. It is not a path designed to minimize effort. Just after starting out, we passed a large wooden sign carved with what looked like a stock price chart. It was a graph of the trail's changing elevation. Today's walk, which gained almost a mile in altitude, rose like the dot-com bubble of 1998; tomorrow's moderate ups and downs looked like normal market turbulence; our fourth and final day on the trail nosedived like the sort of crash that had investors leaping from windows.

"Better use the new heart monitor today," John said as he wrote the numbers down in a little blue notebook.

The path changed from dirt to stone. As we approached a long set of stairs disappearing into the trees above, we caught up to our first fellow hikers. They were stragglers from a big group up ahead, a chubby Frenchman wearing an iPod, and a skinny blond American woman.

"I . . . really . . . thought . . . I was . . . in shape," she panted. "But I guess . . . I'm not."

"Zey did not . . . tell us so many . . . zee steps," shouted the Frenchman, sounding offended, over his personal disco soundtrack.

John pulled alongside the pair. "Now what you'll want to do is slow down and breathe deeply. Are you on the four-day or the five-day itinerary?"

"Four days," the pair said.

"Right, then. Slow and steady. Don't sprint and then stop; you'll waste energy." Once we'd passed them by fifty yards or so, John shook his head and said, "They'll be lucky to get to camp by nine o'clock, those two. What a miserable way to hike the Inca Trail. Hardest part's still up ahead. Then they've got an entire valley to cross after they pass the spot where we'll be stopping for the night. I bet we'll see some porters coming back this way soon."

"What can the porters do?"

"Give them some support, pulling with an arm on each side to start. If that doesn't work they have to push." He mimed a thrusting gesture that coming from almost any other male on the planet would have been lewd.

When we arrived at the prearranged lunch spot, I got my first glimpse of how crowded the trail can be. At least two hundred people, dressed in all the unnatural colors of the moisture-wicking-apparel rainbow, were picnicking. It looked like Woodstock for people with gym memberships. Most of them ate and ran. We were left in peace for the remainder of the afternoon, chewing wads of coca and climbing shaded steps through an eerily quiet valley that Bingham had described as "destitute of even animal life." We slept, fitfully, at a high-altitude site called Llulluchapampa.

By eight the next morning we were walking up a steep, narrow staircase of broken stone steps, climbing toward the day's first light. We were approaching Dead Woman's Pass, the highest spot on the Inca Trail. Two steps from the top, nothing was visible ahead but blue sky. At the summit, the vista opened up to reveal a view like the one at Choquequirao that left Bingham reciting lines from Kipling. Mountain ranges extended for miles like ocean waves.

"This is phenomenal," I said to John, who was videotaping the view.

"When you walk through here you realize that this was the *only* possible route for the Inca to take to Machu Picchu," he said.

John was speaking aesthetically. There's a school of thought that the Inca Trail had been plotted like a good adventure yarn, with twists and turns, rising and falling action, and foreshadowing of the big climax: Machu Picchu. It's a suspenseful tale broken up by surprises. Looked at from a different angle, the Inca Trail is like the narrative of *Alice in Wonderland*—dreamlike and open to interpretation. In which case crossing Dead Woman's Pass was the moment we fell down the rabbit hole. Things only got stranger from this point forward.

"Come on, I want to show you something," Efrain said. We walked down the stairs for a couple minutes, until we were in the shadows again, then turned back toward the sunlit pass. "From here, you can see why they call it Dead Woman's Pass. There's the face, the breast, the belly." It really did look like a woman on her back, her strong facial features aimed skyward.

The trail descended steeply for a while, but John slowed down. His stomach was troubling him.

"Looks like the early score today is Giardia 1, Leivers 0," I said when he caught up.

"More like Giardia 40, Leivers 2," he said, leaning hard on his bamboo pole. "Go on ahead. I'll find you."

Efrain and I walked ahead alone. He started humming. I asked him what the tune was.

"Oh that? It's called 'Apu Yaya Jesucristo.' It's a song you sing in mountain churches."

"What does the name mean?"

"Basically it talks about how the *apus* are connected to Jesus Christ."

Since this suggested a marriage between Catholicism and what the Vatican would probably deem paganism, I asked if this was the sort of thing one discussed publicly in the Andes.

"In Peru, we have two religions, *futbol* and Catholicism. But everybody in Cusco still gives offerings in August." August 1 is Pachamama Day, a major holiday in Cusco. "I'm Catholic, I believe that Jesus Christ is the son of God. And I give offerings." Efrain explained that this was a long-standing tradition in the mountains. If one looked at the most famous paintings in the cathedrals of Cusco, one saw that native painters often combined elements of Catholicism with their traditional beliefs. The Virgin Mary might be painted in the shape of a mountain, or with a snake, or under a moon. "Of course the most famous one is of the Last Supper with the *cuy*—you know, the guinea pig," Efrain reminded me.

According to Efrain, this spiritual hybrid went all the way back to the Spanish Conquest. "Mountain people mix traditional beliefs, Catholicism, and ancestor worship," he said. "My father died when I was very young. After fifteen years, they had to dig up his coffin. So my mother brought his skull back to our house so he could watch over us. Where did this tradition come from? From the Incas."

(I wondered for a moment if Efrain was pulling my leg, but realized that he was far too earnest about Andean traditions to joke about something so important. I later read a news story about a candidate for mayor in a southern Peru town who tried to blackmail his opponent into dropping out of the race by digging up the skull of the man's father and holding it hostage.)

I told Efrain that the Catholic priests I'd known in my life were not always the most open-minded individuals regarding spiritual matters. Pantheism wasn't high on their list of likes. "Are the priests around here okay with this stuff?"

"They have to learn to balance the two," he said. "If a priest says anything bad about the *apus*, two seconds later the church empties out."

"What do you make of the whole mystical energy thing, with the crystals and all that?"

Efrain shrugged his shoulders. "There's energy in everything, Mark. Remember, you can't find everything in a book."

We stopped at the first of Bingham's 1915 discoveries, Runcu Raccay, which looked like a rounded TV dinner tray, with two side-dish compartments surrounding a circular entrée spot. Efrain stepped inside and tapped the dirt floor with my walking stick. It thudded hollow. "After Bingham came through here, lots of people followed—both Peruvian and not Peruvian—looking for gold."

We walked on, and the day grew hot. I looked back occasionally to see how John was faring, but he'd fallen out of view. Almost imperceptibly, the terrain turned to cloud forest. Efrain pointed out curiosities from the plant kingdom. The world's smallest variety of orchid. A type of moss used as a coagulant in World War II. A poisonous fungus that I told Efrain looked like day-old tripe. He grabbed my forearm. "Please don't eat that, Mark," he said.

Around two o'clock, the trail forked. To the right the road continued. To the left it diverted up a set of steps to what from a distance looked like the Rhine castle of an especially antisocial count, perched on a rock outcrop. The building seemed to levitate, as if the Incas had constructed a granite hovercraft. "Sayacmarca," Efrain said. "The name means 'inaccessible town.'"

We ascended the staircase and found ourselves standing inside an elliptical building, open on one end. Contrary to Bingham's interpretation—that it was a fortress—Sayacmarca seems to have been designed for two types of viewing. On the far end, a large platform—perfect for an alpaca-and-chicha barbecue—took in the Aobamba Valley and snowcapped mountains beyond. The horseshoe-shaped building we'd entered at the top of the staircase was configured toward the south and west. "Its windows face to the sunset, for the solstice and equinoxes," Efrain said.

John arrived at the top of the stairs, shuffling slowly and grunting. His face reminded me of construction workers I'd seen waiting in emergency rooms with their hands wrapped in towels. "Very important site, this," he said through his teeth.

After lunch, Efrain and I walked ahead again, passing two small lakes. "You want to see something that probably looks a lot like what Hiram Bingham saw?" Efrain asked. We took a detour through an unspectacular crack in the rock face. This led to a slippery white stone trail that we followed for about five minutes, splashing through a few mud puddles and pushing aside vines and branches. "This place must have been pretty important," Efrain said when we stopped. "Take a look."

We stepped into a two-chambered room carved into a hollow in the mountain. The exquisite stonework had been cut to join seamlessly with a huge overhanging rock like an open clamshell. It was like a slightly less fancy version of the Royal Mausoleum. Niches for holding sacred artifacts were recessed into one wall; the cut-granite stones from another wall had toppled over into a pile. Everything was coated with a thick layer of green moss. A shaft of sunlight shined through a large crack where the roof had once been. Efrain was right. It looked just like one of the buildings in the photographs Bingham had taken in 1911.

"What was this place?" I asked.

"We don't know," Efrain said. "A friend of mine told me he found it when he was looking for somewhere to sneak off and smoke marijuana."

Our final campsite was at Phuyupatamarca, which was Bingham's last discovery in 1915. The name, given by the anthropologist Paul Fejos, means "town above the clouds." The porters had set up my tent in what may be the greatest sleeping spot on the Inca Trail—a small ledge just large enough for one person, with a 180-degree view of mist-shrouded peaks. The cold air was heavy with moisture. John arrived about twenty minutes behind us, grumbling about a group of hikers who had set up their dinner tables on the viewing platform directly above us. "Not *only* are they blocking the way of anyone else who wants to go up there," he said. "They're facing *away* from the mountains. Idiots."

At dinner, everyone was wiped out. After all the day's ups and downs, we were still at about twelve thousand feet. The water for pasta took thirty minutes to boil. I asked Efrain how long it had taken him to get used to sleeping in a tent. He shook his head. "There's nothing like your own bed at home," he said.

"I'll come by and wake you up after sunrise," he told me as he stood up to leave. "If it's clear, the view should be very good. Maybe you'll even see Salcantay."

John popped his last pill of the day. "We'll be at Machu Picchu by this time tomorrow."

"Yep. Pachacutec's country estate."

"Oh, come on, Mark. That theory is fine—and probably correct as far as it goes—but you know it doesn't do justice to what Pachacutec was trying to do here. Machu Picchu was like Mecca, like the cathedral at the end of a pilgrimage." That word again. "These experts all have the same problem Bingham had."

"What's that?"

"Failure of imagination. Too many people think like scientists—mechanically. We've barely scratched the surface here. To really understand Machu Picchu I think you'd need to be someone who could come in with a completely open mind—someone more spiritual and religious. Maybe even arty."

John wasn't alone in thinking this. As I'd been packing to leave

New York for Cusco this time, I came across a new theory attempting to explain why Machu Picchu had been built. Giulio Magli, a professor of archaeoastronomy at the Polytechnic Institute in Milan, Italy, had just published a paper that expanded on Johan Reinhard's sacred center theory. Magli argued that the Inca Trail wasn't just a special VIP access road to Machu Picchu; the two were designed as a single work—a pilgrimage route. This sacred passage had been constructed as a replica of another mythical journey, the one which the very first Incas had made from the Island of the Sun in Lake Titicaca. According to this story, these forefathers had been created on the island and had traveled through a subterranean void, emerging at the far end of their journey at a place called Tampu Tocco.

Having walked most of the Inca Trail, I found Magli's case compelling. As Reinhard had pointed out, the sites along the trail are so different, and so obviously oriented toward watching the sun and stars, that it seems impossible that they didn't have some important ritual use. Magli believed that the trail likely prepared pilgrims for the most important part of the journey, which took place *inside* Machu Picchu. Curiously, the final leg of this pilgrimage roughly mimicked another famous journey, Hiram Bingham's first visit to Machu Picchu in 1911. In both cases, one entered through the main gate, which faced due north to Huayna Picchu (and where Bingham found his rounded stones—which Magli thought had possibly been offerings), walked up past a quarry more symbolic than functional (representing the Pachamama and the journey underground), through the Sacred Plaza, where the Temple of the Three Windows was erected as a tribute to the cave at Tampu Tocco, and up to the Intihuatana, the end point of the pilgrimage, which Reinhard has demonstrated aligns with *apus* in the cardinal directions.

By Magli's reasoning—and he admitted that due to the lack of hard evidence at Machu Picchu, we're never going to be able to make more than an educated guess about this stuff—Bingham's Tampu Tocco theory was wrong. The way I saw it, though, Bingham had also sort of been right. Blinded by ambition, he might have mistaken a handsome three-windowed copy of Tampu Tocco for the real thing. Bingham seems to have made the identical mistake with the Torreon. "If my theory about Tampu Tocco is correct," he'd written in *Lost City of the Incas*, the Koricancha in Cusco "had been built during the reign of the Incas as an echo, on a large scale, of the semicircular temple at Machu Picchu." In his haste to tie up all loose ends, he'd gotten things exactly backward. It was as if he'd seen the Last Supper painting in which Jesus gives the benediction over a platter of roasted *cuy* and proceeded to argue that it must have inspired Leonardo da Vinci.

FORTY-NINE

The Who's Who of *Apus*

At Phuyupatamarca

I got up around 4:30 A.M., feeling oddly refreshed. After I spent an hour reading and shoving things in my pack, the day's first light started to glow weakly through the thin ceiling of the tent. I stepped out onto my private terrace and, with the aid of my ridiculous wristwatch-altimeter-compass, looked roughly in the direction of Machu Picchu. Not much was visible in the obscurity. (Though I did notice that the barometric pressure was rising.) I ducked into the cook tent to grab a cup of coffee. After a few minutes the cloud cover began to lift. Dawn started to break somewhere behind the ranges. It seemed like a good moment to visit the observation platform where the mountain-averse idiots had eaten their dinner the night before. John would really love this, I thought, and momentarily considered waking him before I remembered his stomach troubles. With Nescafé in hand, I exchanged good mornings with the porters sitting outside and turned the corner around the big orange tent, watching my feet as I navigated the cords staked into the ground.

When I looked up, I was face-to-face with a white deity: Salcantay. No wonder people had been talking about this mountain since forever. In the middle of some of the world's tallest peaks, it completely dominated the skyline. I hurried up the path to the platform for a better look. The first thing I saw at the top was the back side of a familiar form, wearing a ski cap and videotaping everything in a slow semicircle.

"Best views in the world and no one's here!" John shouted when he saw me. The panorama was staggering. Almost everything I'd seen in Peru in the last year was visible from this one spot.

"Look at this, Mark! It's just sensational! There's Salcantay, of course. You'll notice a piece missing from that side. That's the part that caused the *alluvion* when it fell into the Aobamba River and wiped out the railway." It looked like someone had taken the tiniest nibble of a snow cone. "To the right is Pumasillo—you might just be able to make out the Choquetacarpo Pass that we crossed. Over there, behind that mountain, is Choquequirao. And if you come over here . . ." We turned to the right and walked to the edge of the platform. "Over there is Llactapata, and beyond that are Vitcos and Espiritu Pampa. And you might recognize that small, green pointy peak down there."

I finally found the one he was trying to single out. "That one?"

"Recognize it? You've been up there. It's Mount Machu Picchu!" It was like a Christmas tree lost in a stand of redwoods. "And if you follow that line along the ridge, that's the Inca Trail leading to the Sun Gate. Just think, at this very moment people are dragging themselves up to the Sun Gate when they should be right here."

Efrain arrived, still rubbing the sleep from his eyes. He took his hat off, faced Salcantay, and held it to his chest. "The older mountain men, sixty or seventy years old, do this when they see a mountain. It's a way of giving respect to the *apus*." He walked to the edge. "From here you can see everything—jungle, highland, the Andes. Everything. There's no question about it—the Incas got to Machu Picchu and said, 'This is a sacred center. We must build here.'"

The sun began to crest over the top of Mount Veronica to the east, a reminder that hundreds of people would also be standing above the Torreon at this moment, for today was the first day of the solstice.

We lingered past our usual departure hour, then moved on toward Machu Picchu, skirting the agricultural ruins of Inti Pata and passing through a tunnel carved through solid rock. We ate bag lunches at Wiñay Wayna, the last of the major sites along the Inca Trail. The massive convex ruins were so overgrown in Bingham's time that he missed them altogether; they weren't discovered until 1941.

As the three of us departed Wiñay Wayna, John bolted ahead; he was eager to get to Machu Picchu. Efrain fell back to chat with a fellow guide, a friend of his. And so on the final leg of the Inca Trail, I was left alone with my thoughts, which naturally turned to Bingham. After almost a year of stalking the man, I thought I'd figured him out.

Regardless of what he implied in *Lost City of the Incas*, Hiram Bingham was definitely *not* the discoverer of Machu Picchu. He may have been the "scientific discoverer," as a plaque inside the entrance to the ruins credits him, but I never came around to that name. The polio vaccine was a scientific discovery. Radium was a scientific discovery. John was right. If you tried to understand Machu Picchu in isolation, from a purely secular viewpoint, you were bound to miss something important.

The truth about Bingham, perhaps the only thing Paolo Greer and Eliane Karp-Toledo would have agreed on, is that he did something less romantic but ultimately much more important than *discovering* Machu Picchu. He saw the ruins, quickly determined their importance (if not their origin) and popularized them to a degree that they couldn't be blown up with dynamite or knocked over in the search for buried gold, as Vitcos had been. Would Machu Picchu exist if Hiram Bingham had never seen it? Of course. Would it be the same Machu Picchu we know today? Almost certainly not.

Similarly, if he'd never published *Lost City of the Incas*, would Bingham have been accused of stealing credit for the discovery? No. Was he the original Indiana Jones? Not exactly. But if he hadn't published *Lost City of the Incas*, would the character of Indiana Jones ever have existed? Probably not, at least not in the form we know.

Did Bingham steal artifacts from Peru? Yes. If he were alive today, would he want the artifacts at the Peabody Museum to be returned to

Peru? Almost certainly, yes. It was hard to argue with that 1916 note he'd written to Gilbert Grosvenor: "The objects do not belong to us, but to the Peruvian government."

A few months later, in a move that took most observers completely by surprise, Yale finally agreed with its most swashbuckling alumnus. A new memo of understanding was signed between the university and the government of Peru, and the most eye-catching pieces on display at the Peabody Museum were packed up to be returned to Cusco in time to be put on display for the hundredth anniversary of Bingham's achievement. The rest of the collection was scheduled to follow not long after, to be housed in a research facility open to Yale scholars as well as Peruvians. Lawsuits were dropped on both sides and everyone pretended that things had turned out exactly as they'd hoped all along. Bingham would have been pleased, both as an explorer and as a politician.

Late in the afternoon of our last day on the Inca Trail, John, Efrain and I passed through the control booth and entered the Machu Picchu Historical Sanctuary. The final stretch of stone trail undulated up and down until it reached a long set of white stairs extending toward the sky. At their summit stood a set of tall stone pillars.

"We call this the gringo killer," Efrain said.

I reached the top of the stairs, winded, and looked around. I was standing in the Sun Gate. Below me stretched a long stone path (upon which a certain Australian was quickly disappearing, GPS in hand), sets of terraces and, at the far end, the familiar green rhino horn of Huayna Picchu. Nestled in between, in the jewelry box of the surrounding mountains, was the still-breathtaking citadel of Machu Picchu.

FIFTY

The Sun Temple

At the Torreon, Machu Picchu

When Efrain and I paused at the Sun Gate to take a drink of water, a *mistico* in a plumed hat and a vest embroidered with astrological signs told us that the morning had been a *major* bummer. Hundreds of harmonically inclined people had assembled above the Torreon and counted down the minutes to sunrise. And then . . . nothing. The clouds never parted and no sunbeam shined.

The *mistico* wasn't the only true believer left at Machu Picchu. John, Efrain and I arrived at the site the next morning before six. Aside from the college kids preparing to run up Huayna Picchu, the ruins were nearly empty. John slipped away by himself; Efrain and I walked up to the Temple of the Three Windows, outside of which a large group of people dressed in white robes stood in a circle, some holding enormous crystals.

"The bigger the crystal, the bigger the power," Efrain told me.

"How'd you know that?"

"My other mom, from the orphanage, she was into that stuff. She was always trying to get us to talk about our chakras." A guy with a beard like Karl Marx's blew a horn and reminded the group to reconvene at ten sharp, so that they might "take advantage of the sacred energy."

We walked down in front of the Royal Mausoleum cavern. "Bingham called this the Royal Tomb, but it wasn't," Efrain said. "It was a temple to the Pachamama, the Mother Earth. Caves are access points to the underground world." The day's first dim light had just begun to illuminate the cave's surreal interior. "The Incas didn't have one church—they had hundreds of places to worship."

At about a quarter to seven, we took our places behind a chest-high stone wall directly above the Torreon, in a spot that faced due east. Below us, John was shooting video of the interior of the new tomb that Paolo had told me about. A minute later, he was next to us, triangulating the perfect position from which to decide once and for all if this sunbeam-through-the-window story had any merit to it. Over the next fifteen minutes, dozens of other people arrived, until we were crowded in like the first arrivals at a sold-out show.

"Looks like we picked a winner of a day, Mark," John shouted from down the row of onlookers. "Nice clear sky."

"We should start to see something right about . . . now," Efrain said.

The day's first illumination arrived to the south, shining like a spotlight on the Sun Gate. A throng of Inca Trail trekkers, who would never know how lucky they were to arrive under perfect conditions, raised their walking sticks and cheered.

At 7:07, the first rays began to appear above the peak known locally as Cerro San Gabriel, the sharply pointed mountain directly in front of us to the east. The luminescence hovered behind the peak for a few moments, then shot its first beams out from the left side of the mountain. For a few minutes, the sun continued to rise slowly, triggering an expanding burst of light from behind the top of San Gabriel, like the glow around Jesus's head in a Renaissance painting.

At 7:15, to our far left, rays of light hit the green horn of Huayna Picchu. The leading edge of the sunlight rolled toward us through the main ruins like a wave.

"Keep your eye on the window," Efrain said.

At 7:20, the sun emerged completely from behind San Gabriel, burning in place momentarily directly above its pinnacle. I concentrated on the window inside the Torreon. A faint rectangle of light appeared on the rock inside the curved wall. Seconds ticked by. The rectangle brightened until its four sides were clearly delineated on the rock, almost perfectly centered on the crack where Paolo thought the golden statue had stood.

"Pa-cha-cu-tec," Efrain said quietly, to no one in particular.

The oldest description I'd been able to find of an Inti Raymi celebration to welcome back the sun was one that Manco oversaw in Cusco in 1535:

> Magnificently robed orejones [nobles] wearing rich silver cloaks and tunics, with brightly-shining circlets and medallions of fine gold on their heads . . . formed up in pairs . . . and waited in deep silence for the sun to rise. As soon as the sunrise began they started to chant in splendid harmony and unison.

There was no chanting this time, but the crowd did, as one, let out a long "Whooooah!"

I shot a look at John, who was busy snapping pictures. Later that day, he showed me his photos on his laptop and explained excitedly how the window did in fact align with the sunrise—"look at that, no shadow at all!"—in part because Inca engineers had angled the sides of the window to funnel the sunlight onto the rock, another Inca special effect. "Further proof that you shouldn't believe everything that you hear and read," he told me. Once again, the experts were wrong, the Incas were right, and John couldn't have been happier.

It would be nice to say that witnessing the sunrise proved for certain that Machu Picchu had been built as the end of a pilgrimage, or that a ghostly image of Pachacutec's gold statue appeared inside the Torreon and gave me a thumbs-up. But the truth is that Machu Picchu is always going to be something of a mystery. Which is, of course, part of its allure. Everyone who visits the citadel in the clouds inevitably follows in Bingham's footsteps—not only by walking the same paths the explorer trod, but by projecting whatever vision it is they hope to see onto the lost city. As for me, the mental image of Machu Picchu that I'll always keep is of John juggling handfuls of gadgets as he tried to capture the sunrise coming through the window, completely oblivious to Karl Marx patting him enthusiastically on the back.

Epilogue

New York

One year after my first visit to Cusco, I met John Leivers at the airport again. For once, I was the person who knew where we were going. John was en route to Australia for his mum's ninetieth birthday celebration and wanted to see an exotic locale that he'd somehow missed in all his travels—New York City. His suitcase, which I offered to carry before I learned that it was filled with materials John was transferring to his master archive in Perth, weighed approximately ten thousand pounds.

When we arrived at my home north of the city, my five-year-old son Magnus, brimming with the confidence he'd gained in two full weeks of kindergarten, opened the front door and asked John, "Is it true you live in a tent?"

"Yes, it is," John said.

"Why don't you have a house like everybody else?"

John leaned in to meet Magnus's dubious stare. "Because I endeavor to remain flexible."

John was not a typical visitor to New York. He showed zero interest in fine dining, shopping or Broadway shows. Instead, he spent the week visiting museums and jotting down notes. He passed several hours at the Museum of Natural History, taking in an exhibition about the Capac Ñan, the royal Inca highway. He wasn't the only out-of-town guest I've had who was put off by the high prices of everything and the

long line for the Empire State Building observatory. But he was undoubtedly the first to complain about his inability to get a GPS signal
at the corner of 42nd Street and Fifth Avenue.

The only time I saw John act like a tourist was when we spent
an afternoon walking through the fashionable winding streets of
Greenwich Village and SoHo. John was dressed exactly like he did in
Cusco. "It looks just like the movies here!" he said, snapping photos of
brownstones and old tenement buildings with iron fire escapes. That
evening, in an e-mail to a former colleague, I described my day: how
I'd brought my Australian guide—who'd led me on an off-the-map
backcountry adventure and was visiting New York for the first time—
downtown to have lunch with my publisher. "You do realize that
you've just given me a plot summary of *Crocodile Dundee*," my friend
wrote back. "He doesn't carry a big knife, does he?"

I remembered John slashing through the cloud forest with his machete and thought, *You have no idea.*

Each night at our family dinner table, John updated me on what was
happening in Peru. Justo, Juvenal and the rest of my pals in the travel
business were hoping for a busy year to coincide with the hundredth
anniversary of Bingham's 1911 expedition. Paolo was continuing, without success, to try to get the government to dig for Pachacutec's
mummy before his bones were forever entombed beneath a strip mall.
Roxana Abril still hadn't heard back about her ownership claim to
Machu Picchu, though perhaps the return of the Yale artifacts would
give her grounds for a new lawsuit. Eliane Karp-Toledo had been quiet
of late—by her standards, anyway—but plenty of other politicians in
Lima and Cusco were lining up to take credit for bringing Bingham's
relics back home.

John's ears had always perked up when I described my visits to the
Yale library and the reams of unpublished—but neatly organized—
information that Bingham had left behind for future historians. So I
guess I shouldn't have been surprised when he managed to talk his
way into the Rare Books and Manuscripts Room. He caught the train
up to New Haven and spent a delirious afternoon reading Bingham's

papers, skipping right over the 1911 Machu Picchu materials to focus on his more obscure expedition journals from the later campaigns. I wondered if the librarians thought they'd seen the explorer's ghost.

"There's some *fantastic* stuff up there at Yale," John told me excitedly that evening over his third bowl of nonfat yogurt. "After seeing those papers I've changed my mind. Bingham was a *serious* adventurer."

"What do you mean?" I asked.

"Everyone knows about Machu Picchu and, less so of course, places like Espiritu Pampa and Choquequirao. That's because Bingham wrote about those things in his books. But he went to *dozens* of places, some that almost no one else has gone to since. He was dealing with corruption, thievery, people of dubious character—and he was under a *lot* of pressure. He still managed to complete those expeditions and record massive amounts of data and information. That took great courage and determination."

For someone who'd recently had his heart rewired, John had some fairly ambitious plans of his own. Evidently, his days humping eighty-pound packs up steep mountainsides weren't over after all. He mentioned an archaeological site deep in the cloud forest of northern Peru, in a region far more remote than anything I'd seen, that he was hoping to explore when he returned from Australia.

"God, I'd love to get in there," he said. "Almost no one's allowed in—there's no tourists, no infrastructure, nothing. You have to petition personally to the local INC office in order to enter the ruins. Who knows how long that'll take, assuming they respond at all."

"You know, I've still got some contacts in the adventure travel business," I said, leaning back in my chair. "Maybe I could make a few phone calls. I'm sure I know someone who knows someone."

I reminded John that I was putting the story of our own peregrinations into a book. But it seemed a shame to hang up my hiking boots and return to the office life just because I'd managed to put my Bingham obsession to rest. Maybe there was some new parallel that I could latch on to to write another story—a story that would, naturally, require me to accompany John on his new expedition.

"I've got it!" I said. "Bingham started out as a martini explorer, and then turned out to be a real adventurer. I started out as a tourist, but then I turned out to be a real traveler, too. Right?"

"Actually . . ." John said, slowly scraping the remnants of yogurt from his bowl. "You remember how things work in Peru, Mark. It all depends on who you ask."

Acknowledgments

The Incas had a three-pronged Golden Rule, still widely repeated in the Andes: *ama sua, ama llula, ama cheklla*. Translated, it means "do not steal, do not lie, do not be lazy." There's not much I can do about my un-Bingham-like laziness at this point in my life—the only way I'm ever going back to Choquequirao is in a helicopter—but I would be lying if I did not admit to stealing hours of valuable time from some very busy people while writing this book. I am deeply indebted to each of them.

My foremost gratitude is to John Leivers, who not only dragged my sorry behind through much of Peru but subsequently answered hundreds of questions, always cheerfully, patiently and in minute detail. Mike Benoist, Cliff Ransom and Steve Byers, all adventurous types, gave invaluable comments on an early draft. The always blunt Gillian Fassel prevented me from indulging my worst authorial instincts, in the nicest way possible. Ryan Bradley ventured into the jungles of Beverly Hills and elsewhere to track down rumors and factoids, then returned to civilization to give insightful notes. The librarians at Yale's Sterling Memorial Library and The New York Public Library (Jay Barksdale in particular) were extremely kind and helpful. My brother Jason Adams, as always, helped me get to the finish line. Paolo Greer delved repeatedly into his personal archives to answer even the most obscure questions I had about Machu Picchu. Dan Ferrara, who hired me at *Outside* magazine in 1992, is still cleaning up my inelegant transitions. Sophy Truslow, Charlie Jolie and Adam Zarkov played uncredited roles in getting this story started. Others who provided support above and beyond the call of duty in New York were Sarah Adams, Caroline Hirsch, Veronica Francis, Mary Anne Potts, Adam Sachs, Peter Zaremba, John Hodgman, Marlon Salazar, Leonor Krawczyk, Melanie James of the sublime General Society Library and pretty much everyone associated with the late, lamented *National Geographic Adventure Magazine*—in particular the preposterously loyal John Rasmus.

Fred and Aura Truslow housed and fed me at their homes in both Washington, D.C., and Lima. The extended Kahatt-Navarrete family—Hilda, Julia, Karim, Sharif and Marta—made me feel welcome during Lima's gloomiest season. (Rocio Lockett and Patrick Manning deserve honorable sunshine mentions.) Nati Huamani put up with my silly inquiries while she cooked dinner for my sons. In Ollantaytambo, Vince and Nancy Lee not only answered my questions but bought me a very nice dinner on their anniversary. Others who provided personal or professional kindnesses big and small included Roberto Samanez, Johan Reinhard, Roxana Abril, Eliane Karp-Toledo, Barry Walker, Alex Chepstow-Lusty, Tati von Kaupp, Robert von Kaupp, Peter Frost, Rosa Cobos, Paul Cripps and the staff of Amazonas Explorer, and the very nice people who run the Hostal San Isidro Labrador, Carlo and Estela in particular. Also, an emphatic *mil gracias* to those who made sure I never lost my way (or my appetite) on the trail: Efrain Valles, Edgar Gudiel, Mateo Gallegos, Julián Bolaños, Juvenal Cobos and Justo Suchli.

My agent, Daniel Greenberg, reworked a half-baked book idea about Machu Picchu into something that people might actually want to read. Brian Tart at Dutton books seemed to understand immediately what I had in mind, probably even better than I did. He and Jessica Horvath helped steer an often wayward narrative back toward the proper path. David Cain drew the beautiful maps, based in part on earlier maps drawn by Bingham, the INC, Kenneth Wright, Peter Frost, Johan Reinhard and John Gilkes.

My greatest debt in all things is to my wife, Aurita, without whom this book could not have been written for about a thousand different reasons. And to my three beloved sons, who have never lied, cheated or betrayed the least sign of laziness—Alex, Lucas and Magnus—I can offer only one hard-earned nugget of wisdom in return for the joy you bring me every day: when hiking downhill, always wear two pairs of socks.

Glossary

These brief descriptions may be useful when you're trying to remember the difference between Huayna Capac (an emperor), Huayna Picchu (the peak at the north end of Machu Picchu) and Huayna Pucará (an Inca fort). For the most difficult names—almost all of them Quechua—I've included an approximate pronunciation as well.

Almagro, Diego de: One of Francisco Pizarro's two original partners in a business syndicate formed to exploit the riches many Spaniards believed (correctly) to exist in Peru. Embittered by his small share of Inca plunder, Almagro later started a war against the Pizarros, lost, and was executed.

Antisuyu: (An-tee-SOO-yoo) The easternmost and most tropical of the four quarters of the Inca empire. Its lands encompassed Machu Picchu and part of the Amazon basin.

Apu: (Ah-POO) A holy mountain, in traditional Andean belief. Often the recipient of religious sacrifices and ceremonies.

Apurimac River: (Ah-POO-ree-mack) Whitewater river that flows below Choquequirao.

Atahualpa: (Ah-tah-WAHL-pah) Inca emperor at the time of Pizarro's conquest of Peru. He had recently defeated his half brother Huascar in a civil war that devastated the empire; his preoccupation with this victory may have led him to underestimate Pizarro's threat. When captured by the Spaniards, Atahualpa paid an enormous ransom for his freedom, but was assassinated.

Ausangate: (Ow-san-GAH-tay) An *apu* that overlooks the Incas' holy city and capital of Cusco. One of the two most sacred mountains in Inca cosmology, along with Salcantay.

Berns, Augusto: Nineteenth-century German prospector, whose papers—located by the researcher Paolo Greer—suggest that he may have been looting Machu Picchu's artifacts long before Hiram Bingham arrived.

Bingham, Hiram: American explorer who located Machu Picchu, Vitcos and Espritu Pampa as the leader of the 1911 Yale Peruvian Expedition.

Cachora: (Cah-CHOR-ah) Small town at the trailhead to Choquequirao.

Calancha, Antonio de la: Augustinian monk and author of the seventeenth-century *Coronica Moralizada*, a history that contains important clues to the location of Vilcabamba.

Capac Ñan: (Cah-POCK-Nyahn) The royal Inca highway system, which, at its peak, stretched more than ten thousand miles.

Choquequirao: (Choh-kay-kee-ROW) An important Inca citadel constructed high above the Apurimac River. It was first visited by Bingham in 1909, when it was believed to be the legendary Lost City of the Incas. It is considered by many to be the sister site of Machu Picchu, because of physical similarities between the two. Several terraces decorated with stone llamas were discovered there in 2005.

Concevidayoc: (Chon-sch-vee-DIE-ock) Small settlement on the trail from Vitcos to Espiritu Pampa. Bingham expected to confront the savage potentate Saavedra there in 1911.

Cura Ocllo: (Koo-rah-OH-klo) Manco Inca's favorite wife and queen (and half sister).

Cusco: (koos-koh) Onetime holy city and capital of the Inca empire, known then as the Tawantinsuyu. Now a hub for tourism.

Espiritu Pampa: (Es-PEER-ee-too POM-pah) Modern name of Vilcabamba, a large Inca settlement in the rain forest and the last capital of the rebel Inca empire.

Hidroeléctrica: (Hee-droh-ee-LECK-tree-kah) Lesser-known train station on the far side of Machu Picchu, named for the nearby hydroelectric plant.

Huadquiña: (Wahd-KEEN-yah) Hacienda near Machu Picchu, where Bingham often visited on his trips to Peru.

Huancacalle: (Wahn-kah-KIE-yay) Small town near Vitcos and Puquiura; location of the Cobos family hostel, Sixpac Manco.

Huascar: (WAHS-kar) Inca emperor from 1527 to 1532. The civil war he fought against his half brother, Atahualpa, weakened the empire's armies just prior to the arrival of the Spanish conquistadors.

Huayna Capac: (WHY-nah KAH-pock) Inca emperor 1493–1527. Died suddenly, making possible the devastating war of succession between his sons Huascar and Atahualpa.

Huayna Picchu: (WHY-nah PEE-chow) Moderate-sized but very sacred peak at the north end of the Machu Picchu site.

Huayna Pucará: (WHY-nah Poo-kar-AH) Defensive fortification constructed by the Incas high above the road from Vitcos to Vilcabamba; their strategy—unsuccessful—was to crush advancing Spanish soldiers by dropping boulders onto them from above.

INC: The Instituto Nacional de Cultura, the Peruvian agency in charge of maintaining the country's ancient heritage.

Inca Trail: Former royal path to Machu Picchu, now famous as a hiking trail. Rediscovered by Hiram Bingham in 1915.

Intihuatana: (In-tee-wah-TAH-nah) This name can refer to almost any carved Inca stone dedicated to sun worship, but the two most famous *intihuatanas* are 1) the angled, sculpted stone at Machu Picchu's highest point, and 2) the larger granite carving below the site, near the Hidroeléctrica train station.

Koricancha: (Kor-ree-CAHN-chah) Primary sun temple of the Inca religion, located in Cusco.

Llactapata: (Yahk-tah-PAH-tah) An Inca site located across the valley from Machu Picchu; found by Bingham in 1912.

Manco Inca Yupanqui: (Man-KOH-Een-KAH Yoo-PAN-kee) Puppet king selected by conquistador Francisco Pizarro in 1533; he soon turned against his patron and led the Inca rebellion against their occupiers. He established Vilcabamba as the new capital of his empire, but was killed at Vitcos in 1544.

Mandor Pampa: (MAN-dor POM-pah) A small flood plain below Machu Picchu, where Bingham camped the night before his famous discovery.

Markham, Clements: President of the Royal Geographical Society at the turn of the twentieth century and an expert on ancient Peru; his work on the Incas greatly influenced Bingham's expeditions.

Mount Machu Picchu: Moderate-size peak that overlooks the southern end of the Machu Picchu site.

Ollantaytambo: (Oy-yan-tie-TAHM-boh) The most important Inca site between Cusco and Machu Picchu, and the location of the greatest Inca military victory against the Spanish conquistadors.

Pacaritambo: (Pah-kar-ree-TAHM-boh) Small town outside of Cusco, believed by many to be the location of the cave called Tampu Tocco, the legendary birthplace of the Incas.

Pachacutec: (Pah-chah-koo-teck) Ruler of the Incas from 1438 to 1471 and founder of the greatest royal dynasty in Inca history. (He is often compared to Alexander the Great.) He launched a building program that created many of the most famous works of Inca architecture, including Machu Picchu and the Koricancha.

Pachamama: (Pah-chah-MAH-mah) The Earth Mother, an important fertility goddess in traditional Andean beliefs.

Patallacta: (Pah-tah-YOCK-tah) A onetime satellite town of Machu Picchu, located near the start of the Inca Trail.

Phuyupatamarca: (Foo-yoo-pah-tah-MAR-kah) A high-altitude set of ruins near the end of the Inca Trail, known for its spectacular 360-degree mountain views.

Pizarro, Francisco: Spaniard who was the conqueror and first governor of Peru. He ordered the execution of the emperor Atahualpa, and was himself killed by supporters of his former partner, Diego de Almagro.

Pizarro, Gonzalo: Younger, nastier brother of Francisco. Infamous for his mistreatment of Manco Inca and for stealing Manco's wife.

Puquiura: (Pa-kee-yoo-rah) Small town near Vitcos and Huancacalle; its location was an important clue to finding the lost city of Vilcabamba.

Quechua: (KETCH-wah) Native language of the Peruvian Andes.

Royal Mausoleum: A cave at Machu Picchu, located directly beneath the Torreon; it is filled with enigmatic stonework, the purpose of which is still a mystery.

Runcu Raccay: (Roon-KOO Rah-KIE) Circular ruin, found by Bingham near the midpoint of the Inca Trail.

Sacred Plaza: A group of three important temples at Machu Picchu, including the Temple of the Three Windows and the Principal Temple.

Sacsahuaman: (Sack-sah-wah-MAHN) Gargantuan walled structure located above Cusco, famous for the size of the carved stones in its walls.

Salcantay: (Sal-kan-TIE) A sacred mountain (*apu*) directly south of Machu Picchu. One of the two holiest peaks in the Inca religion, along with Ausangate.

Sapa Inca: (SAH-pah EEN-kah) Official title of the emperor of the Incas.

Sayacmarca: An enigmatic, fortlike group of ruins near the midpoint of the Inca Trail.

Sayri Tupac: (Say-ree TOO-pock) A son of Manco Inca who ruled the rebel Inca state of Vilcabamba from 1544 to 1560.

Tampu Tocco: (TAHM-poo TOH-koh) According to legend, the three-

windowed hill from which emerged founders of the Inca dynasty. Bingham believed that he had found it at Machu Picchu.

Tawantinsuyu: (Tah-WAHN-tin-soo-yoo) The original name of the
Inca empire.

Temple of the Three Windows: An important building at Machu Picchu. Its signature feature is a wall of three large windows that
face east toward the sunrise.

Titu Cusi: (TEE-too KOO-see) A son of Manco Inca who ruled the
rebel Inca state of Vilcabamba from 1560 to 1571.

Torreon: (Tor-ray-OHN) A large building at Machu Picchu—also
known as the Sun Temple or Semicircular Temple—noted for its
curved wall. A beam of light shines through a small window
there on the June solstice. Located directly above the Royal
Mausoleum.

Tupac Amaru: (TOO-pock Ah-MAR-roo) Last of the rebel Inca emperors. He was captured by the Spaniards in 1572 and beheaded in
the main square in Cusco.

Urubamba River: (Oo-roo-BAHM-bah) The most sacred river in Inca
cosmology, it curves around the spur on which Machu Picchu
sits. Also known as the Vilcanota River near Cusco.

Usnu: (OOS-noo) Raised platform used by the Incas for religious
ceremonies.

Vilcabamba: (Veel-kah-BAHM-bah) The jungle capital of the rebel
Inca state, where Manco Inca went to hide after being chased
from Vitcos in 1537. Sacked by the Spaniards in 1572, the city was
soon reabsorbed into the tropical foliage—leading to the legend
of the Lost City of the Incas.

Vitcos: (Veet-khos) Fortified settlement west of Machu Picchu, near
Puquiura and Huancacalle. Probably built by Pachacutec. Site of
an important religious complex, constructed around a large
carved boulder known as the White Rock.

Vista Alegre: (VEES-tah Ah-LAY-gray) Small settlement on the trail
between Vitcos and Espiritu Pampa, or Old Vilcabamba.

White Rock: A sacred carved Inca boulder located near Vitcos; it was an important clue in Bingham's 1911 investigations. Also known as Yurak Rumi.

Wiñay Wayna: (WEEN-yay WHY-nah) A spectacular set of Inca buildings and terraces near the end of the Inca Trail.

Yanama: (Ya-Nah-mah) A small town on the trail between Choquequirao and Vitcos.

Chronology

Ca. 1200 Founding of what became the Inca dynasty.

1438 Pachacutec becomes Sapa Inca and begins his territorial expansion. He launches a massive building program, which will include the construction of Machu Picchu, the Koricancha sun temple in Cusco and the Capac Ñan.

1492 Christopher Columbus lands at what is now the Bahamas.

1513 Vasco Nuñez de Balboa sees the Pacific.

1519 Hernán Cortés conquers the Aztec empire in Mexico.

1522 A Spanish explorer reports the existence of a land known as Birú, later to be called Peru.

1527 First meeting between Francisco Pizarro and the Incas takes place in northern Peru.

1527–28 Emperor Huayna Capac dies unexpectedly. His son Huascar takes over but is opposed by another of Huayna Capac's sons, Atahualpa. Five years of civil war ensue.

1532 Atahualpa wins the Inca civil war. Pizarro captures Atahualpa. Atahualpa offers a huge ransom for his freedom.

1533 Atahualpa is executed. Manco is crowned Inca by Pizarro.

1536 Manco leads an attack against the Spaniards in Cusco.

1537 Manco flees his rebel headquarters at Ollantaytambo for Vitcos. When Vitcos is sacked by the Spaniards, he escapes to the new jungle capital of Vilcabamba.

1539	Vilcabamba is sacked for the first time. Manco's queen Cura Ocllo is executed by Pizarro.
1541	Francisco Pizarro is murdered in Lima.
1544	Manco Inca is murdered by Spanish refugees at Vitcos. He is succeeded by his sons Sayri Tupac and Titu Cusi.
1570	Spanish friars burn the temple complex near the White Rock of Vitcos.
1572	The Spaniards declare war on the rebel Inca state. Vilcabamba is sacked and burned for a second time. Tupac Amaru, the last Inca emperor, is captured in the jungle and returned to Cusco, where he is executed in the Plaza de Armas.
1781	Would-be revolutionary Tupac Amaru II is executed in Cusco.
1800s	French explorers visit Choquequirao, sparking the legend that it is the site of Vilcabamba.
1847	William Prescott publishes *The Conquest of Peru*.
1895	A new mule road is completed alongside the Urubamba River, passing below Machu Picchu.
1906–07	Hiram Bingham makes his first visit to South America, through Venezuela and Colombia.
1908–09	Bingham attends a scientific conference in Chile, and stays on to make his initial visit to Peru, including Cusco. He visits the ruins of Choquequirao, believed by some to be Vilcabamba—the Lost City of the Incas.
1911	Bingham's *annus mirabilis*. In one summer as the leader of the Yale Peruvian Expedition, he discovers Machu Picchu, Vitcos and Espritu Pampa. He leaves Peru uncertain if he has actually found Vilcabamba.
1912	Bingham returns to Peru, cosponsored by Yale and the National Geographic Society.
1913	The publication of Bingham's first *National Geographic* story makes stars of both Machu Picchu and its discoverer. Bing-

ham begins to formulate his theory that Machu Picchu is Vilcabamba.

1914–15   Bingham's third trip to Peru, during which he finds the Inca Trail. He leaves under a cloud of suspicion.

1948   Bingham publishes *Lost City of the Incas*, makes a final return trip to Machu Picchu.

1956   Bingham dies.

1964   Gene Savoy explores Espiritu Pampa, uncovers new evidence that it is the true Vilcabamba.

1981   *Raiders of the Lost Ark* is released, raising questions about which real-life explorers inspired Indiana Jones.

1982   Yale researchers Richard Burger and Lucy Salazar publish their theory that Machu Picchu had been the royal estate of Pachacutec.

2008   Paolo Greer publishes his article "Machu Picchu Before Bingham," which concludes that the prospector Augusto Berns likely looted Machu Picchu's artifacts long before Bingham arrived.

2011   100th anniversary of Hiram Bingham's first trip to Machu Picchu.

A Few Notes On Sources

A researcher could spend several lifetimes exploring the intertwined histories of Hiram Bingham, Machu Picchu, and the conquest of the Incas. Some of the tales surrounding these subjects have been told again and again, and attempting to trace information back to its original source is often impossible. Whenever possible I've relied on the earliest or most definitive source available, but if you spot an error or have a question about something, feel free to e-mail me at turnrightMP@gmail.com.

While writing this book, I always kept a small stack of key materials close at hand. Anyone interested in learning more about Machu Picchu would find any of them worth reading:

Portrait of an Explorer: Hiram Bingham, Discoverer of Machu Picchu, by Alfred Bingham.

This somewhat critical biography, written by one of Bingham's seven sons, was the first attempt to place Hiram III's career in the context of the golden age of exploration. While I disagree with its author's thesis that Bingham was completely fixated on climbing Mt. Coropuna and required months to realize the importance of Machu Picchu, its account of the 1911 Yale Peruvian Expedition is unparalleled. Also published under the title *Explorer of Machu Picchu*.

The Conquest of the Incas, by John Hemming.

The definitive history of Francisco Pizarro's occupation of Peru, and the starting point for any serious examination of Inca history.

History of the Conquest of Peru, by William H. Prescott.

Published in 1847, this book became the model for all future studies of Inca history. Its bias in favor the gallant Spaniards is offset by Prescott's thrilling narrative style.

Inca Land, by Hiram Bingham.

The explorer's first book-length account of his travels in Peru. Not exactly a page-turner, but it does give a more honest account of his actions and motivations than one finds in the famous *Lost City of the Incas*.

"In the Wonderland of Peru," by Hiram Bingham, *National Geographic*, April 1913.

This is probably the best account of Bingham's first two trips to Peru; it conveys the thrill of discovery better than his later retellings.

Lost City of the Incas, by Hiram Bingham.

Bingham's most readable book about Machu Picchu, in which he builds a case for himself as an important explorer and for his theories regarding the citadel. The best edition includes Hugh Thomson's insightful introduction.

The White Rock: An Exploration of the Inca Heartland, by Hugh Thomson.

A travel book that follows many of Bingham's routes through Peru; its sequel, *A Sacred Landscape* (published in the UK as *Cochineal Red*) describes the 2002 mapping of Llactapata in depth, and features several appearances by Mr. John Leivers.

"Machu Picchu Before Bingham," by Paolo Greer, *South American Explorer Magazine,* Summer 2008.

The article that dragged Bingham back into the news.

Machu Picchu: Unveiling the Mystery of the Incas, by Richard L. Burger and Lucy C. Salazar.

A thorough, scholarly overview of what is known about Machu Picchu, with particular emphasis on the authors' theory that it was one of Pachacutec's royal estates.

The Machu Picchu Guidebook: A Self-Guided Tour, by Ruth Wright.

An excellent guidebook that explains how and why the Incas built the various structures at Machu Picchu.

Cradle of Gold: The Story of Hiram Bingham, a Real Life Indiana Jones, and the Search for Machu Picchu, by Christopher Heaney.

An engaging modern account of Bingham's life and career, with an emphasis on his archaeological work, by a historian who spent an enormous amount of time digging through archives on three continents.

Forgotten Vilcabamba: Final Stronghold of the Incas, by Vincent Lee.
Following clues left by Bingham and others, an architect-explorer ventured into the former rebel Inca kingdom in the 1980s to see if anything remained. As it turned out, quite a bit did.

Machu Picchu: Exploring an Ancient Sacred Center, by Johan Reinhard.
The original, and best, explanation of why Machu Picchu is most likely situated where it is.

Selected Bibliography

Adelaar, Willem, with Pieter Muysken. *The Languages of the Andes*. Cambridge: Cambridge University Press, 2004.

Bauer, Brian. *Ancient Cuzco: Heartland of the Inca*. Austin: University of Texas Press, 2004.

Betanzos, Juan de. *Narrative of the Incas*. Translation by Roland Hamilton. Austin: University of Texas Press, 1996.

Bingham, Alfred M. *Portrait of an Explorer: Hiram Bingham*. Ames: University of Iowa Press, 1989.

Bingham, Alfred M. *The Tiffany Fortune, and Other Chronicles of a Connecticut Family*. Chestnut Hill, MA: Abeel & Leet, 1996.

Bingham, Hiram (I). *A Residence of Twenty-One Years in the Sandwich Islands*. Hartford: H. Huntington, 1848.

Bingham, Hiram (III).

The Journal of an Expedition Across Venezuela and Colombia, 1906–1907. New Haven: Yale Publishing Association, 1909.

Across South America: An Account of a Journey from Buenos Aires to Lima. Boston: Houghton Mifflin, 1911.

"Preliminary Report of the Yale Peruvian Expedition." *Bulletin of the American Geographical Society*. January 1912.

"Vitcos, the Lost Inca Capital." *Proceedings of the American Antiquarian Society*, April 1912.

"A Search for the Last Inca Capital." *Harper's*, October 1912.

"The Discovery of Machu Picchu." *Harper's*, April 1913.

"In the Wonderland of Peru: The Work Accomplished by the Peruvian Expedition of 1912, Under the Auspices of Yale University and the National Geographic Society." *National Geographic*, April 1913.

"The Ruins of Espiritu Pampa, Peru." *American Anthropologist*, April–June 1914.

"Along the Uncharted Pampaconas." *Harper's*, August 1914.

"The Story of Machu Picchu." *National Geographic*, February 1915.

"Further Explorations in the Land of the Incas." *National Geographic*, May 1916.

An Explorer in the Air Service. New Haven: Yale University Press, 1920.

Inca Land: Explorations in the Highlands of Peru. Boston: Houghton Mifflin, 1922

Machu Picchu, a Citadel of the Incas. New Haven: Yale University Press, 1930.

Lost City of the Incas. New York: Duell, Sloan & Pearce, 1948. Reprinted, with an introduction by Hugh Thomson. London: Phoenix House, 2002.

Bingham, Woodbridge. *Hiram Bingham: A Personal History*. Boulder, CO: Bin Lan Zhen Publishers, 1989.

Boorstin, Daniel. *The Discoverers*. New York: Random House, 1983.

Buck, Daniel. "Fights of Machu Picchu." *South American Explorer*, January 1993.

Cobo, Bernabé. *History of the Inca Empire: An Account of the Indians' Customs and their Origin, Together with a Treatise on Inca Legends, History, and Social Institutions*. Translation by Roland Hamilton. Austin: University of Texas Press, 1983.

Dearborn, David and Raymond White, "Archaeoastronomy at Machu Picchu." *Annals of the New York Academy of Sciences*, May 1982.

Dearborn, David, and Raymond White. "The 'Torreon' at Machu Picchu as an Observatory." *Archaeoastronomy*, 1983.

Diamond, Jared. *Guns, Germs and Steel: The Fates of Human Societies*. New York: W. W. Norton, 1999.

Dougherty, Michael. *To Steal a Kingdom*. Waimanaolo, HI: Island Style Press, 1992.

Fejos, Paul. *Archaeological Explorations in the Cordillera Vilcabamba, South-eastern Peru*. New York: Viking Fund Publications in Anthropology, 1944.

Fiennes, Ranulph, Sir. *Race to the Pole: Tragedy, Heroism, and Scott's Antarctic Quest*. New York: Hyperion, 2004.

Frost, Peter. *Exploring Cusco*. Lima: Nuevas Imágenes, 1999.

Gasparini, Graziano and Luise Margolies. *Inca Architecture*. Translated by Patricia Lyon. Bloomington: Indiana University Press, 1980.

Gilfond, Duff. "A Superior Person." *The American Mercury,* March 1930.

Grann, David. *The Lost City of Z: A Tale of Deadly Obsession in the Amazon.* New York: Doubleday, 2009.

Greer, Paolo. "Machu Picchu Before Bingham." *South American Explorer,* May 2008.

Guamán Poma de Ayala, Felipe. *Letter to a King; a Peruvian Chief's Account of Life Under the Incas and Under Spanish Rule.* New York: Dutton, 1978.

Guevara, Ernesto "Che." *The Motorcycle Diaries: Notes on a Latin American Journey.*

Heaney, Christopher. *Cradle of Gold: The Story of Hiram Bingham, a Real-Life Indiana Jones, and the Search for Machu Picchu.* New York: Palgrave Macmillan, 2010.

Hemming, John. *Machu Picchu.* New York: Newsweek, 1981.

Hemming, John. *The Search for El Dorado.* London: Joseph, 1978.

Hemming, John and Edward Ranney (photographer). *Monuments of the Incas.* Boston: Little, Brown and Company, 1982.

Hergé. *Prisoners of the Sun.* Translated by Leslie Lonsdale-Cooper and Michael Turner. London: Methuen Children's Books, 1962.

Hilton, James. *Lost Horizon.* New York: Morrow, 1936.

Lee, Vincent. *Forgotten Vilcabamba: Final Stronghold of the Incas.* Sixpac Manco Publications, 2000.

Lee, Vincent. *Sixpac Manco: Travels Among the Incas.* Self-published, 1985.

Lubow, Arthur. "The Possessed." *The New York Times Magazine,* June 24, 2007.

Lumbreras, Luis. *Peoples and Cultures of Ancient Peru.* Translated by Betty J. Meggers. Washington, D.C.: Smithsonian Institute Press, 1974.

MacLaine, Shirley. *Sage-ing While Age-ing.* New York: Atria Books, 2007.

MacQuarrie, Kim. *The Last Days of the Incas.* New York: Simon & Schuster, 2007.

Magli, Giulio. "At the Other End of the Sun's Path. A New Interpretation of Machu Picchu." Accessed through the Web site arXiv.org.

Malville, J. McKim, Hugh Thomson and Gary Ziegler. "Machu Picchu's Observatory: the Re-Discovery of Llactapata and its Sun-Temple." Self-published, 2004.

Mann, Charles. *1491: New Revelations of the Americas Before Columbus.* New York: Knopf, 2005.

Markham, Sir Clements. *The Incas of Peru.* New York, E.P. Dutton and Company, 1910.

Matthiessen, Peter. *The Cloud Forest.* New York: Viking, 1961.

McBrian, William. *Cole Porter: A Biography.* New York: Knopf, 1998.

McCullough, David. *The Path Between the Seas: The Creation of the Panama Canal*. New York: Simon and Schuster, c1977.

McEwan, Gordon. *The Incas: New Perspectives*. New York, W. W. Norton, 2006.

Meadows, Anne. *Digging Up Butch and Sundance*. Lincoln: University of Nebraska Press, 2003.

Miller, Char. *Fathers and Sons, the Bingham Family and the American Mission*. Philadelphia: Temple University Press, 1982.

Mould de Pease, Mariana. "Un día en la vida peruana de Machu Picchu: avance de historia intercultural." *Revista Complutense de Historia de América*, 2001.

Murúa, Martin de. *Historia General del Perú*. Edited by Manuel Ballesteros. Madrid: Historia 16, 1986.

Poole, Robert M. *Explorers House: National Geographic and the World It Made*. New York: Penguin, 2004.

Prescott, William H. *History of the Conquest of Peru; with a Preliminary View of the Civilization of the Incas*. Philadelphia: J. B. Lippincott & Co., 1861. (First published in New York, 1847.)

Reinhard, Johan. *The Ice Maiden: Inca Mummies, Mountain Gods, and Sacred Sites in the Andes*. Washington, D.C.: National Geographic Society, 2005.

Reinhard, Johan. *Machu Picchu: Exploring an Ancient Sacred Center*. Fourth revised edition. Los Angeles: Cotsen Institute of Archaeology (UCLA), 2007.

Savoy, Gene. *Antisuyo: The Search for the Lost Cities of the Amazon*. New York: Simon and Schuster, 1970.

Starn, Orin, Carlos Iván Degregori and Robin Kirk, eds. *The Peru Reader: History, Culture, Politics*. Durham: Duke University Press, 2005.

Theroux, Paul. *The Old Patagonian Express*. New York: Penguin, 1980.

Thomson, Hugh. *Cochineal Red: Travels Through Ancient Peru*. London: Wiedenfield & Nicolson, 2006.

Thomson, Hugh. *The White Rock: An Exploration of the Inca Heartland*. London: Weidenfield & Nicolson, 2001.

Titu Cusi. *A Sixteenth Century Account of the Conquest*. Translation by Nicole Delia Legnani. Cambridge: Harvard University Press, 2005.

Valencia Zegarra, Alfredo. *Machu Picchu: La Investigación y Conservación del Monumento Arqueólogo Después de Hiram Bingham*. Cusco, 1992.

Vargas Llosa, Mario. *Death in the Andes*. Translated by Edith Grossman. New York: Farrar, Strauss and Giroux, 1996.

Vargas Llosa, Mario. *Making Waves*. New York: Farrar, Straus and Giroux, 1997.

Vega, Garcilaso de la. *Royal Commentaries of the Incas*. Translated by Harold V. Livermore. Indianapolis: Hackett Publishing Co., 2006.

Von Hagen, Victor. *Highway of the Sun*. New York, Duell, Sloan and Pearce, 1955.

Wilson, Jason. *The Andes: A Cultural History*. New York: Oxford University Press, 2009.

Wright, Kenneth and Alfredo Valencia Zegarra. *Machu Picchu: A Civil Engineering Marvel*. Reston, VA: American Society of Civil Engineers, 2000.

Wright, Ruth and Alfredo Valencia Zegarra. *The Machu Picchu Guidebook: A Self-Guided Tour*. Boulder: Johnson Books, 2004.

Ziegler, Gary and J. McKim Malville. "Machu Picchu, Inca Pachacuti's Sacred City: A multiple ritual, ceremonial and administrative center." Self-published, 2006.

Index